College Level Academic Skills Test

PREPARATION GUIDE

by
Richard L. Goldfarb, Ph.D.

and
Ben E. Johnson, M.A.

Series Editor
Jerry Bobrow, Ph.D.

INCORPORATED
LINCOLN, NEBRASKA   68501

ISBN 0-8220-2040-8

© Copyright 1988, 1989

by

Richard L. Goldfarb

and

Ben E. Johnson

ACKNOWLEDGMENTS

We are grateful for the assistance of Laura Link and Susan Goldsworthy during the preparation of this manuscript. A special thanks goes to Elsa Gordon for her work with the mathematics portion of this book. We are indebted to Elsa for her generous gift of knowledge, time, and ability. Without her efforts, the mathematics section of this book would not have been completed.

Thanks also to Susan Goldsworthy for permission to reprint her practice CLAST essay, "Wind is a Necessity of Life," to Dr. Adrienne Perry for information and encouragement, and to the Florida Department of Education for permission to reprint CLAST directions and sample essay topics.

We are especially grateful to Michele Spence, who edited this book, for her unfailing energy, intelligence, and professionalism.

We would also like to thank the copyright holders acknowledged on page 423 for their permission to quote from their material in the reading sections of this book.

*For my wife, Susan, who made it possible
and my daughter, Paris Rose, who made it worthwhile.*

R. L. G.

To Steven, Susan, and Shelley—again.

B. E. J.

CONTENTS

PART IV: PREPARING FOR THE CLAST ESSAY TEST

PART V: PREPARING FOR THE CLAST MATHEMATICS TEST

PART VI: COMPLETE PRACTICE CLAST

PREFACE

If you want an Associate of Arts degree from a Florida community college or admission to the upper division of any state university, then you must pass the College Level Academic Skills Test. The CLAST is a four-part, five-hour test of your reading, writing, grammar, and computation skills.

Cliffs CLAST Preparation Guide, written by Florida college teachers for Florida college students, is designed to help you pass that important test. Even if you have not recently taken an English, reading, or math course—or if you did not earn high grades in those courses—this book can teach you everything you need to know to do well on the CLAST.

Cliffs CLAST Preparation Guide:

- completely explains and demonstrates all skills tested by the CLAST in clear, nontechnical language;
- gives practical, timesaving tips for applying those skills most effectively on the CLAST;
- presents three complete simulated CLAST tests, based on the latest Florida Department of Education specifications, containing more than 400 practice questions;
- provides answer keys, sample essays, analysis of right and wrong answers, and review guides to improve your performance from test to test.

This book takes a lively and efficient approach to test preparation. It will show you how to earn a high CLAST score with a moderate investment of time and concentration.

Part I: Introduction

INTRODUCTION

STRUCTURE OF THE CLAST

TEST	TIME	NUMBER OF QUESTIONS SCORED	PASSING SCORES
Essay	60 minutes	choose 1 of 2 topics	5
Grammar and Reading	80 minutes (combined)	35 36	28✔ 25✔
Mathematics	90 minutes	56	38✔

Passing Scores

Essays are graded by a system that is explained in Part IV of this book. The three multiple-choice subtests are graded on a curve, so the number of correct answers required to pass may vary by plus or minus one each time the CLAST is given. The scores listed above are a guide to the *approximate number of correct answers* required to pass any CLAST.

Number of Questions

The number of questions scored on the three multiple-choice subtests remains constant, but the total number of questions asked may change each time the CLAST is given. This is because extra questions, which are being evaluated for use on future tests, appear on each CLAST. Although these experimental items are not graded, you have no way of distinguishing them from questions that do count toward your score. Approach each question as if it counts. The practice tests in this book all contain extra questions to prepare you for the length of test you will actually take.

CLAST QUESTIONS AND ANSWERS

Q: WHO MUST TAKE THE CLAST?

A: Passing scores on all four subtests are required for the award of an A.A. degree, for admission to the upper division of a state university, and for the award of some types of Florida financial aid.

Q: WHEN IS THE CLAST GIVEN?

A: The test is administered three times each year: in the spring, summer, and fall. Ask your school's student services office for exact dates when you are ready to take the CLAST.

Q: WHERE IS THE CLAST GIVEN?

A: The test is given at all community colleges and state universities as well as some private colleges in Florida.

Q: WHEN AM I ELIGIBLE TO TAKE THE CLAST?

A: Under current regulations, you may take the CLAST whenever you like. This policy, like all CLAST policies, may change at any time, so ask your student services office about the eligibility requirements in effect when you are ready to take the test.

Q: DO I HAVE TO REGISTER FOR THE CLAST?

A: Yes. Registration is required. No late registrations, walk ins, or standby registrations are permitted. Because space in many locations is limited, you should register as soon as possible to reserve a seat at the test. Registration closes four weeks before each CLAST administration.

Q: WHERE DO I REGISTER?

A: Register for and take the CLAST at the school you now attend. If you are transferring to a state university from an institution that does not give the CLAST, register at the university you are applying to.

Q: MUST I PAY TO TAKE THE CLAST?

A: Students at state community colleges and universities may take the CLAST as often as necessary at no cost. Students at private institutions are charged a $10 administration fee each time they take the test.

Q: WHAT IF I FAIL THE CLAST?

A: You can register to retake any or all of the subtests at any time the CLAST is given. You can retake any subtest as often as you choose, either to earn a passing score or to increase a previous score. Only your highest scores will go on your record.

Q: CAN I TRANSFER TO A UNIVERSITY WITHOUT PASSING THE ENTIRE CLAST?

A: Yes. If you pass three of the four subtests and meet all other requirements for admission, you can enroll in upper division courses. You are permitted to take 36 credits at this level before being required to pass the fourth subtest.

Q. WHEN SHOULD I TAKE THE CLAST?

A: As long as state policies allow you to take the CLAST when you want and as often as you need to, you should attempt it early in your college career. Let this book be your guide. If you can pass the sample tests here, you stand a very good chance of passing the CLAST no matter how soon you take it.

Q: HOW LONG DOES THE TEST LAST?

A: About five hours. Here is the timetable:

Time	Activity
7:30–7:45 A.M.	arrive at testing location
7:45–8:00	check in
8:00–8:30	general information
8:30–9:30	essay subtest
9:30–9:35	break
9:45–11:05	grammar and reading subtests
11:05–11:20	break
11:25–12:55 P.M.	mathematics (computation) subtest
12:55	test ends

Q: WHAT SHOULD I BRING TO THE TEST?

A: Bring your registration ticket, your social security card, a watch, two reliable pens with blue or black ink, two sharpened number 2 pencils, and a snack of fresh fruit or candy to eat during the break.

Q: WHAT ELSE MAY I BRING TO THE TEST?

A: Nothing. Books, rulers, dictionaries, calculators, slide rules, and scratch paper are all prohibited.

STRATEGY FOR SUCCESS ON THE CLAST

This book is designed to teach you all the skills tested by the CLAST. Those skills are presented here in the sequence in which they are easiest to learn rather than in the order in which they appear on the CLAST. The Complete Practice CLAST at the end of this book will give you practice with the actual sequence of the test after you have mastered the individual grammar, reading, writing, and computation skills.

In addition to teaching you the required academic skills, this book provides many strategies for making the best use of those skills on the CLAST. Those strategies will show you how to interpret test directions and how to budget your time. Perhaps most important, they will also help you make intelligent guesses. Since *there is no penalty for wrong answers* on the CLAST, you should answer every question on the test. The strategies will increase your chances of success even when you are not sure of an answer.

Because this book presents a necessary skill or a useful strategy on every page, you should read and use everything in it.

COUNTDOWN TO CLAST

This schedule is designed to increase your score on the CLAST while reducing your stress in preparing for the test. You can, of course, prepare adequately in less than the seven weeks called for, but do not skip any of the preparation steps.

Today

Decide which of the three annual CLASTs you want to take. Remember that under current regulations *you* are entitled to decide when you are ready to attempt the test.

CLAST Minus Seven Weeks

1. Register for the CLAST. Early registration will assure you of a seat at the test and will give you ample time to get the greatest benefit from this book.

2. Read the INTRODUCTION (page 13) and take the GRAMMAR PRE-TEST on page 19. Score your performance, recording the

number of correct answers and your time on the CLAST PROGRESS CHART on page 9. The GRAMMAR PRE-TEST ANSWERS, ANALYSIS, AND REVIEW GUIDE (page 25) will help you structure your preparation. Focus on the areas in GRAMMAR COMPETENCIES TESTED (page 27) in which you need improvement, but do not skip any of the material and complete all the practice questions.

3. Take the GRAMMAR POST-TEST on page 85. After recording your score and time on the CLAST PROGRESS CHART, use the REVIEW GUIDE (page 91) and return to GRAMMAR COMPETENCIES TESTED to work on skills that still need improvement.

CLAST Minus Six Weeks

Follow the same procedures with the READING PRE-TEST (page 111), READING COMPETENCIES TESTED (page 139), and READING POST-TEST (page 173).

CLAST Minus Five Weeks

Read PART IV: PREPARING FOR THE CLAST ESSAY TEST (page 201) and write at least four timed essays. Use the topics provided on the SAMPLE ESSAY TEST (page 215), the ESSAY POST-TEST (page 222), or in the list of ADDITIONAL ESSAY TOPICS (page 220). If you decide to use the COLLEGE SKILLS EVALUATION SERVICE (page 220), mail in your essay by the end of this week so that your graded essay and review guide can be returned to you before you take the COMPLETE PRACTICE CLAST.

CLAST Minus Four Weeks

Take the MATHEMATICS PRE-TEST (page 239) and begin to study MATHEMATICS COMPETENCIES TESTED (page 261). Because many skills are presented in the computation section, you may need to devote at least two weeks to mastering them before you are ready to take the MATHEMATICS POST-TEST (page 341). Record your scores and your time on the CLAST PROGRESS CHART.

CLAST Minus Two Weeks

1. Take the COMPLETE PRACTICE CLAST (page 367). Simulate actual conditions as closely as possible by following the instructions that introduce the complete test.

2. Grade your COMPLETE PRACTICE CLAST, recording scores and times on the CLAST PROGRESS CHART. Use the ANSWERS, ANALYSIS, AND REVIEW GUIDE (page 400) to complete your final preparation in grammar, reading, and mathematics.

3. Continue writing timed practice essays, using a new sample topic for each essay.

CLAST Minus One Day

1. Make sure that you know where the test is given and how long it will take you to get there.

2. Get a good night's sleep.

CLAST Day

After eating a nourishing breakfast, arrive at the testing location at 7:30 A.M. with the items described on page 5.

CLAST PROGRESS CHART

Remove this chart and use it
to mark your progress. Circle,
in each column, the number of
correct answers you achieve.

READING

PRE-TEST	POST-TEST	PRACTICE TEST
44	44	44
43	43	43
42	42	42
41	41	41
40	40	40
39	39	39
38	38	38
37	37	37
36	36	36
35	35	35
(34)	34	34
33	33	33
32	32	32
31	31	31
30	30	30
29	29	29
28	28	28
27	27	27
26	26	26
25	25	25
24	24	24
23	23	23
22	22	22
21	21	21
20	20	20
19	19	19
18	18	18
17	17	17
16	16	16
15	15	15
14	14	14
13	13	13
12	12	12
11	11	11
10	10	10
9	9	9
8	8	8
7	7	7
6	6	6
5	5	5
4	4	4
3	3	3
2	2	2
1	1	1

GRAMMAR

PRE-TEST	POST-TEST	PRACTICE TEST
37	37	37
(36)	36	36
35	35	35
34	34	34
33	33	33
32	32	32
31	31	31
30	30	30
29	29	29
28	28	28
27	27	27
26	26	26
25	25	25
24	24	24
23	23	23
22	22	22
21	21	21
20	20	20
19	19	19
18	18	18
17	17	17
16	16	16
15	15	15
14	14	14
13	13	13
12	12	12
11	11	11
10	10	10
9	9	9
8	8	8
7	7	7
6	6	6
5	5	5
4	4	4
3	3	3
2	2	2
1	1	1

CUT HERE

Time: ____ ____ ____ ____ ____ ____

MATHEMATICS

28	28	28
27	27	27
26	26	26
25	25	25
24	24	24
23	23	23
22	22	22
21	21	21
20	20	20
19	19	19
18	18	18
17	17	17
16	16	16
15	15	15
14	14	14
13	13	13
12	12	12
11	11	11
10	10	10
9	9	9
8	8	8
7	7	7
6	6	6
5	5	5
4	4	4
3	3	3
2	2	2
1	1	1

PRE-TEST	POST-TEST	PRACTICE TEST

56	56	56
55	55	55
54	54	54
53	53	53
52	52	52
51	51	51
50	50	50
49	49	49
48	(48)	48
47	47	47
46	46	46
45	45	45
44	44	44
43	43	43
42	42	42
41	41	41
40	40	40
39	39	39
(38)	38	38
37	37	37
36	36	36
35	35	35
34	34	34
33	33	33
32	32	32
31	31	31
30	30	30
29	29	29

PRE-TEST	POST-TEST	PRACTICE TEST

Time: _____ _____ _____   75 min _____ _____

10

Part II: Preparing for the CLAST Grammar Test (Grammar Subtest, English Language Skills Test)

FORMAT OF THE CLAST GRAMMAR TEST
Approximately 37 Questions **Suggested Time: 20 Minutes** **(Combined Time for Grammar and Reading Subtests: 80 Minutes)**

Question Type	Approximate Number of Questions
Word Choice	6
Effective Sentences	9
Sentence Structure	4
Usage	15
Punctuation	3

Note: The English Language Skills Test consists of both a grammar and a reading test. On your first attempt at the CLAST, you will have 80 minutes to complete both tests. Though you may begin with either test, we strongly recommend that you complete the shorter grammar portion first, reserving as much time as possible for the longer, more time-consuming reading test.

If for any reason you retake the English Language Skills Test (see page 5 for information about retakes), you will be allowed 160 minutes to complete either the grammar or reading subtest or both on your second attempt and on any subsequent attempts.

PREPARING FOR THE CLAST GRAMMAR TEST

INTRODUCTION

What the Grammar Test Tests

The Grammar Subtest of the English Language Skills Test, as it is officially named, measures your ability to recognize correct applications of the rules and conventions of standard written American English. Thirty-five multiple-choice questions test fourteen grammar, usage, and word-choice skills. Twenty-three correct answers is a passing score.

Standard Written American English

The CLAST tests your knowledge of a language that both *is standard* and *is a standard*. It is standard because it follows the same rules of sentence structure, punctuation, and spelling everywhere in the United States. It is also the standard by which all writing is judged in every American school and business.

Term papers and job applications written in standard American English communicate clearly because their words and sentences convey the same meaning to every educated reader. They communicate impressively as well: writers who are skillful with standard American English are most likely to earn the "A" and win the job. The language tested on the CLAST is the measure by which your academic and professional writing will be judged for the rest of your life.

How Part II Teaches

The pages that follow will guide you step by step to confident understanding of the rules of standard written American English that are tested by the CLAST. They contain everything you need to know to earn an excellent score on the Grammar Test and nothing you don't need to know.

The CLAST skills are taught here in a form that is probably new to you. You will see very few of the grammatical terms that may have

haunted you since fifth grade. Instead, the rules of standard English
will be presented as steps in a logical system, something like a simple
computer program, which is what language really is. Only the most
basic and useful grammatical terms appear, and those are fully
explained.

The method used here will teach you skills that you need in the
form that you need them. Students who had never mastered tradi-
tional grammar have used this system to earn high scores on the
CLAST and similar tests. Like them, you will have no trouble
understanding and applying it successfully. Give these instructions
your full attention, for whatever time and mental energy you put into
them will come out as points on your CLAST grammar score.

Strategies for the CLAST Grammar Test

In addition to teaching you the skills you need, this section will
show you the most productive ways of using them. Begin to learn
some of these strategies now. Follow these suggestions to improve
your overall CLAST score.

• 1. *Learn the system:* The approach to grammar taught here will
enable you to complete the test both correctly and quickly. Speed
matters because any time you save on the Grammar Test, you can
give to the Reading Test. You will take both these subtests in the
same eighty-minute period. How you divide that time is up to you.
After practicing with this book, you should be able to finish the
Grammar Test in about twenty minutes *without rushing.* This leaves
you an hour for the Reading Test. The extra time you will be able to
give to the reading questions, which require close attention and
careful evaluation, will improve your score on the Reading Test.
Complete the Grammar Test before starting the Reading Test.

• 2. *Learn what to expect:* The fourteen grammar skills are grouped
into six sections on the CLAST. Each section is introduced by
different directions. Some directions name the skills being tested
while others don't. Some instruct you to identify correct uses of
language, and others tell you to mark incorrect uses. Even the
number of answer choices varies from section to section.

Many students have been slowed down and even confused by these
varying directions. But they can have the opposite effect on you. Your
practice in the following sections will show you that these directions

contain useful clues. Fully clarified in the following pages, these clues will enable you to focus your attention entirely on the skills being tested and to tune out any skill not required at that moment. Become familiar with those directions and learn what they can tell you.

• 3. *Work Efficiently:* As you work through the grammar test, mark your answers by circling the appropriate letter *on the test paper.* When you have completed all the questions, transfer your answers carefully to the machine graded answer sheet. There is no danger of your not finishing this test in time to fill out the answer sheet. But there is a possibility of wasting time, losing concentration, and making mechanical errors if you repeatedly shift your attention from the questions to the answer sheet and back again. *Use this marking strategy for the Grammar Test only.* Using the strategy on other sections could leave you out of time without having completed the answer sheet.

How to Begin

Take the Grammar Pre-Test that starts on page 19. Don't be concerned about time, but do note how long you take to complete the test. Use the answers immediately following the test to add up the number of questions you answered correctly. Record that number and your time on page 9.

When you check your answers, you will notice a Review Guide. This guide names the skill tested by each question and directs you to the section which teaches that skill. This analysis will identify the strengths and weaknesses you have now while it shows you where the help you need can be found in this book.

No matter how well you do on the pre-test, do not skip any of the following sections. Every page will give you many kinds of new information that will be vaulable to you on the CLAST Essay Test as well as on the Grammar Test.

Format of the Grammar Tests in This Book

The following pre-test, as well as the two other complete Grammar Tests in this book, are accurate simulations of the test you will see on CLAST day. They are not copies of previous tests because, unlike other testing agencies, Florida does not release actual test questions. The state does, however, provide exact descriptions of skills tested, sample questions, and the wording of directions used on the CLAST. Carefully following the state's specifications, the questions and format presented in this book are as close as possible to the real thing. Students who have recently taken the state test have been unable to tell the difference between Florida's CLAST and the tests in this book.

One similarity is the number of questions. Although only thirty-five questions will be scored, the test you take will contain two or three extra questions. These extras are new questions with which the test's designers are experimenting. To give you an accurate sense of the length as well as the content and format of the CLAST, the practice Grammar Tests in this book all contain thirty-seven questions.

Treat the pre-test as if it were the real thing that it so closely resembles. Begin practicing efficient strategy by circling your answers on the test pages and then transferring those answers carefully to the answer sheet you will find on the following page.

GRAMMAR PRE-TEST

Suggested Time: 20 Minutes
37 Questions

I. DIRECTIONS: Complete each sentence by choosing the most effective word or phrase which conforms to standard written English.

1. Home at last, Sam was happy to _____ his house.
   A. enter into
   B. make an entry into
   C. enter
   D. proceed ahead into

2. Sir Gawain challenged his noble adversary to a _____.
   A. brawl
   B. dual
   C. duel

3. The advertiser offered _____ to the first fifty callers.
   A. a gift
   B. a free gift
   C. an absolutely free gift
   D. a completely free gift

4. The mayor promised fair treatment for all citizens during her _____ of office.
   A. reign
   B. term
   C. r in

5. Jim _____ that dogs make better pets than cats.
   A. rsonally feels
   B. f the opinion
   C. he belief
   D. eves

19

6. The morning fog slowly began to _____ the beachfront town.
   A. envelope
   B. wrap
   C. envelop

II. DIRECTIONS: Choose the sentence that expresses the thought most clearly and effectively and that has no errors in structure.

7. A. Speaking from personal experience, the text for the computer course was adequate.

   B. Speaking from personal experience, I found the text for the computer course adequate.

   C. The text for the computer course, speaking from personal experience, was adequate.

8. A. A free economy has obvious limits, and it produces greater wealth than a planned economy.

   B. A free economy produces greater wealth than a planned economy; it has obvious limits.

   C. Although it has obvious limits, a free economy produces greater wealth than a planned economy.

9. A. Lisa is friendly, efficient, and says witty things.

   B. Lisa is friendly, does her work efficiently, and says witty things.

   C. Lisa is friendly, efficient, and witty.

10. A. Tara, who needed a ride to school, called Sara, who is in her class, and who is her best friend.

    B. Tara, who needed a ride to school, called Sara, her best friend and classmate.

    C. Tara needed a ride to school, so she called Sara, for she is in her class, and Sara is her best friend.

11. A. Exhausted from driving all day, the search for a motel began for Sam.

    B. Sam began to search for a motel exhausted from driving all day.

    C. Exhausted from driving all day, Sam began to search for a motel.

12. A. Many high-school graduates can't decide between going to college and whether to get a job.

    B. Many high-school graduates can't decide between a job and going to college.

    C. Many high-school graduates can't decide between going to college and getting a job.

13. A. Having only enough brain power to respond to their environment, scientists tell us that fish can't think.

    B. Having only enough brain power to respond to their environment, fish can't think, scientists tell us.

    C. Having enough brain power to respond to their environment, only fish can't think, scientists tell us.

14. A. The overworked waiter took orders, greeted guests, cleaned tables, and even dashed into the kitchen to help the cook.

    B. The overworked waiter took orders, greeted guests, cleaned tables, and even dashing into the kitchen to help the cook.

    C. The overworked waiter had to take orders, greeted guests, cleaning tables, and even dashing into the kitchen to help the cook.

15. A. As the sun sank below the horizon, the sky turned green, which amazed onlookers.

    B. The sun sank below the horizon, and the sky turned green, and onlookers were amazed.

    C. Because the sun sank below the horizon, and the sky turned green, onlookers were amazed.

III. DIRECTIONS: Each item below <u>may</u> contain an error in sentence construction: a fragment, a comma splice, or a fused (run-on) sentence. <u>NO ITEM HAS MORE THAN ONE ERROR</u>. Mark the letter which precedes the group of words containing the error. Mark <u>E</u> if there is no error.

16. <u>(A)</u> All living things adapt to dangers in the environment, each in its own way. <u>(B)</u> A fly moves out of the way of a flyswatter, and an octopus changes color when it feels threatened. <u>(C)</u> While staying alive during bad times, one-celled plants form a hard coat. <u>(D)</u> Living things don't live forever, however, each has a limited life span. <u>(E)</u> No error

17. <u>(A)</u> Just a few words in defense of the Muscovy duck. <u>(B)</u> The bird is an excellent flyer; even big old drakes can leap into the air and disappear at amazing speeds. <u>(C)</u> The Muscovy was domesticated, some experts say, by the Central Americans. <u>(D)</u> Because it does not fear humans, the Muscovy is often seen begging food in residential areas. <u>(E)</u> No error

18. <u>(A)</u> Bert Lee, a transplanted New Yorker, claims to make the best key lime pies in the world. <u>(B)</u> After sampling the tasty dessert in 1970, he developed his own recipe, which he says improves on the original Key West version. <u>(C)</u> At first, he sold a few pies each week from an old truck now customers flock to his huge bakery. <u>(D)</u> Sales increase daily. <u>(E)</u> No error

19. <u>(A)</u> A judge awarded a divorcing couple joint custody of their dog after setting out rules for the pet's care. <u>(B)</u> "I gave them the dog for six months each," the judge said, "my decision was as wise as Solomon's." <u>(C)</u> The decision ended a bitter dispute; both husband and wife accepted it gladly. <u>(D)</u> A pet frog died before the case was resolved, however, and an out-of-court settlement was worked out for a parakeet. <u>(E)</u> No error

IV. DIRECTIONS: Mark "A" if the first alternative within the parentheses is correct; mark "B" if the second alternative is correct.

20. Everybody in the English classes (take, takes) the same
                                    A   B
final examination.

21. Spot was the (smallest, smaller) puppy in a large litter.
                   A   B

22. (She, Her) and her brother both attend the same college.
     A   B

23. Local lives are (effected, affected) by distant events.
                     A   B

24. Most nations strive for (independence, independance).
                              A   B

25. After the ceremony, everybody looked for (their,
                                               A

his or her) parents.
     B

26. The football team opened the season playing extremely
(good, well) games.
 A   B

27. Tara wanted Sara and (she, her) to go to the beach together.
                          A   B

28. Many students couldn't understand (their, they're) textbooks.
                                        A   B

29. Lisa played her part in the play (perfect, perfectly).
                                       A   B

30. The rock star couldn't remember (whom, who) he had married.
                                      A   B

31. Her parents had (lead, led) an exciting life together.
                     A   B

32. The band's drummer had amazing (rhythm, rythem).
                                     A   B

33. Either the witnesses or the suspect (are, is) lying.
                                          A   B

34. Sam knew that he (could of, could have) passed the test.
                      A   B

V. DIRECTIONS: The items below <u>may</u> contain errors in punctuation. <u>NO ITEM HAS MORE THAN ONE ERROR UNDERLINED</u>. Mark the letter which locates an error in punctuation. Mark <u>E</u> if there is no error.

35. Having already decreased their alcohol consumption<u>,</u>
                                                        A

    Americans are now being warned of the dangers of even

    moderate drinking<u>;</u> according to a recent report. A study
                       B

    controlled for diet<u>,</u> body weight, and blood pressure reached a
                        C

    surprising conclusion<u>:</u> "Even one drink a day may lead
                          D

    to heart disease." <u>No error</u>
                        E

36. No nation has left as rich a heritage as ancient Greece<u>,</u> many
                                                            A

    historians believe. Its people<u>,</u> though few in number, added
                                   B

    new dimensions to the human spirit<u>;</u> their heroes and ideals
                                       C

    have enlarged our own minds. They excelled at whatever they

    attempted <u>:</u> politics, art, philosophy, and even war. <u>No error</u>
              D   E

VI. DIRECTIONS: The items below <u>may</u> contain an error in capitalization. <u>THERE IS NOT MORE THAN ONE ERROR UNDERLINED</u>. Mark the letter which locates the error in capitalization. Mark <u>E</u> if there is no error.

37. During his <u>Thanksgiving</u> vacation, Jim said to his <u>father</u>,
               A   B

    "From now on, I will do better in Spanish and <u>History</u>."
    <u>C</u>   D

    <u>No error</u>
    E

GRAMMAR PRE-TEST ANSWERS, ANALYSIS, AND REVIEW GUIDE

ANSWERS AND ANALYSIS

QUESTION	ANSWER	SKILL/ERROR CATEGORY
1	C	wordiness
2	C	word choice
3	A	wordiness
4	B	word choice
5	D	wordiness
6	C	word choice
7	B	modification
8	C	subordination
9	C	parallelism
10	B	subordination
11	C	modification
12	C	parallelism
13	B	modification
14	A	parallelism
15	A	subordination
16	D	comma splice
17	A	fragment
18	C	fused (run-on) sentence
19	B	comma splice
20	B	subject-verb agreement
21	A	adjective/adverb
22	A	case
23	B	verb form
24	A	spelling
25	B	noun-pronoun agreement
26	A	adjective/adverb
27	B	case
28	A	noun-pronoun agreement
29	B	adjective/adverb
30	A	case
31	B	verb form
32	A	spelling
33	B	subject-verb agreement

QUESTION	ANSWER	SKILL/ERROR CATEGORY
34	B	verb form
35	B	punctuation
36	E	punctuation
37	D	capitalization

SCORE: _____36_____ (number of correct answers)
TIME: _____8-9? min_____

REVIEW GUIDE

All the skills listed in the Answers and Analysis chart are fully discussed and tested in the sections indicated in this Review Guide. Each of the questions you have just answered appears in those sections either as an illustration in the text or as a sample question at the end of a section. When you see these questions again, they will be accompanied by instructions for locating correct answers and suggestions for avoiding incorrect answers.

IF YOU MISSED QUESTIONS	REVIEW SECTIONS
1–6	6 (p. 76)
7–15	4 (p. 52)
16–19	1, 2, 3 (pp. 27, 37, 48)
20–34	1, 5 (pp. 27, 63)
35–36	1, 2 (pp. 27, 37)
37	5 (p. 63)

GRAMMAR COMPETENCIES TESTED

1: THE X-RAY APPROACH TO SENTENCE STRUCTURE

The better you understand sentence structure, the better you will do on the CLAST Grammar Test. Of the thirty-five questions that count toward your grade on this test, the answers to twenty-five will be obvious to anyone who clearly sees how sentences are put together.

Learning how sentences work is not the same as learning (or relearning) a long list of grammatical terms. Even if you don't know a participle from a predicate, you can still earn an excellent score on the CLAST. What matters on this and other tests of your verbal skills is not your ability to name language but to know how it works. The knowledge that really counts on this test was already yours before you could even pronounce the word *participle*. This section will show you what you already know and how to convert that knowledge into points on your CLAST score.

What You Know

If the first language you learned was English, you already understood its sentence structure before your first day in kindergarten. Of course you did not understand the meaning of every word you heard, but you did have a firm sense of the structures that combined words into sentences. You still have that sense even if you can't explain in technical grammatical terms *how* you know what you know. If you doubt that, try the following experiment.

THE BLAGGLE TEST

Here are eight groups of words. Much of their vocabulary is invented to make the meaning of the statements as mysterious to you as "The Dow Jones index soared to a record high yesterday" would be to a five year old. Despite having no idea of what it means, the child would recognize it as a complete sentence. Put yourself in that child's place. Decide which of these combinations of strange and familiar words have the structure of complete English sentences.

27

	complete	incomplete
1. A gloop blaggles the dorps.	☐	☐
2. We blaggle zugly.	☐	☐
3. The gloop blaggling the dorp.	☐	☐
4. Blaggles zugly.	☐	☐
5. Mim and Dir blaggled zugly.	☐	☐
6. Although she blaggles.	☐	☐
7. To blaggle the dorp.	☐	☐
8. Does Mim blaggle zugly?	☐	☐

Answers: 1, 2, 5, and 8 are complete sentence patterns.

Almost everyone who grew up in an English-speaking family somehow manages to identify most of these statements correctly. It is not knowing the names of "parts of speech" which makes that possible. Instead, structure is revealed through signals built into the language.

Your X-Ray Eye

You learned to recognize language signals when you were a child. As a result, you developed a sense of structure that enabled you to sort out all those jumbled sounds you heard into a language that you could understand and, after a while, speak and read. When you focus that sense on written English, you develop an x-ray eye for structure. Just as a medical x-ray can make a broken bone visible, your x-ray eye can penetrate words to see whether the structure beneath is whole or fractured. The more you understand and practice that skill, the more transparent sentence structure will appear to you. And nothing is more useful on tests like the CLAST than a strong x-ray eye.

• *What the X-Ray Eye Sees:* Looking through words to structure, the x-ray eye sees that almost all English sentences follow the same pattern:

SUBJECT + VERB + COMPLEMENT

Some person or thing (SUBJECT) is causing an action to occur (VERB) in a particular way (COMPLEMENT). The term *complement* means *something that completes* and here describes all the words that complete the meaning of any sentence. *Complement* is a convenient and simplified substitute for many technical grammatical terms that the x-ray eye can safely disregard.

The basic subject + verb + complement pattern—from now on abbreviated as SVC—can be seen beneath the nonsense language of

A gloop/ blaggles/ the dorps.
  S   V   C

Filled in with more familiar words, the same pattern might read

A dog/ chases/ the birds.
  S   V   C

OR:

We/ wash/ the dishes.
  S   V   C

Although most sentences do include a complement, all that is required for a sentence to be complete is a subject, a verb, and a period. Therefore,

A gloop/ blaggles.
  S   V

A dog/ chases.
  S   V

We/ wash.
  S   V

are all complete sentences.

• *How the X-Ray Eye Sees:* Becoming aware of how you instinctively recognize the basic SVC structure of English sentences is the key to unlocking the secrets of sentence structure—and grammar tests— once and for all. In combination, these elements of language form all the sentences possible in English. Separately, each has its own identifying features. Learn to recognize those features consciously and you will strengthen the instinctive pattern-finding of your x-ray eye.

In the Beginning is the Verb

The core of every sentence is its verb, and the first step in x-raying any group of words is to locate that basic element.

- *Meaning:* The most obvious feature of verbs is that they express an action.

- *Examples:* I *run*. It *rains*. We *are*.

Finding the action word in a sentence will usually lead you to its verb. But depending entirely on what verbs say can cause problems, for many words that express actions are not verbs. The x-ray eye avoids these problems by looking for two other features that are characteristic of verbs. Verbs can be identified not only by what they say, but also by where they are and how they look.

- *Position:* The verb is the second element in almost all English sentences.

- *Example:*
$$\underset{\text{S}}{\underset{1}{\text{A dog/}}} \quad \underset{\text{V}}{\underset{2}{\text{chases/}}} \quad \underset{\text{C}}{\underset{3}{\text{the birds.}}}$$

Each element in a sentence may consist of one word:

$$\underset{\text{S}}{\underset{1}{\text{Spot/}}} \quad \underset{\text{V}}{\underset{2}{\text{chases/}}} \quad \underset{\text{C}}{\underset{3}{\text{Tweetie.}}}$$

Or each element may be made up of several words:

$$\underset{\text{S}}{\underset{1}{\text{That mean junkyard dog/}}} \quad \underset{\text{V}}{\underset{2}{\text{has been chasing/}}} \quad \underset{\text{C}}{\underset{3}{\text{those beautiful birds.}}}$$

- *Form:* Verbs change their appearance to communicate many different kinds of information. Changes in form indicate who is performing an action and when it is being performed, among other things. One change in form means most to the x-ray eye. All action words can change form to end in *-ing* or begin with *to*. Action words ending in *-ing* (standing alone) or beginning with *to* are not verbs.

A Program for Identifying Verbs

Meaning, position, or form alone are not dependable indicators of a verb. But these three features can be combined into a program that will enable you to know a verb whenever you see one.

- *Example:*   A dog chases the birds.

Step 1: Look for the action word. Remember that it will almost always be the second element in a sentence.

Step 2: Discard action words introduced by *to* or ending in *-ing*.

Step 3: Identify the verb = *chases*.

Practicing the Verb-Locating Program

Work through the three steps of the program with this sentence.

Find the verb: Jane plays the trumpet in the school band.

Step 1: Look for the action word in the second position.

Step 2: Discard any action words with *to* or *-ing* forms.

Step 3: Identify the verb= _____

The program should have guided you to the word *plays*. If it did, you are now ready to strengthen your x-ray eye by applying the program to a variety of word groups. Begin by working through each step of the program slowly and carefully. Soon the process will seem as natural to you as it really is.

DIRECTIONS: Identify any verbs in the following word groups.

1. Character develops slowly.

2. The tide running high.

3. His car ran over some broken glass.

4. In the years to come.

5. We were swimming all day.

6. Strange things happen.

Answers and Analysis

1. The verb is *develops.* It expresses an action and does not have a *to* or *-ing* form.

2. No verb. *Running* expresses an action but is disqualified by step 2 of the program.

3. *Ran over* is the verb. Remember that verbs can sometimes consist of more than one word. But it is your ability to see a verb that matters. As long as you know that this sentence has a verb—even if you identified it simply as *ran*—then you are using the program correctly and will be able to use it effectively on the CLAST.

4. No verb. *To come,* which looks like a verb, is disqualified by step 2.

5. The complete verb is *were swimming.* Even if you discarded *swimming* because of its *-ing* form, you would still know that this sentence has a verb (*were*).

6. The verb is *happen.* Because it lacks a complement, this sentence may feel incomplete. What matters now is to recognize that it does have a verb.

Subjects in Sentences

Once you have absorbed the verb-locating program, mastering sentence structure is simple. A verb needs only a subject to add up to a complete sentence. Like verbs, subjects can be identified by where they appear, how they look, and what they do.

• *Position:* In most English sentences, the subject is the first element:

$$\begin{array}{ccc} 1 & 2 & 3 \\ \text{A dog}/ & \text{chases}/ & \text{the birds.} \\ \text{S} & \text{V} & \text{C} \end{array}$$

That one element may consist of a list of words:

$$\begin{array}{ccc} \text{Dogs, cats, and hunters}/ & \text{chase}/ & \text{birds.} \\ \text{S} & \text{V} & \text{C} \end{array}$$

Or a single subject may include many descriptive words:

My frisky little dog Spot/ chases/ birds.
S   V   C

• *Form:* Names of persons, places, or things are the usual subjects of sentences. The words that do this naming are called nouns. Frequently, nouns can be recognized because they follow the words *the, a,* or *an.* Just as an amber traffic light warns that a red light will soon follow, these words signal that a noun will soon appear. It was your lifelong familiarity with this system of verbal signals that enabled you to assume that a subject was present in the nonsense example

A gloop/ blaggles/ the dorps.
S   V   C

Nouns can be replaced by shorter words called pronouns: *I, you, he, she, it, we, they.* When one of these words stands in for a subject noun or nouns, then the pronoun is the subject.

They/ chase/ birds.
S   V   C

• *Function:* Whether it takes the form of a noun or a pronoun, the subject is responsible for the action expressed by the verb in a sentence. Because they are partners, subjects are very easily located once the verb has been identified. *Whoever* or *whatever* is responsible for the action of the verb is the subject. This connection can be expressed in a useful formula:

(who/what)? + verb = subject + verb

• *Example:*   Jane plays the trumpet in the school band.

You already know that the verb in this sentence is *plays.*
Plug it into the formula to find the subject.

(who/what)? + *plays* = *Jane* (subject) + *plays* (verb)

Practicing the Subject-Locating Program

You have already identified the verbs in the following sentences. Now using the formula (who/what)? + verb = subject + verb, name the subjects of these sentences.

1. Character develops slowly.

2. It ran over some broken glass.

3. Sam, Bill, and I were swimming all day.

4. All kinds of strange things happen.

Answers and Analysis

1. The subject is *character*. It answers the question "Who or what develops?"

2. The pronoun *it* is the subject. Remember that a subject may appear in many forms.

3. The subject is *Sam, Bill, and I*. Remember that a subject may consist of a list of words.

4. *All kinds of strange things* is the subject. Remember that many descriptive words may be attached to the subject.

When a Sentence Is Not a Sentence

A group of words containing both a subject and a verb can be transformed into something less than a sentence by the addition of a single word. In the nonsense-language experiment, you probably sensed that something was wrong with item 6: *Although she blaggles.* Translating the non-word *blaggles* into English while following the same sentence pattern would produce something like: *Although she wonders.*

This group of words contains a subject (*she*) and a verb (*wonders*), and yet it is not a complete sentence. The difference is the addition of the word *although* before the subject. This word signals that what follows is an incomplete idea, like a joke lacking a punch line. It is one of a class of words known as *subordinators* (abbreviated here as *Sub*). When attached to a sentence in front of the subject, they transform the subject-verb combination into an incomplete sentence. To the x-ray eye, the change look like this:

Complete sentence: She/ runs/ every day.
                                       S   V   C

Incomplete sentence: Because/ she/ runs/ every day.
                                             Sub   S   V   C

Subordinators signal the need for a completing idea.

- *Example:* Because/ she/ runs/ every day/ ,/she/ feels/ good.

          Sub   S   V   C   S   V   C

You use subordinators naturally in your speech. This list of commonly used subordinators will remind you of what they look like.

after	in case	when, whenever
although	now that	where, wherever
as	once	whether
because	since	while
before	unless	who, whoever
if	until	whose

The Complete Sentence Structure Program

You now have all the information you need to recognize correct sentence structure. Keep in mind that this ability is the basis of success on the CLAST and all other tests of your verbal skills. Here in its final form is a program that will sharpen your x-ray vision of sentence structure.

Step 1: Look for the action word (usually in the second position).

Step 2: Discard action words with *to* or *-ing* forms.

Step 3: Identify the verb.

Step 4: Ask (who/what)? + verb to find the subject.

Step 5: Discard SVC units introduced by a subordinator.

Step 6: Any word group that passes all five steps is a *complete sentence*.

Practicing the Complete Sentence Structure Program

Apply each step of the program to all of the following groups of words. Working slowly and carefully now will pay off in speed, accuracy, and confidence on the CLAST.

DIRECTIONS: Identify all word groups as complete or incomplete sentences.

1. While he was away from home at a medical conference.

2. A group of physicians at the next table speaking of serious matters.

3. The troubled doctors spoke quietly, always in control in spite of their anger.

4. Vowing to fight the problem called red tape.

5. Bureaucratic obstacles, senseless regulations, and endlessly rising insurance premiums.

Answers and Analysis

1. *Incomplete.* Although this contains a subject (*he*) and a verb (*was*), the subordinator (*while*) requires a completing idea.

2. *Incomplete.* The action word *speaking* is discarded because of its *-ing* form at step 2 of the program.

3. *Complete.* The subject (*The troubled doctors*) and the verb (*spoke*) add up to a complete sentence that passes all five steps of the program. Everything else in the sentence (*always in control,* etc.) does not change the basic SVC structure.

4. *Incomplete.* In spite of its three action words, this is not a correct sentence. Two of them (*vowing, to fight*) are discarded at step 2 because of their form. *Called* passes that step but does not get beyond step 4. The question (who/what) *called*? could possibly be answered with *the problem.* But though that is a possible answer, it is not a reasonable one, for *the problem* is not able to call. Verbs ending in *-ed* may often function as part of a subject rather than as a verb. The CLAST items will always make clear whether an *-ed* word can reasonably be identified as a verb. Far from trying to trick you, the CLAST designers make every effort to avoid even slightly confusing test questions.

5. *Incomplete.* As you probably saw at once, this group of words lacks a verb.

2: PUNCTUATION

The basic SVC unit communicates a single complete idea. Someone or something (SUBJECT) performs an action (VERB) in a certain way (COMPLEMENT). To communicate more than one idea, the basic SVC units can be strung together like beads, which is the pattern they usually follow in elementary readers:

Dick/ likes/ Jane. She/ prefers/ Spot.
S   V   C.   S   V   C.

Ideas in the real world, of course, are combined in more intricate patterns. Simple elements are joined according to specific rules to form complex new structures. This section will show how basic elements become larger structures with the aid of commas, semicolons, and colons.

Commas

No one with an x-ray eye for sentence structure suffers from comma phobia, that awful uncertainty about where those little marks belong. Your solid grounding in structure frees you from having to depend on the hope, for example, that your breathing will tell you when to insert a comma. Feeling a connection between breathing and punctuation can be useful when you write, expecially when you write expressively or creatively. That feeling, however, will not be of much use to you on objective grammar tests like the CLAST. Breathing is an unreliable guide to punctuation. Comma use is determined by structure.

Commas and the CLAST

The CLAST tests nine uses of the comma. Using the formulas introduced in section 1, this section will account for those nine uses with four general rules. These rules are specifically designed to improve your performance on the punctuation section of the CLAST. Because the Grammar Test does not deal with the optional uses or omissions of commas that are common in good writing, the rules in this section do not deal with them either. Here, as everywhere in this book, the instructions are streamlined in order to teach you everything you need to know to succeed on the CLAST without distracting you with information not useful on the test.

Rule 1: *Commas help to link basic SVC units.* The link is formed by combining a comma with one of seven connecting words known as conjunctions.

- *Formula:* $\text{SVC} + \text{comma} + \left\{\begin{array}{l} \text{and} \\ \text{but} \\ \text{for} \\ \text{or} \\ \text{nor} \\ \text{so} \\ \text{yet} \end{array}\right\} + \text{SVC.}$

- *Example:*   Dick likes Jane, but she prefers Spot.
                             S   V   C   S   V   C

Do not be tricked into thinking that a comma is correct just because it precedes a conjunction. A comma is correct only before a conjunction that is followed by an SVC unit.

- *Example:*   Dick likes Jane but hates Spot.
                             S   V   C   V   C

There is no comma before *but* because the words following that conjunction do not form an SVC unit. Note also that a comma is *not* correct *following* conjunctions that link SVC units.

Rule 2: *Commas link subordinate SVC units to basic SVC units.* When a subordinate SVC unit comes before a basic unit, a comma is necessary.

- *Formula:*   SubSVC + comma + SVC.

- *Example:* Although Dick likes Jane, she prefers Spot.
               Sub   S   V   C   S   V   C

No comma is necessary when the order of these units is reversed.

- *Example:*   Dick likes Jane although he hates Spot.
                          S   V   C   Sub   S   V   C

Rule 3: *Commas join additional information to the basic SVC unit.* Words or groups of words that are not SVC units may be attached with commas at any point in the SVC structure. This additional information (abbreviated here as *Add*) usually serves to explain, expand, or define the single idea communicated by the basic SVC unit.

- *Basic unit:* Susan/ became/ a famous novelist.
  $\qquad\qquad$ S $\qquad$ V $\qquad\qquad$ C

A comma is correct when it appears between added information and the subject of a basic SVC unit.

- *Formula:* $\qquad\qquad$ Add + comma + SVC.

- *Example:* Suprising everyone, Susan became a famous novelist.
  $\qquad\qquad\quad$ Add $\qquad\qquad$ S $\qquad$ V $\qquad\quad$ C

When additional information is inserted between the subject and the verb, *two* commas are required.

- *Formula:* $\qquad$ S + comma + Add + comma + VC.

- *Example:* Susan, who had done poorly in high school English,
  $\qquad\qquad\quad$ S $\qquad\qquad\qquad\qquad$ Add

  became a famous novelist.
  $\quad$ V $\qquad$ C

Two commas are also necessary when additional information is inserted between the verb and the complement.

- *Formula:* $\qquad$ SV + comma + Add + comma + C.

- *Example:* Susan became, her classmates were astonished to learn,
  $\qquad\qquad\quad$ S $\quad$ V $\qquad\qquad\qquad$ Add

  a famous novelist.
  $\quad$ C

Finally, information tacked on to the end of the SVC unit requires a single comma.

- *Formula:* $\qquad\qquad$ SVC + comma + Add.

- *Example:* Susan became a famous novelist, not an obscure poet.
  $\qquad\qquad\quad$ S $\quad$ V $\qquad$ C $\qquad\qquad$ Add

An understanding of sentence structure will guide you unerringly through the punctuation section of the CLAST. If you clearly see the basic skeleton of the SVC unit, you will also see where additional material has been attached to it. *Be sure you know what is basic and what is additional.* Do not forget that any element of the basic SVC unit may consist of more than one word, sometimes many more.

Example:

The woman wearing the ermine coat and driving the expensive car /
S

is / a famous novelist.
V   C

All the words from *The* to *car* make up the subject of this sentence. How can you tell? Return to the basics introduced in section 1:

Step 1: Identify the verb = *is*
Step 2: Ask the question "Who or what *is*? = *The woman . . . car*

In spite of its length, that string of words boils down to the S in a basic SVC unit. Like many students, you may often have trouble deciding whether words near the subject are part of that subject or are additional to it. On the CLAST, however, you can avoid making that decision by reading the test item carefully. If information is intended to be additional, the sentence will contain a comma either before or after the words in question.

Example: The woman, wearing the ermine coat and driving the expensive car   is a famous novelist.
A

Because the item includes a comma after *woman,* another comma is required after *car.* If the test item did not include the first comma, then the second comma would not be correct. These questions are designed to test your knowledge that additional information is set off from the basic SVC unit with two commas, not to force you to guess whether information is additional or part of the subject.

Rule 4: *Commas separate related elements.* Some commas are nothing more than partitions. Because they are simply common sense in action, these commas have probably never been a problem for you. They are required to prevent misreading of four types of sentences.

A: Commas separate items in a series.

• *Example:* Jane likes snakes, rats, and boys.

Remember that the "items" in any series may consist of several words.

• *Example:* The children's voices are as loud as thunder, as constant as rain, and as bright as sunshine.

B: Commas separate quotations from their source.

• *Examples:* Jimmy asked, "What did you say?"
"I asked you," the teacher replied, "to take that banana out of your ear."
"I still can't hear you," the boy whined.

C: Commas separate transitions from the basic SVC unit. Transitions are logical bridges between ideas. Here is a short list of some of the most commonly used transitions. Store them in your memory, for they will serve you well elsewhere on the CLAST.

after all	consequently	meanwhile
also	finally	moreover
as a result	for example	next
at the same time	in addition	on the contrary
besides	instead	therefore

• *Examples:* Finally, this discussion of commas is almost over.
There is, however, one more simple application to review.

D: Commas separate the elements of dates and addresses.

• *Example:* He used to live at 611 Cedar Street, Longboat Key, Florida. He moved on September 5, 1981, to Toronto, Ontario, Canada.

Commas: Yes or No?

Along with two other punctuation skills which we will review soon, the CLAST tests your skill with commas in two ways: you are required to know when necessary commas are missing and when unnecessary commas are present. For you, this task will be less complicated than it sounds. If the comma in question does not follow one of the four basic rules just discussed, then it is unnecessary and, therefore, wrong. If that comma does follow one of the four rules, then it is necessary and, therefore, right. If you see a blank space where one of the four rules calls for a comma, then that blank space is an error.

Format of the CLAST Punctuation Section

The CLAST punctuation items are presented as passages of one to three complete sentences. At four points along these sentences, you will see capital letters under punctuation marks or blank spaces. The letters A, B, C, and D will appear directly beneath correct punctuation, incorrect punctuation, and spaces where punctuation might belong. You will be required to mark the letter that identifies an error. A fifth option, marked by the letter E, states that the sentences contain no errors in punctuation.

Tips for Answering the CLAST Punctuation Questions

Your knowledge of structure saves time that will be valuable to you elsewhere on the CLAST. It sees punctuation as right or wrong rather than better or worse. That means you can stop reading each question as soon as you locate an error in it. *On the test paper* circle the capital letter identifying that error (or E if there is no error) and move on at once to the next question. Transcribe your answers on the answer sheet after you have completed all questions on the Grammar Test.

Practice with Comma Questions

Obviously, your ability to sail through the punctuation questions confidently, quickly, and correctly depends on how well you are absorbing the rules presented in this chapter. Practice with these three comma questions to see how you are doing so far. The directions introducing the questions are exactly the sort of instructions you will see on the CLAST; read them carefully now so they hold no surprises for you on CLAST day.

DIRECTIONS: The items below <u>may</u> contain errors in punctuation. <u>NO ITEM HAS MORE THAN ONE ERROR UNDERLINED.</u> Mark the letter which locates an error in punctuation. Mark <u>E</u> if there is no error.

1. Because robots often lack a human touch<u>,</u> scientists are
   A
   attempting to make them more like people. Some researchers<u>,</u>
   B
   for example, have designed a mechanical hand that can crack
   an egg<u>,</u> stir it into a pan, and scramble it perfectly. The robot
   C
   has not yet learned to make biscuits <u> </u> but it does brew excellent
   D
   coffee. <u>No error</u>
   E

2. "You can get more with a kind word and a gun<u>,</u> " Al Capone
   A
   once said, "than you can with a kind word alone." Admired
   by many for his sense of humor<u>,</u> the famous gangster<u>,</u> who has
   B   C
   been the subject of many movies, was one of America's first
   celebrities<u>,</u> and its most brutal killer. <u>No error</u>
   D   E

3. A very unusual fishing boat<u> </u> was sighted off Key West,
   A
   Florida<u>,</u> in 1925. It was crewed<u>,</u> witnesses claimed, by
   B   C
   lobsters<u>,</u> not people. <u>No error</u>
   D   E

Answers and Analysis

1. The answer is D.
   A follows rule 2.
   B follows rule 4(C).
   C follows rule 4(A).
   D violates rule 1.

2. The answer is D.
   A   follows rule 4(B).
   B   follows rule 3.
   C   follows rule 3.
   D: An unnecessary comma. It *appears* to follow rule 1, *but* the words following the conjunction *and* are not an SVC unit.

3. The answer is E.
   A: Don't be tricked by the space after *boat*. This is essentially an SVC unit with a long subject. If you still insist on using commas to indicate a breath, you will fall for this every time. Structure tells you no comma belongs here.
   B   follows rule 4(D).
   C   follows rule 3.
   D   follows rule 3.

If you made any errors here, review the rules for the comma uses that gave you trouble. You will have a chance to retest your comma skills after a brief look at the two remaining skills tested in the CLAST punctuation questions.

Semicolons

Most people manage to live very full lives without ever using a semicolon; however, the CLAST requires you to know how those marks behave. Remembering two simple rules will enable you to meet that requirement easily.

Rule 1: *A semicolon links two basic SVC units.* One semicolon, in other words, does the same job as a combination of a comma and a conjunction. (See comma rule 1.)

- *Formula:*   SVC + semicolon + SVC.

- *Example:*   Speech is natural; silence must be learned.

Linking semicolons of this sort frequently appear near transitions. (See comma rule 4[C].) The following pattern often turns up on verbal tests of all types, so keep it in mind.

- *Formula:*   SVC + semicolon + transition + comma + SVC.

- *Example:*   Pam studied for the test; as a result, she passed easily.

Rule 2: *Semicolons may replace commas that might create confusion.*

• *Example:*

The exam results included Pam, A; Sam, D; and Ham, C.

•*Semicolon tip:* To decide whether a semicolon is correct, x-ray the units it separates. Both must have similar structures. It helps to picture a semicolon as the fulcrum (midpoint) of a seesaw. The game works only when equal weight sits on both ends of the board:

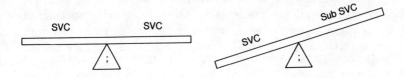

This image will help you see the incorrectness of a common test item which misuses a semicolon for a colon.

NOT: Jane likes three things; snakes, rats, and boys.
BUT: Jane likes three things: snakes, rats, and boys.

Colons

Like a drum roll before a circus act, a colon signals that something is about to happen. It introduces a list, as in the "Jane" sentence above, as well as quotations and explanations.

• *Examples:* Sam keeps muttering the same words: "I will study harder."
Friends worry about Sam: they fear he may be cracking up.

• *Colon tips:* Two common misuses of colons frequently appear on tests. You can avoid colon traps by remembering two DONTs:

1. Colons *do not* belong immediately after any form of the verb *to be.*

NOT: Three things Jane likes *are:* snakes, rats, and boys.

2. Colons *do not* belong after introductory words like *to, that, of,* or *such as*.

> NOT: The king urged his knights *to:* eat, drink, and be merry.
> NOT: The king had many virtues, *such as:* honesty, loyalty, and charity.

All these words are themselves signals that something is going to happen, thus making colons unnecessary.

Practice with Punctuation Questions

You will see up to three punctuation questions on the CLAST, each testing up to three punctuation skills. Test your competence at recognizing correct comma, semicolon, and colon placement with these three sample CLAST items. Circle your answers on the question page.

DIRECTIONS: The items below <u>may</u> contain errors in punctuation. <u>NO ITEM HAS MORE THAN ONE ERROR UNDERLINED</u>. Mark the letter which locates an error in punctuation. Mark <u>E</u> if there is no error.

1. Having already decreased their alcohol consumption , Americans
                                                     <u> </u>
                                                      A
   are now being warned of the dangers of even moderate
   drinking; according to a recent report. A study controlled for
            <u> </u>
             B
   diet , body weight, and blood pressure reached a suprising
        <u> </u>
         C
   conclusion : "Even one drink a day may lead to heart disease."
              <u> </u>
               D
   <u>No error</u>
       E

2. Laura finds her economics class demanding , for it introduces
                                              <u> </u>
                                               A
   many concepts that are new to her. She had never thought
   much about the stock market ; however, she is rapidly becoming
                               <u> </u>
                                B
   an expert on the subject. Her professor , a former stock-
                                           <u> </u>
                                            C

broker has made the course profitable for her in many ways.
     D

No error
  E

3. No nation has left as rich a heritage as has ancient Greece ,
                                                              A
many historians believe. Its people , though few in number,
                              B
added new dimensions to the human spirit ; their heroes
                                           C
and ideals have enlarged our own minds. They excelled at
whatever they attempted : politics, art, philosophy, and even
                           D

war. No error
       E

Answers and Analysis

1. The answer is B.
   A follows comma rule 3.
   B violates the "seesaw" rule. The words immediately before the
      semicolon are an SVC unit; the words after it are not.
   C follows comma rule 4(A).
   D: The colon correctly introduces a quotation.

2. The answer is D.
   A follows comma rule 1.
   B follows semicolon rule 1.
   C follows comma rule 3.
   D incorrectly omits the second comma required by rule 3.

3. The answer is E.
   A follows comma rule 3.
   B follows comma rule 3.
   C follows semicolon rule 1.
   D: The colon correctly introduces a list.

3: SENTENCE STRUCTURE ERRORS

Now that you know what basic sentences are made of and how punctuation links them together, you have all the skills and information necessary to identify the sentence structure errors presented by the CLAST. This section will explain how to recognize those errors.

Sentence Structure Errors and the CLAST

A minimum of four questions will test your ability to recognize three types of faulty sentences: fragments, comma splices, and fused (or run-on) sentences. You will not have to label incorrect sentences, but since those names appear on the test, you will feel more confident if you know what they mean.

Recognizing Sentence Fragments

As the name suggests, a fragment is a piece of a sentence. It pretends to be a sentence because it starts with a capital letter and ends with a period, but it lacks at least one of the essential elements of an SV unit. Groups of words punctuated as if they were sentences are fragments when:

1. They lack a verb.

• *Example:*   A group of physicians speaking of serious matters.

Remember that action words introduced by *to* or ending in *-ing* are not verbs.

2. They lack a subject.

• Example: For hours discussed the problems facing their profession.

Remember the subject-locating program: (who/what) ? + verb = subject + verb. In this fragment, the question "who *discussed?*" produces no reasonable answer.

3. They lack a completing idea after a subordinator.

• Example: While he was away from home at a medical conference.

Remember that subordinated units require a completing basic unit: SubSVC + comma + SVC.

Recognizing Comma Splices

Comma splices attempt to link complete SVC units without the required conjunction.

• *Example:*   The spirit is willing, the flesh is weak.

Remember comma rule 1: SVC + comma + *conj* + SVC.

Recognizing Fused Sentences

Sentences are said to be fused when neither a conjunction nor a comma links two SVC units.

• *Example:*   The spirit is willing the flesh is weak.

Format of the CLAST Sentence Structure Error Section

Each of the four questions in this section appears as a short passage made up of four apparent sentences. One of the sentences may contain an error discussed above. You will be required to identify any sentence structure errors that appear in the passage by marking a capital A, B, C, or D. Mark the letter E when a passage contains no error.

Tips for Answering the CLAST Sentence Structure Error Questions

On the CLAST, sentence structure is either right or wrong, and only one error can appear in each question. As soon as you find one of the three sentence structure errors, stop reading, circle the capital letter preceding the faulty sentence, and move on to the next question. Don't invent an error where you can't see one. *No error* is as likely to be the correct answer as any of the other four options in each passage.

Practice with Sentence Structure Error Questions

Use this practice to get to know the directions as well as the questions they introduce. When you see the actual exam, the words *fragment, comma splice,* and *fused (run-on) sentence* should tell you exactly what to look for.

DIRECTIONS: Each item below <u>may</u> contain an error in sentence construction: a fragment, a comma splice, or a fused (run-on) sentence. <u>NO ITEM HAS MORE THAN ONE ERROR</u>. Mark the letter which precedes the group of words containing the error. Mark <u>E</u> if there is no error.

1. <u>(A)</u> All living things adapt to dangers in the environment, each in its own way. <u>(B)</u> A fly moves out of the way of a flyswatter, and an octopus changes color when it feels threatened. <u>(C)</u> While staying alive during bad times, one-celled plants form a hard coat. <u>(D)</u> Living things don't live forever, however, each has a limited life span. <u>(E)</u> No error

2. <u>(A)</u> Just a few words in defense of the Muscovy duck. <u>(B)</u> The bird is an excellent flyer; even big old drakes can leap into the air and disappear at amazing speeds. <u>(C)</u> The Muscovy was domesticated, some experts say, by the Central Americans. <u>(D)</u> Because it does not fear humans, the Muscovy is often seen begging food in residential areas. <u>(E)</u> No error

3. <u>(A)</u> Bert Lee, a transplanted New Yorker, claims to make the best key lime pies in the world. <u>(B)</u> After sampling the tasty dessert in 1970, he developed his own recipe, which he says improves on the original Key West version. <u>(C)</u> At first, he sold a few pies each week from an old truck now customers flock to his huge bakery. <u>(D)</u> Sales increase daily. <u>(E)</u> No error

4. <u>(A)</u> A judge awarded a divorcing couple joint custody of their dog after setting out rules for the pet's care. <u>(B)</u> "I gave them the dog for six months each," the judge said, "my decision was as wise as Solomon's." <u>(C)</u> The decision ended a bitter dispute; both husband and wife accepted it gladly. <u>(D)</u> A pet frog died before the case was resolved, however, and an out-of-court settlement was worked out for a parakeet. <u>(E)</u> No error

Answers and Analysis

1. The answer is D.
   A follows comma rule 3.
   B follows comma rule 1.
   C follows comma rule 3.
   D is a comma splice. Don't confuse transitions (*however*), which are logical bridges between ideas, with conjunctions, which are structural links between SVC units. This is a comma splice you can depend on seeing, either on the CLAST or some other verbal test. If it tripped you up, review semicolon rule 1.

2. The answer is A.
   A is a fragment because it lacks a verb.
   B follows semicolon rule 1.
   C follows comma rule 3.
   D follows comma rule 2.

3. The answer is C.
   A follows comma rule 3.
   B follows comma rules 2 and 3.
   C is a fused, or run-on, sentence. The word *truck* ends one SVC unit; *now* begins the second.
   D by the way, is a complete sentence. Your ear might hear this as incomplete because it is so much shorter than the other sentences in the passage, but you should see its basic SVC structure. If you picked D as the error, review section 1.

4. The answer is B
   A follows comma rule 1.
   B is a comma splice. No matter what additional information is inserted between SVC units, a conjunction is still needed to link them. Like the error in 1(D), this is a favorite of test writers. When you see a quotation on a test, make sure it is not concealing a comma splice of this sort.
   C follows semicolon rule 1.
   D follows comma rule 1. Notice the conjunction (*and*) after the transition (*however*). Compare this correct link with the comma splice in 1(D).

4: EFFECTIVE SENTENCES

On one section of the CLAST, correct sentence structure is not enough. This section tests your ability to recognize sentences that are effective because they communicate ideas not only correctly, but also clearly and logically. The CLAST focuses on three aspects of structure that produce effective sentences. What follows will describe how those structures work and how to identify them.

Structure and Meaning on the CLAST

Just as a car is easier to steer when its wheels are aligned, a sentence is most likely to get where it is going—to the reader's understanding—when its form and content point in the same direction. At least nine questions on the CLAST test your ability to see this alignment of meaning and structure. To answer them confidently and correctly, you will need to understand how structure contributes to meaning when:

1. words or groups of words are added to basic SVC units;
2. basic SVC units are combined;
3. related words are combined in a list.

Adding Words to SVC Units (Modification)

The partnership between structure and meaning is easiest to see when sentences are expanded by the addition of a single word. That one word can change the meaning expressed by the basic SVC unit in many ways.

• *Example:*   Jane likes Spot. → *Only* Jane likes Spot.

The original sentence announces a girl's affection for a dog. That meaning changes when the word *only* is added, for the new sentence says that Spot has no admirers *other than* Jane. That much is obvious. What may be less obvious is that *where the added word is placed is as important as what it says.*

• *Example:*   Jane likes *only* Spot.

Shifting *only* from the beginning of the sentence to the slot between verb and complement creates an entirely new meaning: Jane likes no creature other than Spot. Moving the added word to the other side of the verb completely changes the original idea yet again.

• *Example:*   Jane *only* likes Spot.

Now the sentence tells us that the girl's feelings for the dog don't go beyond liking.

Each new placement of the added word changes the basic SVC unit's structure, thereby creating a new meaning. Changes in structure also produce changes in meaning when the additions are groups of words.

• *Example:*   The dog with the spotted coat likes the girl.

Placed next to the subject (*The dog*), the added words tell us something new about it. When placed next to the complement (*the girl*), they say something new about the girl, thus conveying an entirely new meaning.

• *Example:*   The dog likes the girl with the spotted coat.

A small change in structure has resulted in a big change in the idea expressed by the same basic SVC unit.

Because these added words change—or modify—the meaning of a sentence, they are called modifiers. They change meaning by altering structure. How their placement in the basic SVC unit changes its meaning can be expressed in a simple rule.

• *Modifier rule:* Modifiers change the meaning of the element closest to them in the SVC structure.

You have been seeing this rule in operation. In the last two examples, when the modifier (*with the spotted coat*) is closest to the subject, it tells us that the dog has a spotted coat; when it is closest to the complement, it tells us that it is the girl who has the spotted coat.

Modification Errors

Errors in modifier placement create errors in meaning. Now that your x-ray eye is tuned to see how modifiers affect the meaning of an SVC unit, such errors will be obvious to you. They may even provide some comic relief during the test, for misplaced modifiers often produce absurd statements.

• *Example:* Sitting alone in the playground, Dick's feelings were hurt.

The basic SVC unit in this example begins, as you can see, after the comma. Its subject is, as you know, *Dick's feelings*. Since the modifier changes the meaning of the closest element, which in this example is the subject, the complete sentence makes the ridiculous statement that Dick's feelings were sitting alone in the playground. Obviously, the sentence wants to say: "Sitting alone in the playground, Dick felt hurt." But what it wants to say is changed to nonsense by the effects of structure on meaning.

Practice with Modification Error Questions

DIRECTIONS: Choose the sentence that expresses the thought most clearly and effectively and that has no errors in structure.

1. A. Speaking from personal experience, the text for the computer course was adequate.

   B. Speaking from personal experience, I found the text for the computer course adequate.

   C. The text for the computer course, speaking from personal experience, was adequate.

2. A. Obviously too small, the wicked stepsister could not fit the glass slipper on her fat foot.

   B. The wicked stepsister could not fit the glass slipper on her obviously too small fat foot.

   C. Obviously too small, the glass slipper could not fit on the wicked stepsister's fat foot.

3. A. Short, stocky, and usually friendly, a pit bull's jaws can exert 1,800 pounds of pressure per square inch.

   B. Short, stocky, and usually friendly, a pit bull can exert 1,800 pounds of pressure per square inch with its jaws.

   C. Short, stocky, and usually friendly, with its jaws a pit bull can exert 1,800 pounds of pressure per square inch.

Answers and Analysis

1. The answer is **B**.
   A: Structure makes this say that the text is speaking.
   B correctly places the subject (*I*) closest to the modifier.
   C is not as silly as A, but still the text seems to be speaking.

2. The answer is **C**.
   A: Structure causes this to mean that the stepsister was too small; the rest of the sentence says otherwise.
   B: Here again structure contradicts logic. These questions will provide obvious clues to the thought that needs to be effectively expressed. In this case, a fat foot is not likely to be too small for a slipper of any kind.
   C correctly places the modifier (*Obviously too small*) next to the subject (*the glass slipper*) to which it logically belongs.

3. The answer is **B**.
   A: Structure makes the unlikely statement that the jaws are friendly.
   B: Of course it is the dog that is all the things listed in the modifier beginning this sentence. The structure here makes that clear and is therefore effective.
   C is not as obviously wrong as A, but still the structure here does not correctly place the modifier next to the words whose meaning it logically changes. Remember to select the *most effective* sentence.

Combining SVC Units (Subordination and Coordination)

As you saw in section 2, basic SVC units can be combined in a variety of structural patterns. Effective sentences are produced when the structure used to combine SVC units is aligned with their meaning.

Coordination, for example, is more than a technique for linking ideas. The structure described by comma rule 1 not only joins two ideas, but it also says something about their relationship. Structure has meaning, and the meaning of coordination is that the two ideas linked in this way are equally important.

• *Example:*   Jane was cruel, *yet* Dick still loved her.

Subordination, on the other hand, is a structural signal that two ideas are of unequal importance. Subordinators both show and tell how two ideas are related: the structure (see comma rule 2) shows an unequal relationship, and the meaning of each subordinator (*before, although,* and so on) tells what that relationship is.

• *Example:* *After* Jane grew bored with Spot, she looked for Dick.

OR: Dick was elated *when* Jane found him.

Still more information can be woven logically into a sentence when modifiers are added.

• *Example:* No longer alone, Dick was happy because Jane now loved him.

No matter how many ideas they contain, effective sentences are never confusing or awkward because their structure both organizes those ideas and highlights their meaning.

Effective Sentences and the CLAST

As a writer, you decide which of these structures will communicate your ideas most clearly and smoothly. *Remember to use them to do just that when you write the essay portion of the CLAST.* When you are taking the Grammar Test, however, all you can decide is whether structure and meaning are aligned in sentences written by somebody else. Don't waste time trying to do a writer's job when you are a test-taker. Trying to decide, for example, whether ideas are equal or unequal will only confuse you. Instead, look for sentences that combine two or more ideas correctly, logically, and clearly. The following sample CLAST questions will help you understand what is expected of you on the test.

Practice with Coordination and Subordination Questions

DIRECTIONS: Choose the sentence that expresses the thought most clearly and effectively and that has no errors in structure.

1. A. A free economy has obvious limits, and it produces greater wealth than a planned economy.

B. A free economy produces greater wealth than a planned economy; it has obvious limits.

C. Although it has obvious limits, a free economy produces greater wealth than a planned economy.

2. A. The sun sank below the horizon, and the sky turned green, and onlookers were amazed.

B. As the sun sank below the horizon, the sky turned green, which amazed onlookers.

C. Because the sun sank below the horizon, and the sky turned green, onlookers were amazed.

3. A. After carefully selecting a bat, Jim, who was the team's best hitter, walked confidently to home plate.

B. Jim was the team's best hitter who carefully selected a bat and walked confidently to home plate.

C. First Jim carefully selected a bat, and then walked confidently to home plate, and he was the team's best hitter.

Answers and Analysis

1. The answer is C.

   A is a good example of why to avoid weighing the importance of the ideas presented in these questions. The weakness here is not the use of coordinated structure, but the choice of *and* as the conjunction in that structure. The ideas imply a contrast between *obvious limits* and *greater wealth*. The conjunction *and* does not express that contrast effectively; *but* would make sense here.

   B is ineffective because the structure does not clearly state a relationship between the contrasted ideas.

   C is effective in making *limits* seem less important than *wealth*. A person who experienced more of a free economy's limits than its wealth would have arranged these ideas differently. Remember that you are choosing effective sentences, not statements that you entirely agree with.

2. The answer is B.

   A is ineffective because its repetition of *and* supplies only the barest connections between ideas. Excessive coordination is very often a sign of an incorrect option on verbal tests.

   B: The subordinators *as* and *which* effectively show the sequence of these events.

   C: This resembles B structurally, but the meaning of *because* does not make sense here. That subordinator belongs in front of the statement about the green sky.

3. The answer is A.

   A effectively describes both the sequence and meaning of these events. It states first what Jim did first. Then it explains who Jim is, which in turn explains why he walks confidently.

   B is less effective if only because it fails to describe the sequence of events.

   C is another example of excessive and unhelpful coordination.

Listing Related Words (Parallelism)

All soap boxes look alike. Even competing manufacturers put similar products in similar packages to let consumers know what type of product to expect. To let readers know what relationships to expect, effective sentences present similar ideas in words of similar form. Sentences containing lists of two or more related things or actions are effective when the words in the list, like soap boxes on a supermarket shelf, look like they belong together.

• *Examples:*	Spot likes eating, sleeping, and barking.
OR:	Spot likes to eat, sleep, and bark.
BUT NOT:	Spot likes to eat, sleep, and bark*ing*.

This method of listing related words is known as *parallelism* because structure, in this case the form of words, is aligned with, or parallel to, meaning.

Parallelism and the CLAST

If you are looking for them, nonparallel structures are as easy to notice as soup cans among soap boxes. Your ability to recognize inconsistent word forms in lists is tested on the CLAST by three questions scattered throughout the effective sentence structure section. The parallelism questions stand out because, naturally, they contain some sort of list. When they appear apart from other types of items, these questions are too obvious to be a useful test of your skills. The real trick is to see them when they are mixed in with the two other types of effective sentence questions.

Format of the CLAST Effective Sentence Section

At least nine questions, divided about equally among the three skills discussed in this section, test your ability to recognize effective sentences. Modification, subordination, and parallelism items are all combined in the same section, introduced by the same directions, and presented in the same form. Each question expresses the same general thought in three different sentences. One option in each question will be structurally correct and more effective than the other two options. Choose the most effective sentence by marking its identifying letter.

Tips for Answering the CLAST Effective Sentence Questions

Become familiar with the directions in this section. Because they appear nowhere else on the CLAST, they alert you to focus on three specific skills. Don't try to decide which skill each question is testing: often the modification and subordination items look very much alike, and the difference between these and the parallelism items will stand out without any special effort on your part. Read each question in this section carefully and completely, for here the incorrect options may differ only slightly from the correct one. Many "wrong" options will be structurally correct, so be prepared to choose the most effective expression of the idea offered by each question.

Practice with Effective Sentence Questions

DIRECTIONS: Choose the sentence that expresses the thought most clearly and effectively and that has no errors in structure.

1. A. Having only enough brain power to respond to their environment, scientists tell us that fish can't think.

   B. Having only enough brain power to respond to their environment, fish can't think, scientists tell us.

   C. Having enough brain power to respond to their environment, only fish can't think, scientists tell us.

2. A. A country gets a reputation for settling its internal disputes with rocks and bombs, and tourists and their money stay away.

   B. When a country gets a reputation for settling its internal disputes with rocks and bombs, tourists and their money stay away.

   C. Whenever tourists and their money stay away, a country gets a reputation for settling its internal disputes with rocks and bombs.

3. A. Lisa is friendly, efficient, and says witty things.

   B. Lisa is friendly, does her work efficiently, and is witty.

   C. Lisa is friendly, efficient, and witty.

4. A. Unless their spawning grounds are protected, Florida's fish will disappear.

   B. Florida's fish will disappear, so their spawning grounds must be protected.

   C. Florida's fish will disappear; therefore, their spawning grounds must be protected.

5. A. Many high-school graduates can't decide between going to college and whether to get a job.

   B. Many high-school graduates can't decide between a job and going to college.

   C. Many high-school graduates can't decide between going to college and getting a job.

6. A. Exhausted from driving all day, the search for a motel began for Sam.

   B. Exhausted from driving all day, Sam began to search for a motel.

   C. Sam began to search for a motel exhausted from driving all day.

7. A. The overworked waiter took orders, greeted guests, cleaned tables, and even dashed into the kitchen to help the cook.

   B. The overworked waiter took orders, greeted guests, cleaned tables, and even dashing into the kitchen to help the cook.

   C. The overworked waiter had to take orders, greeted guests, cleaning tables, and even dashing into the kitchen to help the cook.

8. A. Freshly painted, Kim thought her old car looked almost new.

   B. Kim almost thought that her freshly painted car looked new.

   C. Freshly painted, her old car looked almost new, Kim thought.

9. A. Tara, who needed a ride to school, called Sara, who is in her class, and who is her best friend.

   B. Tara, who needed a ride to school, called Sara, her best friend and classmate.

   C. Tara needed a ride to school, so she called Sara, for she is in her class, and Sara is her best friend.

Answers and Analysis

1. The answer is B (modification).
   A is typical of the absurdities a misplaced modifier can create. The structure makes this say that scientists have only enough brain power to respond to their environment.
   B correctly places the modifier closest to the subject that it logically applies to.
   C misplaces the single word modifier *only* to create an untrue statement. Many things besides fish can't think.

2. The answer is B (subordination).
   A: Even though the conjunction between SVC units is not entirely wrong, it gets lost among all the other *and*'s in this sentence.
   B immediately states the connection between the two ideas combined here; from the first word, the reader knows how to organize all the details that follow.
   C reverses the obvious logical sequence of events.

3. The answer is C (parallelism).
   A: The last item in this list is in a different form than the first two.
   B puts the inconsistent word form in the middle of the list.
   C expresses all three related ideas in similar form.

4. The answer is A (subordination).
   A effectively states the necessary cause-and-effect relationship between the two ideas.
   B indicates a relationship, but not as precisely as A.
   C also fails to be as specific as A.

5. The answer is C (parallelism).
   A: *going to* and *whether to get* express similar ideas in dissimilar forms.
   B: *a job* and *going to college* are not parallel.
   C: *going* and *getting* have the same form.

6. The answer is B (modification).
   A incorrectly applies the modifier to *the search* . . .
   B makes it clear that it was Sam who had been driving all day.
   C illogically says that the motel was exhausted.

7. The answer is A (parallelism).
   A correctly expresses all the items in similar word forms.
   B inconsistently switches to *dashing*.
   C is hard to read because it uses several word forms in the same list.

8. The answer is C (modification).
   A states that Kim was freshly painted.
   B says confusingly that she almost had a thought.
   C effectively says that the paint was on the car.

9. The answer is B (subordination).
   A is an example of excessive subordination; all those *who*'s are as confusing as too many *and*'s or *but*'s.
   B effectively combines subordination (*who needed*) with modification (*her best friend*) in a clear, crisp sentence.
   C confusingly strings ideas together with too many conjunctions.

5: USAGE

Like stop signs, many English words communicate through their form as well as their meaning. Verbs, for example, not only express an action, but they also signal—by means of their form—whether one or more people or things are performing that action.

- *Example:*   Spot *runs*. → Spot and Fifi *run*.

Such changes in form help readers to keep track of which actor is connected to which action. Other kinds of words change form in other ways to show how they fit into the meaning of a sentence. The rules that regulate all these changes in form are known as the rules of *usage*, for they signal how a word is being used in a sentence.

You employ many usage rules quite naturally. Even in your most casual conversation, you put them to work as threads that tie bits and pieces of language into a web of meaning. Some of these rules, however, come less naturally to you. As you might expect, verbal tests concentrate on these less "natural" aspects of usage. This section will briefly review standard English usage, concentrating on the unusual aspects of it that are likely to appear on the CLAST.

Format of the CLAST Usage Section

The bad news is that the CLAST tests seven "unnatural" aspects of usage, most of which involve several specific rules, with a minimum of fifteen questions. The good news is that—unlike all other sections of the test—these items present only two options for each question, one right and the other wrong. Even without improving your present usage skills, you might (with luck!) do fairly well on this section of the CLAST. But if you put some energy into learning what these instructions can teach you about usage, you will feel more confident and score much higher.

Subject-Verb Agreement

Usage requires verbs to change their form in order to indicate whether one or more actors are responsible for the actions they express. When this rule is followed, verbs are said *to agree with* their subjects. When you put together most sentences, you follow this rule without even thinking about it. However, three types of problems may arise for you.

Problem A: *Failing to identify the subject.*

• *Sample question:* The gleam in Fifi's eyes (excite, excites) Spot.
                                                    A   B

• *You may go wrong if* you mistake the word nearest the verb for the subject. When that word is plural (*eyes*), you may be tricked into using a plural verb form (*excite*).

• *Solution:* Use your x-ray eye to locate the actual subject. Remember that the subject is usually the first element in a sentence (*The gleam*). Remember also that a complete subject may consist of several words ("*The gleam* in Fifi's eyes"). The answer is B. When you are sure of the subject, the verb is obvious. If this solution is a problem in your mind, you need to review section 1.

Problem B: *Mistaking singular for plural subjects.*

• *Sample question:* Mathematics (are, is) Dick's favorite subject.
                                        A   B

• *You may go wrong if* you assume that all nouns ending in -*s* are plural or that all words that sound plural really are.

• *Solution:* Memorize this list of words frequently used as subjects in test questions. Some look plural, and others are used as plural in most *spoken* English, but all are really singular.

SINGULAR WORDS THAT LOOK PLURAL	SINGULAR WORDS THAT SOUND PLURAL
economics	anyone
electronics	each
mathematics	every
mumps	everybody
news	everyone
physics	neither
politics	

- *Examples:* Economics is easy for June, and physics is fun for

  Dick. Neither of these subjects is interesting to Sam,

  who believes that everyone is entitled to decide his or

  her own major.

The answer is B.

Problem C: *Confusion about* either/or *and* neither/nor.

- *Sample question:* Neither the dog nor the children
  (are, is) at home.
      A   B

- *You may go wrong if* you never learned the rules that apply here.

- *Solution:* Memorize these two rules.

1. Two singular subjects joined by *either/or* or *neither/nor* take a singular verb; two plural subjects joined in this way take a plural verb.

- *Examples:* Neither money nor praise *wins* their love. (singular)
  Either kisses or hugs *win* their love. (plural)

2. When one subject is singular and one is plural, the verb agrees with the nearer subject.

- *Examples:*   Either kisses or a hug *wins* their love.
  Neither a fortune nor praises *win* their love.

The answer is A. The plural subject is nearer the verb, so a plural verb is required.

Noun-Pronoun Agreement

Like verbs, pronouns also change form to signal how they are being used in a sentence. Pronouns indicate whether the nouns they are replacing are singular or plural.

- *Example:*   Dick lost *his* hat. → The boys lost *their* dog.

Pronouns also change form to indicate whether the nouns they replace are masculine, feminine, or neuter.

- *Example:*   Jane lost *her* coat. (feminine)
                     Dick lost *his* hat. (masculine)
                     The car lost *its* shine. (neuter)

When it replaces a noun, a pronoun must indicate through its form whether that noun was singular or plural *and* whether it was masculine, feminine, or neuter. When a pronoun does convey this information correctly, *the pronoun agrees with the noun.*

Noun-Pronoun Agreement Problems

Three types of pronoun agreement create problems for many students. The first two types will cause you no trouble because they resemble the subject-verb agreement problems that you have already mastered.

Problem A: *Mistaking singular for plural nouns.*

- *Sample question:* Everyone took (their, his or her) turn.
                                    A   B

- *Solution:* Review the list of words that look and sound plural. It will show you that *everyone* is singular and therefore requires a singular pronoun. In addition, since you don't know from the sentence whether *everyone* is male or female, current standard usage requires that both masculine *and* feminine forms of the singular pronoun be used here. The answer is B. Stay alert for this usage; you are bound to see it on one verbal test or another.

Problem B: *Confusion about* either/or *and* neither/nor.

- *Sample question:* Neither Dick nor his friends knocked before
                     (he or she, they) opened the door.
                              A   B

- *Solution:* Review the usage of *either/or* and *neither/nor* in the subject-verb agreement section. The same principle applies to noun-pronoun agreement. When a singular and a plural noun are combined by these structures, the last noun determines the form of the pronoun.

Since *friends* is plural, the pronoun must be plural. The answer is **B**.

Problem C: *Mistaking contractions for pronouns.*

• *Sample question:* Water seeks (it's, its) own level.
A   B

• *Solution:* Remember that *it's* is a shortened form of *it is* and that *its* is a pronoun meaning *belonging to it*. Remember also that *their* is a pronoun meaning *belonging to them* and that *they're* is a shortened form of *they are*. The answer is **B**.

Adjectives and Adverbs

Adjectives change the meaning of (modify) the words that name people, places, or things (nouns).

• *Example:* Dick is a *happy* boy becaue of Jane's *sudden* change.

Adverbs change the meaning of (modify) the words that express actions (verbs).

• *Example:*   Dick sings *happily* because Jane *suddenly* changed.

Problems with Adjectives and Adverbs

Adjectives and adverbs may create problems for you in two situations.

Problem A: *Adverbs are separated from the verbs they modify.*

• *Sample question:* Jane took Dick's marriage proposal
(serious, seriously).
A   B

• *Solution:* Correctly placed adjectives almost always look right to you: *serious* proposal; *happy* marriage; *good* grades. They look right because they are close to the nouns that they modify. Adverbs, however, may often appear to float in a sentence, not clearly attached to any word. If you are not certain whether a word is an adverb or an adjective, then it is probably an adverb. Adverbs usually end in *-ly*. So when in doubt about adverb/adjective usage, choose the word ending in *-ly*. The answer is **B**.

Problem B: *Making comparisons.*

• *Sample question:* Alaska was the (coldest, colder) of all the
                                                    A   B
                          states we visited.

• *Solution:* Remember that the form used to compare only two items is different from the form used to compare more than two items. Review this list if you are not sure of the differences between these two forms of comparison:

TWO ITEMS	MORE THAN TWO ITEMS
better	best
bigger	biggest
colder	coldest
less	least
more	most
taller	tallest
worse	worst

The answer is A because more than two items (*all the states*) are being compared.

Pronoun Form (Case)

Of all the aspects of usage tested by the CLAST, some pronoun uses are likely to be least "natural" to you. Pronouns change their form (or case) to indicate what role they are playing in a sentence. For example, pronouns used as subjects have a different form than pronouns that appear as part of a complement.

• *Example:* Dick kissed Jane. → He kissed her.
                                    S   V   C
              Jane kissed Dick. → She kissed him.
                                    S   V   C

Changes of this sort are natural in your speech, and so they present no problem. But some pronoun forms may be unfamiliar to you because they seldom appear outside of formal writing.

Problem A: *When to use* who *or* whom.

- *Rule: Whom* cannot be the subject of a verb.

- *Sample question:* Dick is the boy (who, whom) Jane likes.
$$\qquad\qquad\qquad\qquad\qquad\quad \text{A} \qquad \text{B}$$

- *Solution:* Decide if the pronoun in question is the subject of a verb.

       Step 1: Locate any verb that may apply to (*who, whom*) = *likes*

       Step 2: Identify the subject of that verb: Who or what *likes?* = *Jane*

       Step 3: If (*who, whom*) is used as a subject, then *who* is correct; If (*who, whom*) is *not* used as a subject, *whom* is correct.

The answer is B because (*who, whom*) is not used as a subject in this example.

- *Compare:* Dick is the boy (who, whom) likes Jane.
$$\qquad\qquad\qquad\qquad\qquad\quad \text{A} \qquad \text{B}$$

       Step 1: The verb nearest the pronouns in question is again *likes*.

       Step 2: In this example, the answer to "who or what *likes?*" = (*who, whom*). Therefore, the pronoun in question is being used as a subject.

The answer is A because *whom* cannot function as a subject.

Problem B: *When to use* I/me, *etc., in longer sentences.*

- *Rule: Me, her, him, us, them* cannot be subjects of verbs.

- *Sample question:* By June, all the students except Sam and
$$\qquad\qquad\qquad\qquad\qquad (\text{I, me}) \text{ had left town.}$$
$$\qquad\qquad\qquad\qquad\qquad \text{A} \quad \text{B}$$

- *Solution:* Decide if the pronoun in question is the subject of a verb.

       Step 1: Locate any verb that may apply to (*I, me*) = no verb The verb *had left* applies to the subject *all the students.*

       Step 2: If (*I, me*) is used as a subject, then *I* is correct; If (*I, me*) is *not* used as a subject, *me* is correct.

The answer is B because (*I, me*) is not the subject of a verb.

•*Compare:* Sam and (I , me) will go on vacation in July.
                    A   B

•*Solution:* The verb *will go* applies to (*I,me*). Therefore, (*I,me*) is a subject. The answer is A.

Verb Meanings and Forms

At least three questions in the usage section of the CLAST test your ability to recognize correct verb use. These questions present two types of problems.

Problem A: *Confusing the meaning of verbs.*

• *Sample question:* Jane likes to (lay, lie) on the beach.
                            A   B

• *Solution:* Memorize this list of frequently misused verbs.

VERB	MEANING	OFTEN MISUSED FOR	MEANING
to advise	to offer ideas	advice	a suggestion
to affect	to influence	to effect	to bring about
to compliment	to praise	complement	something that completes
to imply	to suggest	to infer	to deduce
to lay	to place	to lie	to recline
to lead	to guide	led	past tense of *lead*

The answer is B. Since the sentence clearly implies that Jane likes to recline on the beach, you can easily infer that the correct verb is *lie*.

Problem B: *Confusing standard and nonstandard verb forms.*

• *Sample question:* Dick (should have, should of) asked Jane
                                    A   B
                        to dance.

• *Solution:* Simply be aware that verbs made up of several words are often simplified when they are spoken. Do not confuse the forms of casual speech with those of standard written English. The answer is A.

Spelling

Two or more items will require you to choose between the correct and an incorrect spelling of the same word. Since you will be faced with only two options, guesses based on a vague memory of what the tested words usually look like in print may get you by. To increase your chances of success significantly, however, memorize the following list. These words turn up with amazing frequency on all types of verbal tests.

		WORDS FREQUENTLY MISSPELLED		
accommodate	cemetery	forty	prominent
acquaint	consistent	fourth	pursue
acquire	course	government	receive
address	coarse	independence	recommend
apparent	decision	irrelevant	repetition
appearance	defendant	license	rhythm
argument	definitely	loneliness	separate
athlete	disastrous	noticeable	succeed
beginning	embarrass	occurring	surprise
believe	environment	occurrence	thorough
benefit	exaggerate	possession	vicious
beneficial	existence	principal	weather
business	existent	principle	whether
category	fascinate	privilege	writing

Practice with Usage Questions

DIRECTIONS: Mark "A" if the first alternative within the parentheses is correct; mark "B" if the second alternative is correct.

1. Everybody in the English classes (take, takes) the same
                                           A   B

   final examination.

2. Spot was the (smallest, smaller) puppy in a large litter.
                       A   B

3. (She, Her) and her brother both attend the same college.
     A   B

4. Local lives are (effected, affected) by distant events.
                   A   B

5. Most nations strive for (independence, independance).
                           A   B

6. After the ceremony, everyone looked for (their, his or her)
                                    A   B
parents.

7. The team opened the season playing extremely (good, well)
                                       A   B
football.

8. Tara wanted Sara and (she, her) to go to the beach together.
                         A   B

9. Many students couldn't understand (their, they're) textbooks.
                                 A   B

10. Lisa played her part in the play (perfect, perfectly).
                            A   B

11. The rock star couldn't remember (whom, who) he had married.
                               A   B

12. Her parents had (lead, led) an exciting life together.
                 A   B

13. The band's drummer had amazing (rhythm, rythem).
                              A   B

14. Either the witnesses or the suspect (are, is) lying.
                           A B

15. Sam knew that he (could of, could have) passed the test.
                        A   B

Answers and Analysis

QUESTION	ANSWER	SKILL	WHAT TO LOOK FOR
1	B	subject-verb agreement	*Everybody* is singular
2	A	adjective/adverb	more than two items are compared
3	A	case	*She* is part of a subject
4	B	verbs	*affected* means *influenced*
5	A	spelling	review spelling list
6	B	pronouns	*everyone* is singular
7	A	adjective/adverb	*good* modifies the noun *football*
8	B	case	(*she, her*) is not used as a subject because *to go* is not a verb
9	A	pronouns	*they're* means *they are*
10	B	adjective/adverb	*perfectly* modifies the verb *played*
11	A	case	(*who, whom*) is not a subject
12	B	verbs	review verb list
13	A	spelling	review spelling list
14	B	subject-verb agreement	verb agrees with nearer subject
15	B	verbs	*could of* is nonstandard

Capitalization

Capitalization is an aspect of usage. Because it is tested in a different format than are the six other usage skills, it is being presented separately.

In standard written English, capital letters are signals of two types of information:

1. *Capitals signal the beginning of a sentence.* This is true also when the sentence is a quotation within another sentence.

- *Example:* The boy asked, "Where did I go wrong?"

2. *Capitals signal a distinction between specific and general people, places, and things.*

- *Examples:*

People: My instructor, Professor Fogbound, is an excellent
                             (specific)
        professor.
        (general)

Places: The South is any state south of   Ohio.
          (specific)   (general) (specific)

Things: My favorite sociology course is Sociology 2121.
              (general)   (specific)

- *You may go wrong if* you are misled by the examples of capitalization seen in nonstandard writing. Here are two common uses of capitals that would be errors in standard English. On the CLAST, capitals are not correct when they:

1. seek to grab attention. *Not:* Grunge soap is New and Improved!

2. attempt to express strong feelings. *Not:* My Mother is my dearest Friend.

Format of the CLAST Capitalization Questions

Most CLAST tests contain only one capitalization item. It is presented as a passage made up of one to three sentences which *may* contain one error in capitalization. Errors include the absence of required capitals as well as the presence of unnecessary capitals. The locations of possible errors are marked by the letters A, B, C, D. A fifth option, no error, is marked by E.

Practice with Capitalization Questions

DIRECTIONS: The item below <u>may</u> contain an error in capitalization. <u>THERE IS NOT MORE THAN ONE ERROR UNDERLINED.</u> Mark the letter which locates the error in capitalization. Mark <u>E</u> if there is no error.

During his <u>Thanksgiving</u> vacation, Jim said to his <u>father</u>,
      A   B

"<u>From</u> now on, I will do better in Spanish and <u>History</u>."
 C   D

<u>No error</u>
 E

Answer and Analysis

The answer is D.
A correctly capitalizes the name of a specific holiday.
B: The general term *father* is not capitalized. As part of a specific person's title, it would be *My priest, Father Connelly*.
C correctly capitalizes the initial letter of a quoted sentence.
D: *History,* a general term, is incorrectly capitalized. As part of a specific course name (*History 2020*) it would be capitalized.

6: WORD CHOICE

The CLAST tests your ability to recognize effective word choice with a minimum of six questions. Two types of questions appear in this section of the test. One type requires you to identify expressions that convey information effectively in the fewest words. The other, more challenging, questions ask you to choose the most effective words for a given context.

The first word skill—recognizing wordiness—is essentially a logical one. On the other hand, knowing which is the best word for a particular context requires more memory than logic. A good vocabulary, which is what the word choice items test, is the result of thousands of hours of attentive reading. This section will not attempt to add much to your memory bank of words. It will, however, show you how to make the best use of what you already know and how to use your preparation time most efficiently.

Recognizing Wordiness

Although you might never guess it from listening to the speech of many politicians and other "experts," language is most effective when it gets to the point quickly. The following list gives ten widely used overstuffed expressions and their more streamlined equivalents. Studying it will prepare you for the wordiness items you will see on the CLAST.

WORDY	EFFECTIVE
at this point in time	now
by means of	by
due to the fact that	because
has the ability to write	can write
in a helpful manner	helpfully
in order to	to
in this day and age	now/today
located in the vicinity of	near
of the opinion that	think/believe
very unique	unique

Format of the CLAST Wordiness Questions

The wordiness items are short sentences from which one or more words have been omitted. Under each sentence appear four words or groups of words, one of which most effectively completes the thought expressed by the sentence. The choice that most effectively completes these sentences is both correct and brief.

- *Sample question:* Home at last, Sam was happy to _____ his house.
  - A. enter into
  - B. make an entry into
  - C. enter
  - D. proceed ahead into

- *Solution:* Wordy options are, as you see, longer than effective ones. When the shortest option is not obviously wrong for the sentence it completes, it will almost always be the correct answer to a wordiness question.

The answer is C.
A: *enter* means *to go in,* so this gives the same information twice.
B needs four words to accomplish the work of one.
C makes sense in the context and is short.
D: *proceed* means *to go ahead;* incorrect options typically repeat ideas needlessly.

Recognizing Effective Word Choice

Effectively chosen words communicate on two levels at the same time. They *state exactly* as they *suggest appropriately.*

1. Exact Statements

The meaning of many words may be unclear to you even if you have been an active reader. Confusion often surrounds words that look or sound like other words with different meanings. Here are some examples of such frequently confused words that often appear on verbal tests.

WORD	MEANING	FREQUENTLY CONFUSED WITH	MEANING
allusion	indirect reference	illusion	false impression
conscience	sense of right/wrong	conscious	awake; aware
formally	in established form	formerly	in the past
moral	ethical; story's message	morale	confidence level
notable	worthy of notice	notorious	unfavorably and widely known
personal	belonging to a person	personnel	group of workers

• *Example:* Sam bought a new (vice, vise) for his workshop.
                                    A   B

• *Solution:* Although these words sound alike, they have very different meanings.

A is an immoral habit;
B is a tool used to hold objects being worked on.

Since the incomplete sentence refers to a workshop, the meaning required by the context must be *vise.* (If the relation between meaning and context is not clear to you, see the "Tips" below.)

2. *Appropriate Suggestions*

Even words that have similar meanings often suggest different attitudes or feelings—the quality of words that enables writers to make unspoken judgments about the events they describe. *Example:* I am *assertive,* you are *aggressive,* and he is *pushy.* Those three words are very close in meaning: *to put oneself forward insistently.* But notice how the suggestions of each become slightly more insulting as the act of *putting oneself forward* moves from *I* to *he. Remember to choose your words for their suggestions as well as their meaning when you write the CLAST essay.*

When taking the Grammar Test, you will be evaluating, not choosing, the suggestions of words. To decide whether the words presented to you are appropriate, make sure that they fit the context you are given.

• *Example:* Sir Gawain challenged his noble adversary to a
    (duel, brawl).
    A   B

• *Solution:* Both these words describe a kind of fight. But *duel* suggests rules whereas *brawl* suggests lawlessness. Since the context refers to noble knights behaving honorably, the word suggesting polite bloodshed is more appropriate.

Format of the CLAST Word Choice Questions

Presented under the same directions, the wordiness and effective word choice questions have a similar format. Short sentences from which a word or words have been omitted provide the context. The effective word choice items differ in one important respect: they provide only *three* options to choose from. One of these will usually be a word with a *meaning* that does not fit the context; another option will carry inappropriate *suggestions* even when its meaning fits the context.

• *Sample question:* Sir Gawain challenged his noble adversary to a
    _____.

    A. brawl
    B. dual
    C. duel

The answer (of course) is C.

A carries inappropriate suggestions.

B looks and sounds like the correct answer but has a different meaning.

Tips for Answering the CLAST Word Choice Questions

Notice first the number of options in each question. *A list of four possible answers identifies a wordiness item; three options signal an effective word choice question.* When answering a four-option question, choose the shortest reasonable answer.

Three-option questions require more attention. Read them carefully, looking for the clues offered by the phrasing of the incomplete sentence. Those clues—like the reference to noble knights in the example above—should tell you what kind of suggestions will be appropriate to the context.

If those clues don't help you very much, then you need to sharpen your sense of how words suggest attitudes. If you do that with the reading section of this book (Part III), you can double the benefits of your preparation time. Study the passages that the reading questions are based on. As you read carefully, ask yourself why the professional authors of these passages chose the words they did. Keep a list of any unfamiliar words: work out their suggestions from the context in which you find them and look up their meanings in a dictionary. In addition to increasing and sharpening your vocabulary for the Grammar and Essay Tests, this review will also improve your reading skills.

Practice with Word Choice Questions

DIRECTIONS: Complete the sentence by choosing the most effective word or phrase which conforms to standard written English.

1. Because they have such great _____ for each other, Jack and Jill are considering marriage.
   A. affectation
   B. love
   C. endearment

2. The advertiser offered _____ to the first fifty callers.
   A. an absolutely free gift
   B. a free gift
   C. a gift
   D. a completely free gift

3. The mayor promised fair treatment for all citizens during her _____ of office.
   A. reign
   B. term
   C. rein

4. Jim _____ that dogs make better pets than cats.
   A. personally feels
   B. is of the opinion
   C. has the belief
   D. believes

5. The morning fog slowly began to _____ the beachfront town.
   A. envelope
   B. wrap
   C. envelop

6. The new car _____ 8,000 miles without an oil change.
   A. can travel
   B. is capable of traveling
   C. has the capacity to travel
   D. can continue on for

Answers and Analysis

1. The answer is B (word choice).
   A sounds like *affection,* which might fit here, but actually means *false appearance.*
   B means *a feeling of warm personal attachment,* which fits here.
   C is "a *statement* of affection," not the feeling itself.

2. The answer is C (wordiness).
   A gift means *something given,* so everything except C is wordy.

3. The answer is B (word choice).

   A: Queens, not elected officials, *reign.*
   B is a *specified period of time,* which is how long a mayor serves.
   C sounds like A, but means *a leather strap.*

4. The answer is D (wordiness).
   Everything other than D says the same thing in too many words.

5. The answer is C (word choice).
   A looks like the correct answer but means *a flat paper container.*
   B describes a similar action, but one that is done to *enclose and tie* an object.
   C means *to surround entirely,* which is what the context suggests the fog is doing.

6. The answer is A (wordiness).
   A says what B and C say but in fewer words.
   D: *continue* means *to go on,* so this repeats itself.

ANSWER SHEET FOR GRAMMAR POST-TEST
(Remove This Sheet and Use It to Mark Your Answers)

1 A B C D E	11 A B C D E	21 A B C D E	31 A B C D E
2 A B C D E	12 A B C D E	22 A B C D E	32 A B C D E
3 A B C D E	13 A B C D E	23 A B C D E	33 A B C D E
4 A B C D E	14 A B C D E	24 A B C D E	34 A B C D E
5 A B C D E	15 A B C D E	25 A B C D E	35 A B C D E
6 A B C D E	16 A B C D E	26 A B C D E	36 A B C D E
7 A B C D E	17 A B C D E	27 A B C D E	37 A B C D E
8 A B C D E	18 A B C D E	28 A B C D E	
9 A B C D E	19 A B C D E	29 A B C D E	
10 A B C D E	20 A B C D E	30 A B C D E	

GRAMMAR POST-TEST

Suggested Time: 20 Minutes
37 Questions

I. DIRECTIONS: Complete each sentence by choosing the most effective word or phrase which conforms to standard written English.

1. Too excited to sleep, they talked until _____.
   A. the clock struck two in the morning
   B. two A.M. in the morning
   C. two o'clock in the early hours of the next dawn
   D. two A.M.

2. The children were so _____ that most people thought they were twins.
   A. a like
   B. alike
   C. exact

3. He was happy to begin the flight, but after ten hours in the air, _____ diminished.
   A. Dave's excitement
   B. the excitement of Dave
   C. the excitement Dave had
   D. Dave's excitement slacked off and

4. She enjoyed the story and was inspired by its _____.
   A. moral
   B. parable
   C. morale

5. Although she was healthy, the child was _____ for her age.
   A. small in size
   B. of small dimension
   C. small
   D. minute in stature

6. His good study habits enabled him to pass the _____ with an excellent grade.
   A. class   B. course   C. coarse

II. **DIRECTIONS:** Choose the sentence that expresses the thought most clearly and effectively and that has no errors in structure.

7. A. The part that he bought for his car nearly cost eighty dollars.

   B. The part that he bought for his car cost nearly eighty dollars.

   C. The part that he bought for his car cost eighty dollars nearly.

8. A. The child learned to crawl and lift his head, and his parents began to enjoy him.

   B. Although the child learned to crawl and lift his head, his parents began to enjoy him.

   C. After the child learned to crawl and lift his head, his parents began to enjoy him.

9. A. During the term, she learned to write clearly, correctly, and expressively.

   B. During the term, she learned to write with clarity, correctly, and expressively.

   C. During the term, she learned to write clearly, in a correct way, and expressively.

10. A. The college students' cars were driving up and down Main Street hanging their heads out the windows and singing.

    B. Driving in their cars, the college students were hanging their heads out the windows and singing up and down Main Street.

    C. The college students were hanging their heads out their car windows and singing as they drove up and down Main Street.

11. A. Some students believe that homework is more a punishment than helpful.

   B. Some students believe that homework is more a punishment than a help.

   C. Some students believe that homework punishes more than it is a help.

12. A. A girl approached the stage, and she was carrying roses, and she gave them to the singer.

   B. A girl carrying roses approached the stage, so she gave them to the singer.

   C. A girl approached the stage carrying roses that she gave to the singer.

13. A. The actor was tall and muscular, had long hair, and was about thirty-five.

   B. The actor was tall and muscular with long hair and about thirty-five.

   C. The actor was tall and muscular, who wore long hair, and was about thirty-five.

14. A. Torn and smelling of mothballs, Susan helped her mother mend and wash the old blankets.

   B. Susan helped her mother mend and wash the old blankets, which were torn and smelled of mothballs.

   C. Susan helped her mother mend and wash the old torn blankets smelling of mothballs.

15. A. Jeff and Steve have similar physical characteristics, and they also have similar personalities.

   B. Jeff and Steve, who have physical characteristics that are similar, also have personalities that are similar.

   C. Jeff and Steve have similar physical characteristics, but they also have similar personalities.

III. DIRECTIONS: Each item below <u>may</u> contain an error in sentence construction: a fragment, a comma splice, or a fused (run-on) sentence. <u>NO ITEM HAS MORE THAN ONE ERROR.</u> Mark the letter which precedes the group of words containing the error. Mark <u>E</u> if there is no error.

16. <u>(A)</u> After high school, many young adults continue their education at a community college or university. <u>(B)</u> This is a difficult transition for some. <u>(C)</u> When they first walk on an unfamiliar campus, the new students are nervous, their hearts flutter and pound. <u>(D)</u> Soon, however, they feel at home in the new setting, and they begin to enjoy higher education. <u>(E)</u> No error

17. <u>(A)</u> The most beautiful feline in the world. <u>(B)</u> Dana is part domestic cat and part bobcat. <u>(C)</u> Her fur is multicolored, with spots of orange, white, and grey. <u>(D)</u> Also, she has the wild cat's black-tipped ears and short tail. <u>(E)</u> No error

18. <u>(A)</u> Terry joined her new ship, the *U.S.S. Dupar,* in Mayport, Florida. <u>(B)</u> Her first night on board was a long one, for she was unable to sleep in the narrow bunk that had been assigned to her. <u>(C)</u> Even worse was her first day at sea; it was rough and stormy. <u>(D)</u> Still, the voyage was interesting she met many new people and learned about life aboard a ship. <u>(E)</u> No error

19. <u>(A)</u> The east entrance of the Student Center is a place of many moods. <u>(B)</u> When it is quiet, it is a peaceful refuge, a setting for many relaxing activities. <u>(C)</u> For example, students reading and thinking in silence. <u>(D)</u> It can also be very busy when it is filled with clusters of friends discussing the day's events. <u>(E)</u> No error

IV. DIRECTIONS: Mark "A" if the first alternative within the parentheses is correct; mark "B" if the second alternative is correct.

20. After the dance lesson, the instructor had the students (lay, lie) on the floor to rest.
     A   B

21. How (do, does) your doctor's charges compare with the
     A   B
average fee in your area?

22. The boy remembered how distinguished his father was
    and how (impressively, impressive) he spoke.
                    A   B

23. Mary always wondered whether John (would have, would of)
                                          A   B
    married her if she had proposed to him.

24. The stain is large, but in the candlelight it is hardly
    (noticable, noticeable).
      A   B

25. The sight of new shoes, freshly ironed clothes, and
    tear-stained faces always (remind, reminds) Mary of her
                                  A   B
    first day of school.

26. The childless couple decided to (adopt, adapt) a baby.
                                        A   B

27. The ham was delicious last week, but it doesn't taste very
    (good, well) now.
      A   B

28. Everyone in the crowded theater stumbled about looking for
    (their, his or her) seat.
       A   B

29. Todd rarely meets anyone who is as tall as (he, him).
                                                  A   B

30. The sun (omits, emits) its most dangerous rays between
              A   B
    10 A.M. and 2 P.M.

31. Neither John nor Sam remembered to bring a towel for
    (himself, themselves).
        A   B

32. Paula always enjoyed the story of the kitten that lost
    (it's its) mittens.
      A   B

33. He won the prize, but it was (her, she) who did the work.
                                    A   B

34. Of the two sisters, Lisa has the (better, best) grades.
                                         A   B

V. DIRECTIONS: The items below <u>may</u> contain errors in punctuation. <u>NO ITEM HAS MORE THAN ONE ERROR UNDERLINED.</u> Mark the letter which locates an error in punctuation. Mark <u>E</u> if there is no error.

35. Smiling shyly<u>,</u> Anne accepted the gift from Buddy<u>,</u> who sat
    A   B
    at the desk next to hers. The happy girl<u>,</u> was almost too
    C
    excited to see what the box contained<u>:</u> a small ring.
    D
    <u>No error</u>
    E

36. The motor we had just tuned started at once<u>;</u> vibrating and
    A
    roaring. Mike said<u>,</u> "That's music to my ears." But before
    B
    he had even finished speaking<u>,</u> the motor sputtered<u> </u> and
    C   D
    stopped. <u>No error</u>
    E

VI. DIRECTIONS: The item below <u>may</u> contain an error in capitalization. <u>THERE IS NOT MORE THAN ONE ERROR UNDERLINED.</u> Mark the letter which locates the error in capitalization. Mark <u>E</u> if there is no error.

37. Jane spoke to her advisor, <u>Professor</u> Marx. Helping her
    A
    decide on her program for the following term, the <u>professor</u>
    B
    suggested that <u>English</u> literature would be illuminated by a
    C
    sociology course. <u>No error</u>
    D   E

GRAMMAR POST-TEST ANSWERS, ANALYSIS, AND REVIEW GUIDE

ANSWERS AND ANALYSIS

QUESTION	ANSWER	ANALYSIS	REMINDER
1	D	wordiness	*A.M.* means *morning*.
2	B	word choice	Read these questions closely because small details, such as the space between *a* and *like* in choice A, are important.
3	A	wordiness	In four-option word choice questions, the shortest answer is usually correct.
4	A	word choice	See the word list in section 6.
5	C	wordiness	See reminder 3 above.
6	B	word choice	*Class* means *a group*.
7	B	modification	Choice A could mean that he didn't buy the part at all.
8	C	subordination	Choice C effectively emphasizes the cause-effect relationship.
9	A	parallelism	All items in choice A have the same *-ly* form.
10	C	modification	In choice B, *up and down Main Street* sounds like a song title.
11	B	parallelism	Both items are in the same form: (*a* + noun).

QUESTION	ANSWER	ANALYSIS	REMINDER
12	C	subordination	The string of *and*'s in choice A is the mark of an incorrect answer; the *so* in B is illogical.
13	A	parallelism	The related characteristics are presented in parallel verbs.
14	B	modification	Choice B makes it clear that the *blankets* were torn and smelled.
15	A	coordination	Choice A makes both ideas equally important; B is awkward; C's *but* requires a contrast.
16	C	sentence errors	The *nervous, their* is a comma splice.
17	A	sentence errors	Lacking a verb, choice A is a fragment.
18	D	sentence errors	The *interesting she* creates a fused sentence.
19	C	sentence errors	Choice C is a fragment: *-ing* words are not verbs.
20	B	verb form	See the verb list in section 5.
21	A	subject-verb agreement	The plural subject *doctor's charges* requires *do*.
22	A	adverb	The word *impressively* modifies *spoke*.
23	A	verb form	Don't confuse casual speech with written English.
24	B	spelling	Review the spelling list in section 5.

QUESTION	ANSWER	ANALYSIS	REMINDER
25	B	subject-verb agreement	The singular subject *The sight* requires *reminds*.
26	A	verb form	*Adapt* means to *adjust*.
27	A	adjective	The term *well* says that the ham was doing the tasting.
28	B	noun-pronoun agreement	*Everyone* is singular.
29	A	case	*He* is the subject of *is*.
30	B	verb form	*Omits* means *leaves out*.
31	A	noun-pronoun agreement	See the *neither/nor* rule in section 5.
32	B	case	*It's* means *it is*.
33	B	case	*She* is the subject of *did*.
34	A	adjective	See the comparison list in section 5.
35	C	punctuation	Choice C is an unnecessary comma.
36	A	punctuation	The semicolon is misused.
37	E	capitalization	Academic subjects are capitalized only when they name a specific course.

SCORE: _____ (number of correct answers)
TIME: _____

REVIEW GUIDE

IF YOU MISSED QUESTIONS	REVIEW SECTIONS
1–6	6 (p. 76)
7–15	4 (p. 52)
16–19	1, 2, 3 (pp. 27, 37, 48)
20–34	1, 5 (pp. 27, 63)
35–36	1, 2 (pp. 27, 37)
37	5 (p. 63)

Part III: Preparing for the CLAST Reading Test
(Reading Subtest, English Language Skills Test)

FORMAT OF THE CLAST READING TEST

Approximately 44 Questions
Suggested Time: 60 Minutes
(Combined Time for Grammar and Reading Subtests: 80 Minutes)

Approximately 3 or 4 Questions for Each of the Following Question Types

Literal Comprehension	*Critical Comprehension*
central idea	author's purpose
details	organizational pattern
word meaning	fact/opinion
	bias
	tone
	relationship within sentence
	relationship between sentences
	valid/invalid
	conclusion

PREPARING FOR THE CLAST READING TEST

INTRODUCTION

The reading section of the CLAST tests twelve specific reading abilities. The forty-four questions in this Reading Subtest are generally divided so that each of the twelve abilities is tested with four questions scattered randomly through the test. Twelve of the questions will test literal comprehension, and the other thirty-two will test critical comprehension. These terms are explained below. The Reading Test contains a series of readings of varying lengths, but each under 500 words, followed by questions you are expected to answer or incomplete statements you are expected to complete correctly. Each question is a multiple-choice question with either two or four answer choices.

Passages

The reading passages on which the questions are based are quite varied in terms of content difficulty and readability. The passages will be

1. quoted or paraphrased from subject-area texts (for example, science, art, social studies, humanities, business, literature, music, physical education, economics); or
2. quoted or paraphrased from newspapers, magazines, or public documents; or
3. written by the test developer.

CLAST developers tell us that the reading level of the passages is equivalent to that of a standard college-level textbook. Unfortunately, the "standard" college-level textbook doesn't exist. What we all know from experience is that some "standard" college texts are easy reading, while others are hard reading. You should not expect, however, any passages which have a technical vocabulary or require any specialized knowledge. In short, expect variety in the passages and treat them accordingly—that is, hurry through the easy reading, move slowly through the tough passages, and pay close attention to both.

97

What the Reading Test Tests

Fortunately, the twelve reading competencies tested by the Florida CLAST exam are very specific, making it fairly easy to study for this subtest of the exam. You will be expected to demonstrate your ability in two broad areas: *literal comprehension* and *critical comprehension.*

Literal Comprehension

Literal comprehension refers to the ability to identify ideas and facts that are *directly* stated in a reading passage. Literal comprehension skills are generally considered to be the easiest reading skills to master because questions of literal comprehension refer to words, facts, and ideas which are usually clearly stated on the page. These questions do not require that you do much evaluating—just locating—and involve information that you can locate, underline, or identify in the reading passage if necessary. Literal comprehension skills require that you simply remember and understand what the author actually said.

Critical Comprehension

Critical comprehension refers to the ability to identify an author's inferences, implied meanings, relationships, tone, and method of argument. Critical comprehension also involves the ability to actively and creatively question, comparing and evaluating what may not be stated specifically. While literal comprehension questions test what is written "in the lines" of a passage, critical comprehension questions test what is written "between the lines." On the CLAST (and most reading tests), critical comprehension questions are usually more difficult than literal comprehension questions.

Of the forty-four questions on the CLAST Reading Test, approximately 25% test for literal comprehension abilities and 75% test for critical comprehension abilities. The twelve specific literal and critical comprehension skills you will need to master (if you haven't already) in order to pass the CLAST are clearly identified here. In this section, you will learn not only what skills are tested but also how you can become *proficient* at each of them.

Literal Comprehension Skills

Literal comprehension skills are divided into three areas. You will be expected to:

1. Recognize the main idea/ideas in a passage
2. Identify supporting details
3. Determine meanings of words on the basis of context clues

Critical Comprehension Skills

Critical comprehension skills are divided into nine areas. You will be expected to:

1. Recognize the author's purpose
2. Identify the author's overall organizational pattern
3. Distinguish between statements of fact and statements of opinion
4. Detect bias in the passage or by the author
5. Recognize the author's tone
6. Recognize explicit and implicit relationships *within* sentences
7. Recognize explicit and implicit relationships *between* sentences
8. Recognize valid/invalid arguments
9. Draw logical inferences and conclusions

These are the twelve skills you must master in order to score well on the CLAST Reading Test. The forty-four question Reading Pre-Test which you will take shortly is designed to simulate the questions and the conditions of the real CLAST and to help you identify skill areas in which you need to improve. You will then be able to concentrate on explanations of those skills and practice them in this book until you feel comfortable that you know how to correctly answer similar questions on the CLAST. A word of advice: be certain that you study all twelve of the skill explanations, not just the explanations for the skills you may have had difficulty with on the Pre-Test. Practice in a strong skill area can often positively affect your competence on a weak one.

GENERAL READING SKILLS ADVICE

There are several techniques that will help you score well on the CLAST Reading Test. Study them *before* you take the Reading Pre-Test and *before* you study the twelve specific reading skills. Make the following information a part of your plan to *master* what you read. The best students know and successfully use the following efficient reading techniques on all their reading, *including test passages,* without regard for specific content area. These general reading skills are equally applicable to everything they (and you) read. If you follow these tips as you use this book to prepare for the CLAST, you will find your reading skills improved not only on the CLAST but also in your day-to-day college studying and assignments.

Tip 1: Read with a Pencil in Your Hand—Always

When you take the CLAST, you will be required to use a number two pencil so that your answer sheet can be machine scored. That pencil should not be overlooked as a tool for increasing your reading speed and comprehension. Keep that pencil in your hand as you read the passages about which the questions are asked.

Tip 2: Pace Yourself as You Read

Rapid readers (and more important, *efficient* readers) know the value of pacing themselves as they read so that they increase not only their speed but also their concentration, and as a result, their comprehension. Pacing is simply creating a left-to-right movement with your finger (or pencil) across the page, along each line you are reading and from line to line. In reading improvement classes, expensive reading machines are often employed as pacers, but you can just as effectively use the pencil in your hand to accomplish the same thing. The pacing movement directs and "pulls" your eyes along each line at a steady speed (or *pace*). Your eyes will follow the motion at a faster than normal (but still comfortable and efficient) speed.

Pacing is really very simple, and perhaps you are already doing it. If not, try it now as you are reading this book. Simply hold the pencil in your hand as if you were getting ready to write, but instead of writing, use the pencil as a pointer when you read. Don't touch the paper with the pencil, but move the tip of the pencil along the line slightly ahead of your eyes. This steady left-to-right motion will have a tendency to steadily pull your eyes along the line in order to keep up with the moving pencil point. But remember, you aren't just moving your eyes; you are *reading*. So don't pace yourself faster than your ability to comprehend. If you are zipping along but you don't know what you're reading, you are going too fast. Slow down. Let your comprehension determine if you should speed up. When you reach the end of each line, simply flick the pencil point back to the beginning of the next line and start moving along the line again. This very quickly develops into a rhythmic pattern of reading that does a lot to eliminate the choppy, start-stop, backtrack pattern of reading that most of us have developed over the years. After a few weeks of practicing with a pacer while reading, many students *double* their reading speeds and still maintain normal comprehension.

You will find that if you begin reading with the pacing movement described here, in just a few hours of practice, your comprehension improves. That shouldn't be a surprise. Reading without a pacer is a mental process subject to many distractions. Reading with a pacer becomes a mental and *physical* process. When you are physically involved (pacing yourself) in your reading, you concentrate much more on what you are reading.

Tip 3: As You Read, Don't Underline—Mark the Margin

Now that you are pacing yourself with a pencil, you will find that you are in a wonderful position to mark the passage *as you read it.* Should you? Yes and No. Yes, you should get in the habit of marking everything as you read it. This is not only an aid to your comprehension *if done correctly* but also a help if you have to refer back to the passage later—and you will have to often on the CLAST or any other reading test you take. Don't be afraid to mark your test booklets or question sheets. They will not be used again, so feel free to mark them up. However, you should not *underline* as you read (as you may be doing right now) because it can be a hindrance to efficient reading, especially on a test which times your performance.

In high school you probably got in the habit of dragging a felt-tip pen along the lines as you read. Usually you read halfway through a sentence (you always had to read halfway through to get some idea of what the sentence was about), decided that it might be an important sentence, and stopped reading in order to underline what you just read. You interrupted your concentration on what you were reading to do something else, reducing your comprehension and retention. You may even have used a straightedge of some sort so that your underlining would look neat and straight. You ended up doing so much at the same time that you probably retained very little of what you read. When you finished, you had a passage with lots of ink on it, and you had little comprehension of what you had just read. In addition, with all that activity, it took you much longer to read the material than it needed to. *But there is a way to read faster and mark at the same time without losing comprehension.*

Don't underline while you are reading, but instead mark the whereabouts of important information in a passage by putting a mark or symbol in the *margin* at the end of the line where the information is located. This is easily done, especially since you are now pacing yourself with a moving hand which is holding a pencil. It requires very little effort, and no loss of reading comprehension, to simply dot or otherwise mark the margins as you read. You read faster, you don't ruin your comprehension, and later you can find important information at a glance.

Tip 4: Use a Symbol System for Marking Margins

Marking the margins of a passage as you read is a very good idea, but with just a little bit of effort, you can use an even better way to mark the margins, indicating specifically *what* is in the line opposite the mark: *use symbols that represent specific things.* After you identify what you generally are looking for in a reading selection, create a specific symbol for each thing and use that symbol as a mark in the margin. You will then be able to "read" the margins at a glance to find important information without searching haphazardly. This quick "read" is especially important when you are taking reading tests like the CLAST in which you often will need to refer back to the reading passage in order to answer a question.

To do well on the CLAST Reading Test, you need to know and use only eleven symbols. You may wish to create your own eleven marks or use the symbols shown below (ten margin marks and one interior mark). The twelve competencies tested by the CLAST will be discussed a little later in this book. For now, just associate (memorize) the symbols that go with the CLAST competencies.

MARGIN MARKS

Competency	Margin Mark
Literal Comprehension	
1. central idea	— (solid line)
2. details (may be many)	--- (broken line)
3. word meaning (circle unusual words)	○ (circle)
Critical Comprehension	
1. author's purpose ("the goal is," etc.)	* (asterisk)
2. organizational pattern (cause/effect, etc.)	P (the letter *P*)
3. fact/opinion (note only opinion)	O (the letter *O*)
4. bias (when obvious)	B (the letter *B*)
5. tone (words that indicate attitude)	T (the letter *T*)
6. relationship *within* sentences	( ) (parentheses)
7. relationship *between* sentences	+ (plus sign)
8. valid/invalid argument (note only invalid)	^ (inverted *V*)
9. logical inference (if inferred, it is not written, so no mark)	

After you have memorized these margin marks and have related each one to the competency being tested, start using this system. NOW. While you are reading this book, make certain that you read with a pencil in your hand, pace yourself, and start marking the margins with the symbols you've learned. All eleven of these symbols can be employed on what you are reading now, and the more you use your new system, the easier it gets. You will soon be able to mark a passage without consciously thinking about each symbol. It's a valuable skill to have, especially when you are racing the clock taking the CLAST. Later, as you better understand the twelve reading competencies and how to spot them, margin marking can be quickly employed on the CLAST Reading Test.

The following marked passage shows how some of these margin marks may be employed.

One important way to build comprehension is to *question* P✱
before reading. You must always be conscious of comprehension
as you read, and this can best be accomplished by reading with a
questioning mind. You've been in situations in which you've
been asked to read specific pages in preparation for a class. And
you did the reading. But in class, when you were questioned on +
the contents of those pages, it may have seemed that you didn't +
know much. Has this happened to you? Sure.

But how different it was those times that the teacher asked
you to read specific pages and also indicated what it was that you
should look for: "Discover the route that Marco Polo took on his
journey." "What were the major cities he visited?" "What were
the bodies of water he had to cross?" And so on. What a
tremendous difference it made when you were questioned on the +
material. You knew three times as much as you ordinarily knew ○
after reading an assignment.

What was the difference? You were reading with a questioning mind. You were reading with a purpose, and not just
(passively) passing your eyes over pages. You must raise questions
about your reading material *before* you begin reading. What do
you want to get from your reading? What is the thesis or
problem in the passage? What is the sequence of ideas? By
raising questions like these before you read, you will recognize —
the answers when you come across them, and you will remember
them.

The reader/marker of this passage has indicated the location of
main ideas, author's purpose, an unusual word (to him or her),
opinion, and relationship clues. *Note: Use margin marks only for
information you'll need to answer the questions* (see Tip 5).

Tip 5: Be Test Wise

Following are standard practices that you should always employ
when you take the CLAST Reading Test.

• *First:* Check to see how much time you have remaining after
completing the Grammar Test. Then allot your time for each of the
forty-four reading questions so that you can tell if you are spending
too much time on any one passage or question.

• *Second:* Read the *questions* for each reading passage first *before* you read the passage. *Don't read the answer choices for each question;* the many options will only confuse you. By reading the four or five questions before you read the passage, you will *actively* read, looking for specific answers to questions rather than passively plodding through a passage in which everything seems to be of equal importance. When you read the questions first, your mind actively processes what you read—and you remember it longer. Add your new margin-marking skills to your active processing and you have a highly effective test-taking ability.

• *Third:* Skim, scan, and glance as you read the selections and answer the questions. If you have a reading selection of more than one paragraph, you should begin by skimming it.

To *skim* read the first sentence of each paragraph (often the first sentence is the topic sentence) in order to get the main idea of the passage. Skimming takes only a few seconds but is valuable as an overview of what you are about to read and often isolates the main idea (one of the things you are often asked), giving you a framework within which the details later can make sense. Such an overview also helps you read faster (because as you read, the passage seems familiar, and you naturally speed up). Too, by skimming, you can later locate information you need to recheck to answer a question without rereading the entire passage.

Scanning is also a very effective reading technique. Often the terms *skimming* and *scanning* are used interchangeably, but here they mean two different things. In skimming, you look for the main idea. In scanning, you look for a word (or number, or other detail) in a *methodical* way. In order to scan, you must know what you are looking for. In order to scan properly, move your pencil in a steady zigzag motion from the beginning of the paragraph down through the lines. At the same time, silently repeat to yourself the word or phrase you are looking for. This repetition will heighten your visual perception, and as you pass near the word, it will seem to jump out at you. You will be *passing* words (*not reading*) at very high speed. Several of the test questions will require that you scan the reading selections in this manner.

Glancing is a third skill that will be useful as you take the CLAST. Glancing involves flicking your eyes over a passage with no particular movement pattern in order to get an impression of the internal structure of the passage. Glancing is useful when you are asked to determine whether a passage is time ordered, cause and effect, or other organizational pattern. Often a glance will enable you to spot words such as *first, second, third* or *Monday, Wednesday, Friday,* organizational pattern indicators (in this case, indicators of time order).

• *Fourth:* Eliminate immediately from consideration any answer choices that appear to be unreasonable, irrelevant, or contradictory. Often the test questions include answer choices which are too extreme or give themselves away as being illogical or impossible. By removing them from consideration immediately (and crossing their letters off in your test book), your chances of success at picking the correct answer are greater. A guess between two choices stands a better chance of being correct than a guess among four choices. If you are left with two choices, you can approach them as true-false answers, asking, "In the light of the question, would this answer be true or false?" This approach often makes the correct answer clear. Note: Always make sure that you read *all* the answer choices before you pick the correct one, even if you feel strongly that the *first* answer you read is correct. You are looking for the *best* answer, not simply a possible answer.

• *Fifth:* Answer all the questions for each reading selection before you move on to the next reading selection. If you don't know the answer, don't waste time struggling with it. Take an educated guess and select one of the answers. At the same time, however, put a question mark in the margin next to the question. If you have extra time, you can easily spot it and come back to it. But be sure not to put the question mark on the machine-scored answer sheet. It could be counted as a wrong answer. Remember, you are not penalized for guessing, so answer all the questions.

How to Begin

Take the Reading Pre-Test that starts on page 111. Don't be concerned about time, but do note how long you take to complete the test. Use the answers immediately following the test to add up the number of questions you answered correctly. Record that number and your time on page 9.

When you check your answers, you will notice a Review Guide. This guide names the skill tested by each question and directs you to the section which teaches that skill. This analysis will identify the strengths and weaknesses you have now while it shows you where the help you need can be found in this book.

No matter how well you do on the Pre-Test, do not skip any of the following sections. Every page will give you many kinds of new information that will be valuable to you on the CLAST Reading Test.

Format of the Reading Tests in This Book

The following Pre-Test, as well as the two other complete Reading Tests in this book, are accurate simulations of the test you will see on CLAST day. They are not copies of previous tests because, unlike other testing agencies, Florida does not release actual test questions. The state does, however, provide exact descriptions of skills tested, sample questions, and the wording of directions used on the CLAST. Carefully following the state's specifications, the questions and format presented in this book are as close as possible to the real thing. Students who have recently taken the state test have been unable to tell the difference between Florida's CLAST and the tests in this book.

Treat the Pre-Test as if it were the real thing that it so closely resembles. Begin practicing the efficient strategies for reading that you have just learned.

READING PRE-TEST

Suggested Time: 60 Minutes
44 Questions

Passage 1

On the afternoon of May 18, 1983, three ten-year-old girls
on a class camping trip in a Connecticut state park acciden-
tally took a left turn instead of a right and became missing
children. The girls' parents spent a windy, wet night at a
5 state-police command post in the park, listening to searchers
radio back about their progress through the dense, rocky
terrain and imagining what they might find. It was easily the
worst night of their lives. Ambulances were waiting nearby
at dawn, and a hundred or more fresh volunteers were ready
10 to renew the search. Among this group was an ancient
bloodhound, red-eyed and loose-fleshed, who was called
Clem. The dog's handler, a state trooper named Andrew
Rebmann, slipped on its harness at the last place the girls
had been seen. The dog then sniffed at an article of clothing
15 one of the girls' parents had brought from home. "Find 'em,"
Rebmann said.

Clem worked silently, pulling hard on the lead when the
scent was strong, hesitating and casting from side to side
when it faded. After three miles, he dropped his nose on a
20 purple barrette. A mile farther down the trail, sniffing the air
now instead of the ground, the dog came to the edge of a
swamp. The searchers shouted and from across the swamp,
they got a reply. Rebmann followed the hound through
waist-deep water and on the other side, on high ground,
25 found the girls safe. Rescuers carried them out on their
shoulders to greet their parents, medical attendants, and
finally, the press. Back home again, the youngsters did the
right thing: they sent Clem a bone.

In the annals of the breed, it was an unextraordinary case.
30 The bloodhound, a large, doleful-looking creature bred specifically to recognize people by scent alone, has saved
countless missing children and adults as well, often where

111

large numbers of human searchers have failed. The bloodhound is not the most intelligent dog in the world or the
35 easiest to train. The German shepherd is better at sniffing
out certain kinds of objects—bombs, for example. The black
Labrador retriever excels at searches that call for sweeps
across a given area of land. But when it comes to following
the specific trail of a particular person, the bloodhound is in a
40 league by itself. "It'll work and work, in any kind of weather,
until it can't stand up anymore," says Jerry Newcomb, a Los
Angeles photographer and long-time bloodhound handler
who belongs to the California Rescue Dog Association. "A
bloodhound just won't quit on a trail."

1. The main idea in this passage is that
   A. Clem, the bloodhound, became a hero for finding the lost
      children.
   B. bloodhounds are not intelligent or easy to train.
   C. bloodhounds are in a league by themselves at following the
      specific trail of a particular person.
   D. different breeds of dogs excel at different kinds of searches.

2. The sentence beginning in line 40 ("It'll work and work . . .") is a
   statement of
   A. fact.
   B. opinion.

3. In line 29, the word <u>annals</u> means
   A. breeding record.
   B. medical record.
   C. local record.
   D. historical record.

4. The author uses the example of the barrette (line 20) to illustrate
   which of the following?
   A. Bloodhounds are good at finding lost items.
   B. The bloodhound was on the right track of the missing girls.
   C. Bloodhounds trail with their noses close to the ground.
   D. Bloodhounds need to have an item of clothing in order to
      track someone.

Passage 2

Under the July semiconductor pact, Tokyo agreed to abide
by so-called fair market values for microchips set by the U.S.
Department of Commerce. Japanese manufacturers could
not undercut those prices in the U.S. market without violat-
5 ing American antidumping laws. Tokyo also made a com-
mitment to prevent dumping by Japanese semiconductor
producers in other, so-called third-country (non-U.S. and
non-Japan) markets and to encourage Japanese companies
at home to buy more foreign-made chips, meaning, by and
10 large, those made in the U.S.

Yet almost as soon as the agreement was signed, the U.S.
began charging that it was being violated. The main culprits,
in Washington's view, were Japanese manufacturers who
continued to dump semiconductors, either directly or
15 through middlemen, in such Asian markets as Hong Kong,
Taiwan, and Singapore. Washington was as sure of that
activity "as I'm sitting here," declares Commerce Secretary
Malcolm Baldrige. In January the Reagan Administration
privately warned Japan that some kind of retaliation was
20 likely unless the practice stopped. Washington finally conducted an investigation and satisfied itself that dumping had
taken place. The Administration's preliminary finding is that
there has also been no increase in Japanese purchases of
foreign microchips.

• • • • • •

25   Much about the semiconductor pact is indeed question-
able in economic terms. Among other things, it raises the
costs of American manufacturers who use the devices to
build computers and other products, thus making them more
vulnerable to foreign competition. But to U.S. trade officials,
30 the evidence of alleged Japanese dumping and Japan's
refusal to open domestic semiconductor markets were the
last straw. For one thing, the ink on the semiconductor
agreement was barely dry before, in Washington's view, it
was being ignored. For another, that Japanese behavior
35 seemed to U.S. officials to be part of a familiar Japanese
attitude toward trade issues: delay followed by nominal
agreement followed by intransigence.

5. The author's primary purpose in writing this passage is to present
   A. an impartial account of U.S.-Japanese trade practices.
   B. a case in favor of Japanese trade practices.
   C. a case against Japanese trade practices.
   D. one viewpoint on the theory that Japanese trade practices are more advanced than those of the U.S.

6. How is sentence 3, beginning in line 5 ("Tokyo also made . . ."), related to sentence 4, beginning in line 11 ("Yet almost as soon . . .")?
   A. Sentence 4 contradicts sentence 3.
   B. Sentence 4 draws a conclusion from sentence 3.
   C. Sentence 4 gives a specific example of sentence 3.
   D. Sentence 4 presents a cause-effect relationship to sentence 3.

7. One conclusion that can be drawn from this passage is that the author
   A. questions the honesty of all Japanese.
   B. believes the U.S. has not violated any trade agreement with the Japanese.
   C. questions whether any future trade agreement can be entered into with the Japanese.
   D. believes the July semiconductor agreement is not being adhered to by some Japanese.

8. The author has created in this passage a tone that could be described as
   A. amused.
   B. objective.
   C. outraged.
   D. uneasy.

Passage 3

   I see trouble ahead. Big trouble. Because of the fall hemlines. They're going to be shorter. This has been decreed by Paris, France, and ratified by New York, N.Y. You will be receiving your formal notification via mail within the next
5 few weeks.
   I am worried because, inevitably, we're going to have

tragic cases wherein women who are not ideally suited for this fashion are going to wear it anyway. I'm talking about women who, although they have many other fine attributes,
10 do not happen to have great thighs, or even thighs that you could fit simultaneously onto a flatbed truck. Some such misguided soul will show up at a major social occasion encased in an 18-inch skirt that no doubt looked terrific on the anorexic model with great legs who wore it in the Vogue
15 advertisement, but which now looks like the tutu on Francine the Ballerina Rhinoceros.

And the horror of it is, NOBODY WILL TELL HER. Her friends will squeal large artificial squeals and examine her skirt as though it were the ceiling of the Sistine Chapel,
20 making remarks such as: "Marge! It's absolutely DARLING!" And Marge will waddle off, oblivious, to the buffet, while her "friends" race to the ladies' room to laugh until their makeup forms stalagmites on the floor.

It has already started to happen. I have just received a
25 report from New York, where a friend of mine named Kae observed what she describes as "a VERY large woman wearing a VERY short skirt."

"It was so bad," Kae reports, "that EVEN THE CONSTRUCTION WORKERS WERE LOOKING AWAY."
30 What this woman is, of course, is a Fashion Victim—a person who, in a desperate effort to be part of a Trend, makes a fool of herself. Or himself. Men can be fashion victims, too. Have you ever seen a man wandering around a party with his collar carefully turned up, apparently thinking he looks like
35 the sullenly handsome, brooding model staring out from those vaguely threatening Calvin Klein advertisements, when in fact he looks like some weenie who forgot to put his collar down? This man is a victim. So is the man who goes around with several days' growth of beard, thinking he is
40 reminding everybody of Don Johnson, although he is actually reminding everybody of Yasser Arafat.

9. In this passage, the author shows bias against
   A. advertisements.
   B. short skirts.
   C. construction workers.
   D. fashion trends.

10. For this passage, the author uses an organizational pattern known as
   A. simple listing.
   B. chronological.
   C. topical.
   D. generalization and example.

11. The author has created in this passage a tone that could be described as
   A. gentle.
   B. mocking.
   C. reverent.
   D. serious.

DIRECTIONS: The following passage has several words deleted. For each blank, choose the word or phrase which best completes the passage. Choices for each item are given below the passage.

Passage 4

Continual short-term use of nasal sprays can enlarge blood vessels in the nasal tissue and obstruct breathing, ___12___ people who use them over long periods of time risk becoming addicted, warns one otolaryngologist.

Although nasal sprays can temporarily reduce swollen nasal tissues, they do not treat the root cause of the swollen tissues. In the long-term, use can cause irreparable damage to the mucous membranes inside the nasal cavity, says Dr. Jeffrey Hausfeld, a clinical professor of otolaryngology at George Washington University Medical Center in Washington. ___13___, says Hausfeld, nasal spray junkies may need surgery to trim enlarged nasal tissue that resists shrinking with medication.

Rather than resort to the quick relief promised by a nasal spray, Hausfeld recommends that stuffed-up sufferers consult a physician to find out what is causing the congestion. It could be caused by a structural blockage, in which case a nasal spray is useless, or an allergic reaction. ___14___ nasal sprays can provide limited relief, he stresses that the sprays are merely palliative, not cures.

12. The missing word in space 12 is
    A. but.
    B. yet.
    C. and.
    D. however.

13. The missing word or phrase in space 13 is
    A. In fact.
    B. Yet.
    C. On the other hand.
    D. Similarly.

14. The missing word in space 14 is
    A. And.
    B. Although.
    C. Since.
    D. Because.

Passage 5

The United Nations must be a biased organization because each of its individual members is strongly biased.

15. Is the author's argument logically valid or invalid?
    A. valid
    B. invalid

DIRECTIONS: The following passage has words deleted. Choose the word which best completes the passage. The choices are given below the passage.

Passage 6

A psychiatrist who has studied women with eating disorders has found that those who obsessively pursue slenderness have more sexual problems than overweight women.

Examining 121 women with eating disorders who attended Loyola University of Chicago's Sexual Dysfunction Clinic over the past 15 years, Dr. Domeena Renshaw found that those with weight-loss disorders were so concerned with their bodies that they had little inclination or time for sex. These women also had fewer sexual fantasies and fewer dates, she says.

The vast majority of the women, 111 of the 121, had problems with obesity; ____16____, eight had bulimia, the binge-purge syndrome, and two had anorexia nervosa, a pathological fear of gaining weight that causes its victims to severely restrict their food intake.

Renshaw, who directs the clinic, found that obese women were much more likely than their thinness-obsessed counterparts to have accepted their bodies and were more likely to date and marry.

Obesity can contribute to sexual dysfunction too, she says, ____17____ the problem is more often the result of other conflicts, ____18____ losing a job.

16. The missing word or phrase in space 16 is
    A. consequently.
    B. usually.
    C. nevertheless.
    D. of the remainder.

17. The missing word or phrase in space 17 is
    A. but.
    B. such as.
    C. and.
    D. or.

18. The missing word or phrase in space 18 is
    A. but.
    B. such as.
    C. still.
    D. meanwhile.

Passage 7

Last summer the report of the Carnegie Forum on Education and the Economy contained a key recommendation for
the creation of a national board for professional teaching
standards. It was argued that the existence of such an
5 organization would enhance the teaching profession by

establishing high standards for teacher competence. The Carnegie Forum convened a 33-member planning group, which is currently developing the structure, governance, and financing of the national board. While no absolute deadline
10 exists, it is anticipated that the board would be chartered by the end of summer 1987—a remarkable accomplishment if it does happen.

Initially the board would have no power, only the potential to influence. Certification would be voluntary and would not
15 replace state licensure. However, many new and practicing teachers would be expected to seek a certificate because it would probably represent an unambiguous statement that its holder is a highly qualified teacher. Teacher preparation programs are expected to undergo revision to agree with the
20 newly established standards when they are announced. Over time states might either wave licensure requirements for those teachers possessing a board certificate, or, in what is a more probable scenario, they would incorporate the board's standards into their own licensing requirement. Also, the
25 board is expected to develop an ethics code for the profession and a system for disciplining those who violate it.

In a parallel effort, researchers at Stanford University are half-way through a project to assess school teachers. The assessment methods evolved would be used by the board as it
30 develops its certification system. The basic strategy of the development of the Stanford assessment methods first involves a delineation of the areas to be evaluated. Early efforts involve assessments on the teaching of basic subjects, for example, elementary school mathematics and secondary
35 school social studies. It now appears that the board will expect to assess teachers in a variety of ways over a period of years. One phase of the examination would require tests of knowledge and skill. A second would involve assessments of performance through "high-fidelity simulations" of class-
40 room activities. Another would involve documentation and attestation of a candidate's educational background and classroom performance.

19. Identify the statement below which gives the most accurate statement of the central idea of this passage.
   A. The Stanford University project to assess school teachers will be part of the national project for creation of a national board.
   B. Teacher preparation programs are expected to undergo revision.
   C. The national board will assess teachers in a variety of ways.
   D. The creation of a national board for professional teaching standards is expected to enhance the teaching profession by establishing high standards.

20. The example of the Stanford University project to assess school teachers was used to illustrate that
   A. prestigious universities back this Carnegie Forum project.
   B. work is currently being done to develop assessment methods.
   C. a lot of the work of the national board has already been done.
   D. the half-completed Stanford project now will be taken over by the national project.

21. In this context, the phrase "high-fidelity simulations" (line 39) means
   A. accurate reenactment of classroom activities.
   B. audio recordings of classroom activities.
   C. videotaping of classroom activities.
   D. documentation of classroom activities.

22. In the sentence "Last summer the report of the Carnegie Forum on Education and the Economy contained a key recommendation for the creation of a national board for professional teaching standards." the author indicates that his or her purpose is to
   A. describe an educational recommendation.
   B. state a problem in national education.
   C. define an educationally weak area.
   D. analyze the pros and cons of an educational recommendation.

23. In developing the passage, the organizational pattern used by the author could be described as
    A. summary.
    B. cause and effect.
    C. definition.
    D. time order.

24. The author's statement "It was argued that the existence of such an organization would enhance the teaching profession by establishing high standards for teacher competence." (lines 4–6) is a statement of
    A. fact.
    B. opinion.

25. Which of the following statements reveals a biased attitude expressed by the author in this passage?
    A. "Teacher preparation programs are expected to undergo revision . . ."
    B. "Initially the board would have no power, only the potential to influence."
    C. "Early efforts involve assessments on the teaching of basic subjects . . ."
    D. ". . . the board would be chartered by the end of summer 1987—a remarkable accomplishment if it does happen."

26. If the author were delivering this passage orally, his or her tone of voice would probably be
    A. amused.
    B. malicious.
    C. detached.
    D. excited.

27. From this passage you could conclude that the creation of a national board for professional teacher standards
    A. is a desirable goal.
    B. is an undesirable goal.
    C. will be easily accomplished.
    D. will gain immediate acceptance by all states.

DIRECTIONS: In the following sentence, a certain relationship between parts of the sentence can be identified. Read the sentence carefully; then choose the word or phrase which identifies the relationship between parts of the sentence.

Passage 8

Under Illinois law this episode fits the definition of insanity: the person did not know the difference between right and wrong.

28. What is the word or phrase which identifies the relationship between parts of the sentence?
    A. summary
    B. cause and effect
    C. comparison and/or contrast
    D. statement and clarification

Passage 9

Reagan is not to be blamed for the Iran/Contra scandal; other presidents have allowed worse scandals.

29. Is the author's argument logically valid or invalid?
    A. valid
    B. invalid

Passage 10

Are you one of the 15 million Americans who regularly skips lunch? If so, you're not doing yourself any favors, according to a recent report in *American Health.*

True, by going without lunch, you're preventing your body's natural tendency to slow down soon after a midday meal. But, getting through the rest of the afternoon may be tough because your energy supply's so low.

Dieters, especially, shouldn't go without lunch. "A common pattern among overweight women is to skip breakfast, eat a light lunch, and consume 80 percent of their calories in the evening," says obesity expert C. Wayne Callaway of George Washington University, Washington, D.C. "Such women have lower metabolic rates than people who eat three meals a day." Result: unwanted weight gain.

So, instead of skipping lunch, try eating a light, 300-calorie meal, such as a turkey sandwich, followed by a midafternoon snack of fruit or raw vegetables. These foods won't cause you to slump and are nutritious enough to fuel your body until dinner.

30. From this passage, you could conclude that eating lunch
    A. leads to weight loss.
    B. causes low metabolic rates.
    C. is important for getting through the day efficiently.
    D. will not lead to weight gain.

31. In developing the passage, the organizational pattern used by the author could be described as
    A. time order.
    B. contrast and comparison.
    C. definition.
    D. statement and clarification.

Passage 11

Peer pressure can be amazingly powerful. It can prompt teenage girls to get up before dawn to wash and style their hair and get their makeup just right—or at least so that they look like their friends. It can make good students ashamed of
5 their high grades. It can make kids demand the right to sexual freedom long before parents think they're ready, and can tempt kids to ignore warnings about drugs and alcohol. What's behind it all is the need to belong, which is most intense in the teen years.
10 There are actually two kinds of peer pressure. On the one hand, there is what could be called active peer pressure, which is the kind one child applies to another with promises of an immediate payoff if a deed is done—or taunts about being a scaredy-cat if it's not. Kids do this because they feel
15 more justified in their behavior if they can get friends to join in doing the forbidden.
On the other hand, passive peer pressure—which is the more powerful of the two—stems from the child's almost desperate need to fit in with his or her friends. No one wants
20 to feel left out or different.
But peer pressure isn't always a negative influence. I believe that it is an aspect of a child's normal rebelliousness

against parents, which is part of growing up. It is the driving
force that makes young people eventually want to strike out
25 on their own. Otherwise, they might remain indefinitely in a
state of childlike dependence on their parents. But we human
beings are belongers. We can't give up one form of dependence without replacing it with another. In fact, clinging to
one's peers is a sort of mental-health measure that keeps
30 young people from feeling lost.

How can parents maintain maximum influence over their
children during the rebellious years so that the children are
least likely to be thrown off course by peer pressures that are
harmful?
35   The first thing parents need to realize is that their
influence on their adolescent children does not come as a
result of vigilance over their activities or warnings or
threats—it comes from the children's own admiration of
their parents and a desire to be like them, which is deter-
40 mined way back in early childhood, particularly in the three-
to six-year-old period. From six or seven onward, children
don't think of their learned values as having come from their
parents; they think of those values as their own. So the most
effective method of influencing teenagers is through the
45 example parents set in their attitudes and manners.

32. Identify the statement below which gives the most accurate
statement of the central idea of this passage.
   A. Parents need to maintain maximum influence over their
   children during the rebellious years.
   B. Peer pressure and parental influence can both be constructive
   and destructive influences in children's lives.
   C. Peer pressure is a sort of mental-health measure that keeps
   young people from feeling lost.
   D. Most parents realize that their love for one another will be
   the strongest influence on their children.

33. The example of teenage girls getting up before dawn to wash and
style their hair was used to illustrate the
   A. foolishness of modern hair styles.
   B. amount of time it takes for teenage girls to get ready for
   school.
   C. amazing power of peer pressure.
   D. legitimate need for starting classes later in the morning.

34. In this context, the word <u>taunts</u> (line 13) means
    A. threats.
    B. mocking challenges.
    C. insinuations.
    D. laughter.

35. What is the relationship between the sentence beginning in line
    10 ("On the one hand . . .") and the sentence beginning in line 17
    ("On the other hand . . .")?
    A. cause and effect
    B. comparison and contrast
    C. statement and clarification
    D. generalization and example

Passage 12

    Dogcatchers, like police officers, must read people their
constitutional rights when questioning them about crimes,
the Iowa Court of Appeals has ruled, overturning the first-
degree robbery conviction of a Des Moines man.

5   The court said Monte L. Johnston should have been
warned of his right to remain silent as soon as he told an
animal control officer that he was severely bitten by a dog
after he held up a store.

    According to court documents, Johnston talked with the
10 dogcatcher at a hospital about the bite and revealed his role
in a robbery. The animal control officer did not warn him to
remain silent, asked further questions, and later testified
about the confession at a trial. Johnston was convicted of the
crime.

15   On appeal, he argued that the conviction was invalid
because he had not been advised of his rights, and the court
said the animal control officer was "allied" with "his fellow
peace officers" and his testimony about the confession was
inadmissable because he failed to follow legal procedures.

36. In the sentence "Dogcatchers, like police officers, must read
    people their constitutional rights when questioning them about
    crimes . . ." the author indicates that his or her purpose is to
    A. repeal a law.   B. analyze a problem.
    C. define a job role.   D. state a fact.

37. In developing the passage, the organizational pattern used by the author could be described as
   A. time order.
   B. summary.
   C. simple listing.
   D. clarification.

38. The author's statement "The animal control officer did not warn him to remain silent, asked further questions, and later testified about the confession at a trial." (lines 11–14) is a statement of
   A. fact.
   B. opinion.

Passage 13

An Alabama woman who seeks $25 million from a Roman Catholic priest and his superiors for injuries she allegedly received during his 1983 raid on an abortion clinic has won a default judgment because the priest refused to name a member of his parish with whom he discussed the raid in advance.

Madison County Circuit Judge S. A. Watson rejected the argument that traditions of clerical confidentiality prevented the Rev. Edward Markley from naming the person with whom he discussed the foray against the Women's Community Health Center in Huntsville. Markley was placed on court supervised probation for his role in that raid and one on a Birmingham abortion clinic. He is serving a five-year sentence for continuing to participate in antiabortion protests, in violation of the terms of his probation.

The priest is also the target of a lawsuit by Kathryn Wood, an employee of the Huntsville clinic at the time of the raid, who claims she has required daily pain medication and had nightmares since Markley allegedly charged into her during the raid. She also seeks damages from church officials she claims condoned his activity.

Watson said the amount Markley owes will be determined by a jury trial.

39. Which of the following statements most likely contains a biased attitude expressed in this passage?
   A. ". . . was placed on court supervised probation for his role . . ."
   B. ". . . she has required daily pain medication and has had nightmares . . ."
   C. "She also seeks damages from church officials she claims condoned his activity."
   D. ". . . has won a default judgment because the priest refused to name a member of his parish . . ."

40. If the author were delivering this passage orally, his or her tone of voice would probably be
   A. gentle.
   B. mocking.
   C. incredulous.
   D. detached.

Passage 14

Abraham Lincoln became a famous statesman and revered president because it was his destiny to do so.

41. Is the author's argument logically valid or invalid?
   A. valid
   B. invalid

Passage 15

People chart unknown and frightening territory when they experience a heart attack. As they recuperate, they rely on their physician's expertise to comfort and guide them. Surprisingly, however, patients seem to know more about how fully they'll recover than their physicians do.

To learn what health professionals might be missing, Israeli psychologist Dan Bar-On interviewed 89 first-time heart attack patients (all men) and their physicians. Just before their release from the hospital and six months later, Bar-On asked the patients and physicians why the attack occurred and what would aid the patient in coping with it. Patients also indicated what changes they planned to make in their lives.

Physicians and patients, Bar-On found, often gave different

Read sentence
some of the
physicians
were also
men

precipitating reasons for the heart attack and different "pre-scriptions" for recovery. Poor physical condition or habits, such as obesity or smoking, seemed the most likely cause to physi-cians, and they recommended relevant changes in the aftermath of the attack. Many of the men, on the other hand, attributed the attack to troubling circumstances in their lives, such as an undesirable position at work.

The patient's perspectives seemed to affect their recuperation. Those who thought that a combination of controllable and uncontrollable circumstances caused the attack made the greatest recovery. They agreed, for example, that they are "angry people" who experience a lot of "pressure at work." To help themselves get better, they planned to draw on their own strengths and the advice and support of others. Those least likely to return to work and other activities cited "fate" as the cause of the attack as well as the determinant of their chance for recovery. These people, for example, thought that being "un-lucky" might have led to the attack and being "lucky" would aid their rehabilitation.

Regardless of the amount of progress patients made, they were better at predicting how fully they would resume the life they had known prior to the attack than the physicians were. Bar-On attributes this to the physicians' limited view of the heart trouble in the first place.

Physicians were not even generally aware of the attitudes their patients had toward their illness, Bar-On says. Though he sympathizes with "the overload of information" physicians take in daily, he feels they still lack important knowledge. "Without taking patient outlook into account," Bar-On says, physicians will be "hampered in their ability to help their patients."

42. Identify the statement below which gives the most accurate statement of the central idea of this passage.
    A. Patients seem to know more about how fully they'll recover than their physicians do.
    B. Physicians and patients often give different precipitating reasons for a heart attack.
    C. Physicians and patients often have different "prescriptions" for recovery.
    D. Physicians were not even generally aware of the attitudes of their patients.

43. The example of "obesity or smoking" is used to illustrate
    A. what both patients and physicians consider "bad."
    B. that those who smoke and are overweight are considered high insurance risks.
    C. what physicians consider likely causes of heart attacks.
    D. what "lucky" people don't permit.

44. In this context, the word prescription (third paragraph) means
    A. an order from a physician to a pharmacist for medicine.
    B. a plan for getting better.
    C. a description of what ails you.
    D. a piece of paper with a medical signature.

READING PRE-TEST ANSWERS, ANALYSIS, AND REVIEW GUIDE

ANSWERS AND ANALYSIS

QUESTION	ANSWER	ANALYSIS	REMINDER
1	C	central idea	Since the first sentence didn't contain the thesis sentence, you were wise if you asked yourself the key questions "What is this about?" (bloodhounds) and "What is the main idea the author wants us to know about bloodhounds?" This questioning automatically eliminates A, B, and D.
2	B	fact/opinion	The probable exaggeration here should suggest to you that this is opinion.
3	D	word meaning	*Historical record* is the only choice that fits the context.
4	B	details	No other choice fits the meaning.
5	C	author's purpose	D is not mentioned in the passage, and B is not suggested. A is not a good choice as nothing is mentioned concerning *U.S.* trade practices.

QUESTION	ANSWER	ANALYSIS	REMINDER
6	A	relationship within sentence	*Yet* is a clue word that suggests an opposite is coming, choice A.
7	D	conclusion	Don't be tricked by A. The passage does not question the honesty of *all* Japanese but does question Japanese behavior concerning a specific semiconductor agreement and attitude toward trade issues.
8	B	tone	You can eliminate A and C immediately. Nothing in the passage suggests such extremes as amusement or outrage. C is not as extreme, but the tone here actually is very straightforward and objective.
9	D	bias	The entire passage suggests a negative reaction to fashion trends.
10	D	pattern	This passage starts with a general statement and then adds examples.
11	B	tone	The tone is quite caustic and derisive. The best answer is B.

QUESTION	ANSWER	ANALYSIS	REMINDER
12	C	relationship within sentence	Both the first part of the sentence and the second part are negative. The word *and* suggests this parallelism.
13	A	relationship between sentences	Again, two negative ideas are reasonably connected by the *In fact*. D is not the best choice because the *surgery* may be a *result* of *overuse* and cannot be said to be similar to it.
14	B	relationship between sentences	*Although* signals a contrast, *limited relief* as opposed to *cures*.
15	B	valid/invalid	Together these individually biased members may be unbiased.
16	D	relationship within sentence	The information following the blank involves 10 people, the *remainder* of the group.
17	A	relationship within sentence	The word *other* signals a contrast. *But* is the only choice that provides that contrast.

QUESTION	ANSWER	ANALYSIS	REMINDER
18	B	relationship within sentence	*Losing a job* is obviously meant to be an example of *other conflicts*. The phrase *such as* correctly introduces the example.
19	D	central idea	This choice summarizes the main point. The other choices are details concerning the standards to be established.
20	B	details	A quick rereading of the section mentioning Stanford reveals this as the correct choice.
21	A	word meaning	A simulation is a representation similar to actual performance.
22	A	author's purpose	B is incorrect because no problem is stated. C is incorrect because nothing is defined. No pros and cons are mentioned as given in D. The sentence is describing, choice A.
23	C	pattern	The passage defines the function of the proposed national board.

QUESTION	ANSWER	ANALYSIS	REMINDER
24	A	fact/opinion	If this statement started with *The existence of such an . . . ,* this would be an opinion. It is, however, a fact that *It was argued . . .*
25	D	bias	This is the only choice that has *any* bias, although mild.
26	C	tone	There is nothing in the passage to suggest the emotional tone of amusement, maliciousness, or excitement.
27	A	conclusion	The general impression of the board is of something desirable. The act of creating the board seems complex, not easy (choice C), and the state reactions are presented as possibilities only, not definite immediate acceptance (choice D).
28	D	relationship within sentence	The first part of the sentence is a statement, and the second part clarifies the *definition of insanity* mentioned in the first part.

QUESTION	ANSWER	ANALYSIS	REMINDER
29	B	valid/invalid	The two parts of the statement logically have nothing to do with one another.
30	C	conclusion	A and D *may* be true but are not necessarily true. *What* is eaten at lunch and other times will affect weight as well. B is not suggested by the passage; in fact, its opposite is implied.
31	D	pattern	The statement that skipping lunch may not be a good thing is clarified by the following paragraphs.
32	B	central idea	The passage states that peer pressure isn't *always* a negative influence and suggests that parental influence can help in preventing harm but could also be overly strong, resulting in *childlike dependence*. A and C are supporting details rather than the central idea. D may be true but is not mentioned.

QUESTION	ANSWER	ANALYSIS	REMINDER
33	C	details	This is specifically stated in the first paragraph as an example of the power of peer pressure.
34	B	word meaning	The clue word is *scaredy-cat*.
35	B	relationship between sentences	Clue words are *On the one hand* and *On the other hand*.
36	D	author's purpose	This is a simple statement of fact.
37	D	pattern	This is a fairly difficult judgment to make. There is some time order involved (although not strictly chronological), and there is some summary involved in that events related to this case are summarized. However, you should recognize that the *best* answer is *clarification* because the intention of the author is to clarify, explain, the ruling mentioned in the first sentence.
38	A	fact/opinion	This tells *what happened*. It can be verified.

QUESTION	ANSWER	ANALYSIS	REMINDER
39	C	bias	This is a claim that may or may not be provable and is likely to be based on emotion. The other choices offer specific, provable assertions.
40	D	tone	*Detached* is appropriate here. The passage is written in the manner of an objective news story.
41	B	valid/invalid	What Abraham Lincoln's destiny might have been is not a provable item; thus, an argument commenting on that destiny is invalid.
42	A	central idea	This is the thesis sentence. It is the last sentence in the first paragraph. The other choices are details that support the central idea.
43	C	details	The third paragraph states specifically how physicians view obesity and smoking.
44	B	word meaning	The quotation marks mean that the word isn't used in its usual sense.

SCORE: __34__ (number of correct answers)
TIME: __25__

REVIEW GUIDE

IF YOU MISSED QUESTIONS	REVIEW SECTIONS
	Literal Comprehension
1, 19, 32, 42	1. central idea (p. 139)
4, 20, 33, 43	2. details (p. 142)
3, 21, 34, 44	3. word meaning (p. 144)
	Critical Comprehension
5, 22, 36	1. author's purpose (p. 148)
10, 23, 31, 37	2. organizational pattern (p. 150)
2, 24, 38	3. fact/opinion (p. 153)
9, 25, 39	4. bias (p. 155)
8, 11, 26, 40	5. tone (p. 158)
12, 16, 17, 18, 28	6. relationship within sentence (p. 161)
6, 13, 14, 35	7. relationship between sentences (p. 162)
15, 29, 41	8. valid/invalid (p. 164)
7, 27, 30	9. conclusion (p. 168)

READING COMPETENCIES TESTED

The general reading skills discussed earlier will be of great help to you in all of your reading and test taking, but it is time now to focus on the twelve specific reading competencies that will be tested on the CLAST. Paying careful attention to the discussion of each of these competencies, and the illustrations and sample questions, will pay off in a higher test score.

LITERAL COMPREHENSION SKILLS

There are three literal comprehension skills tested.

1: RECOGNIZING THE CENTRAL IDEA (—)

There will probably be four questions on the exam that will ask you in some way to select the central, or main, idea of a reading passage. The questions may be stated in any of the following ways:

—Identify the statement below which gives the most accurate statement of the central idea of this passage (or paragraph _____).
—The main idea expressed in this passage (or paragraph _____) is
—the most accurate expression of the central, or controlling, idea of this passage (or paragraph _____) is

The key phrases to note in these question "stems" are *central idea, main idea,* and *controlling idea.* They all mean the same thing. You are expected to identify what the passage is about in a brief sentence or statement without being misled by supporting details or ideas. The main idea is simply the point the author is trying to get across to the reader. You may recognize the main idea in a number of ways:

• Frequently the *topic sentence* (often the first sentence of a paragraph) or the *thesis sentence* (the sentence that summarizes the content of the passage) contains the main idea. Is it summarized and offered as an answer choice? That's probably the correct answer.

• Write a mental headline as if to summarize the passage and the most important thing being said. Is your mental headline close to one of the answer choices? Chances are that that's the correct response.

139

• What idea is restated or reinforced in the passage? Check the final sentence. Does it summarize, restate, an (the) important point? Is that point one of the answer choices?

• Ask three key questions about the reading passage:
1. What is the subject of the selection?
   For example, you might conclude that the subject of a reading passage is *dogs*.
2. What is the purpose of discussing this subject (*dogs*)?
   You may determine that the author's purpose is to *describe* a specific kind of dog—*golden retriever*.
3. What is the main idea that the author wants you to know about this specific subject (*golden retrievers*)?
   "Golden retrievers are ideally suited as pets for families with small children." (the main idea)

At first, you may find that raising these three questions is cumbersome and time consuming—but only at first. Soon you will find that these three questions become second nature, and you will find yourself answering these questions *as you read*.

What To Look Out For

Often the answer choices given make the main idea more difficult to find. The following misleading answer choices are used to make things hard for you:

• A *misinterpretation* (often slight) of information in the passage such as of the main idea itself, of a supporting detail, or of an idea other than the main one.

• An *allusion* to the main idea, but *not* the main idea.

• An *allusion* to an idea in the passage which is expanded in the answer with information *not* in the passage.

• An *incomplete* statement of the main idea.

Read the two following passages and see how well you can answer the questions asking for the main idea. Remember to pace and margin mark as you read. The symbol for main ideas is a straight line (—).

Sample Passages and Questions: Central Idea

Humankind has known about tides and their relationship to the phases of the moon since the time of the ancient Egyptians. Tides, the periodic rise and fall of the waters of the earth, are highest at the new-moon and full-moon phases and lowest when the moon is in its first and last quarter. People in ancient times had no explanation for this mysterious connection between the phases of the moon and the tides. It is not hard to understand how astrology came into being. After all, if a phenomenon as impressive as the tides is somehow influenced by the position of the moon, it was an easy step for people to believe that events in their everyday lives could be influenced by the positions of the stars.

1. The main idea expressed in this passage is that
   A. the moon, and its effect on tides, has been observed for centuries.
   B. astrology is demonstrated by the moon/tide relationship.
   C. it was easy for astrology to come into being because of the moon/tide phenomenon.
   D. ancient peoples had no explanation for the tides.

Covering just about everything on the lunar surface is a layer of fine, powderlike soil or dust. In some places it is mixed with rocks and pebbles. It varies in depth from place to place, and when it is mixed with the rocky rubble, it can be as deep as 65 feet (19.5 m). The fine soil is actually the result of billions of years of meteorites hitting the lunar surface and breaking up the rocks. It is ground up, or pulverized, rock. The astronauts were not hampered by its presence on the surface, since they never sank more than a few inches into it. However, it did cling to their space suits as they moved about on the lunar surface.

2. The most accurate expression of the central, or controlling, idea of this passage is
   A. the astronauts were not hampered by the moon dust because they didn't sink in very far.
   B. the moon soil is the result of meteorite showers.
   C. lunar soil is made up of pulverized rock.
   D. the lunar surface is covered with a layer of fine, powderlike soil or dust.

Answers

1. (D) All of the other choices are true, but they are details. This is an example of the main idea's being located (and emphasized) in the last sentence of the passage.

2. (D) This passage begins with a topic sentence (the main idea), and the other sentences add detail to it.

2: IDENTIFYING SUPPORTING DETAILS (— — ⌣)

Supporting details are all those facts, secondary ideas, and illustrations which an author uses to develop and support the main idea or ideas. These details are necessary in order to explain thoroughly the idea the author is trying to get across. But there is no way to remember, or margin mark, all the details as you read. Therefore, you ought to identify only major details—those which support the main idea. The minor details may be interesting, but they don't change what the author is saying. The questions most frequently found on the CLAST which test for supporting details take the following forms:

—The example of _____ is used to illustrate
—All of the following are factors in (or causes of) _____ except
—The passage (or paragraph) compares (or contrasts)
—_____ is different from (or similar to) _____ in that
—The author quotes _____ to

The test question does not have to *quote* specifically from the passage read but may often be a restatement or paraphrase of a supporting detail. Don't be tricked into making the wrong choice because the question is a paraphrase of a portion of the reading selection and the correct response is also a paraphrase. Often, correctly answering a detail question is simply a matter of remembering what you read or of quickly referring to the reading passage to verify or eliminate an answer. Your margin marks will help you locate details quickly.

What To Look Out For

Selecting the correct answers when you have questions that ask you to identify supporting details is often complicated by three things:

• The detail, which in fact may be given in the reading passage, is not related to the question being asked.

• A closely related detail may be *known* by the reader but is *not* contained in the passage.

• In the case of a negatively stated stem (such as, "All of the following *except* . . ."), the correct response is the option which is *not* a supporting detail given in the passage. Often we get so anxious to answer the question quickly that we select the first answer that we see that we remember as being in the passage, forgetting that we are looking for an answer not mentioned.

Read the following passages and answer the questions. Remember, you're looking for detail, but it is good practice to also be aware of main ideas. Are you remembering to *read the questions first?* Are you pacing yourself with a pencil and marking the margins as you read? Remember, the margin mark that indicates important details is a broken line (— — —).

Sample Passages and Questions: Supporting Details

It is easy to describe acids in terms of what they do. Chemists have been familiar with the properties of these substances for many years. Among other things, they are sour and they corrode metals. For example, the acetic acid found in vinegar is responsible for the tart taste that imparts flavor to salads and other foods. It is easy to show that acetic acid corrodes metals. If you leave a steel knife immersed in vinegar, the knife will quickly corrode. The acetic acid in vinegar is only moderately strong, but at full strength the acid blisters the skin. Sulfuric acid is so corrosive that it is seriously damaging to the human skin. In some very weak acids, the properties of sourness and corrosion are hardly noticeable, and these substances may even be used in medicines. Thus acetylsalicylic acid (better known as aspirin) is a valuable drug, used to relieve pain. Boric acid is used in ointments and in eye washes.

1. The example of the steel knife in vinegar is used to illustrate
   A. one way to clean a corroded knife.
   B. one way not to clean a corroded knife.
   C. that acetic acid corrodes metal.
   D. that vinegar has several strong properties.

Whales are the largest creatures ever to inhabit the earth and are among the most powerful, the most intelligent, the most far-ranging, the most majestic. There are approximately eighty known species. Sizes range from 4 to 100 feet (1.2 to 30 meters) in length and 160 pounds (73 kilograms) to 150 tons (136 metric tons) of weight. Whales have always been respected, admired, revered, even by those who hunted them. Their irrevocable and indiscriminate slaughter, however, has been among modern humanity's most undignified activities and has, in our times, sparked whale protection movements around the world. In fact, few conservation issues have provoked as much public outrage and concern. The change in attitude, however, was a long time coming.

2. All of the following are descriptions of whales except that they
    A. are powerful.
    B. are intelligent.
    C. weigh 150 tons.
    D. communicate with each other.

Answers

1. (C) The example of the knife in vinegar follows the statement that "acetic acid corrodes metal" and is an illustration of that property.

2. (D) D is the only fact *not* mentioned, even though it is true.

3: DETERMINING WORD MEANING FROM CONTEXT (◯)

The last of the literal comprehension competencies tested is the one which demonstrates that you can determine the meaning of a word by noting context clues. Here you will be expected to identify the correct meaning of a specific word by recognizing and interpreting other words in the surrounding context. This really is a lot easier than it sounds because most authors realize that readers often have problems with word recognition and deliberately put in clues that will define or at least suggest the correct meaning of the word.

On the CLAST, questions that are designed to test your ability to determine word meaning from context are stated in the following ways:

—In this context, the word _____ (line ____) means
—As used in line ____, the word _____ most nearly means
—What is the meaning of _____ as used in line ____?

Context Clues

There are six clues that enable us to determine correct meanings from context: synonyms, restatements, antonyms, definitions, explanations, and situations.

• *Synonyms:* When an author uses a difficult word, he or she often will use a more familiar word or words *with the same meaning* to make the difficult word understood.

The child was *cantankerous.* She was quarrelsome, irritable, and ill-tempered.

• *Restatement:* A restatement is close to a synonym but differs in that the restatement of a difficult word is usually made in *simpler terms.* The restatement is often set off by commas.

The *perimeter,* or the distance around the yard, was 3200 feet.

• *Antonyms:* Sometimes a writer uses a contrast to clarify a word meaning, and an antonym, a word of opposite meaning (Did you notice the restatement here?), is used to accomplish this. Often, *contrast* clue words such as *but, however,* and *in contrast to* are used. These words are good clues that an antonym is being used.

The giant sea turtle is a *cumbersome* creature on land, but in the ocean it is positively graceful.

• *Definition:* Very often an author will simply include a definition of a difficult word.

An *insidious* plan is a plan that is working or spreading in a subtle or stealthy manner.

• *Explanation:* An explanation often looks like a definition. As an aid to the reader, the difficult word is explained, usually very simply, in order to make the meaning clearer. The explanation might be found in the same sentence (like the definition) but usually is found in a different sentence.

John is a *versatile* carpenter. He not only builds houses, but he also builds furniture and repairs broken items.

Note: Sometimes the meaning of a word is explained *before* it is given.

He not only builds houses, but he also builds furniture and repairs broken items. John is a *versatile* carpenter.

• *Situations.* Sometimes a major section or the entire passage acts as a definition or illustration of a word. This context clue is a little harder to spot initially and requires more reasoning on the reader's part.

The athletes were *jubilant* when they learned that their team had placed first in the competition, had taken the league title, and had been invited to play in a bowl game.

What To Look Out For

These word meaning questions can be a little tricky at times. Watch out for the following:

• A definition given of the word would be correct if it were used in a different context. Do not assume that you know the meaning of the word if you know *one* meaning. The context may require (and suggest) a different meaning.

• *Another* word or phrase, often close in meaning, appearing in the passage may be mistaken for the definition.

• Other answer choices "look good" and a snap decision is made.

Now try the practice passages and questions below. As you read the brief passages, circle obvious words that may need definition. Get in the habit of doing this as you read. Don't forget to pace yourself.

Sample Passages and Questions: Word Meaning from Context

His remarks were infrequent as well as short and to the point. He was certainly not a loquacious man.

1. As used in this context, the word <u>loquacious</u> means
    A. friendly.
    B. resentful.
    C. talkative.
    D. frequent.

    The Orient offers myriad sights of interest to travelers. It would take days to see the sights in Tokyo alone.

2. What is the meaning of the word <u>myriad</u> as used in this passage?
    A. very many
    B. very inexpensive
    C. very interesting
    D. very expensive

Answers

1. (C) The context clue is in the words *infrequent* and *to the point.*

2. (A) The context clue is *it would take days*, implying that there are *many* sights to see.

CRITICAL COMPREHENSION SKILLS

There are nine critical comprehension skills tested.

1: RECOGNIZING THE AUTHOR'S PURPOSE (✳)

This first critical comprehension skill of recognizing the author's purpose—or intention—is closely related to a skill that we've already discussed: finding the main idea. In any reading passage an author may or may not state outright his or her purpose for writing. If the purpose is not stated, the main idea and the way it is developed should provide clues. Questions asking you to identify the author's purpose are more difficult than those involving the main idea because you must select an answer that is usually not stated in the passage. This process is open to errors. Nevertheless, by grasping the author's main point, you should be able to *reject* answers which point to purposes which the author does *not* have.

Occasionally, but not often on this exam, an author will say directly something like "my purpose is," but more likely the purpose will be implied. When an author implies purpose, often you can determine that purpose by taking into consideration two things:

• *Other clues:* Phrases like *This discussion will center on, My intention is,* and *You should realize* all point to the author's intent.

• *Author's tone:* The tone, or mood, of the writing may also give you a clue as to the author's purpose. If, for example, the tone is serious and formal, then the author's purpose is not likely to be one that is lighthearted.

Questions which test your ability to select the author's purpose are usually stated like the following question stems. Note that these stems suggest very specific purposes and that they usually point to or quote specific sentences that you have read.

1. The first sentence of this paragraph ("_____
   _____.") indicates that the author's purpose is
   to
   A. describe _____.
   B. state a problem regarding _____.
   C. define _____.
   D. analyze _____.

2. In this sentence "_____." the author indicates
   that his or her purpose is to
   A. compare _____.
   B. classify _____.
   C. offer a solution to _____.
   D. evaluate _____.

What To Look Out For

The CLAST will give you four answers to choose from. Three of
the answers will be *misstatements* or *misinterpretations* of the
author's purpose. If you are clear about what the author is saying, the
correct answer should stand out.

See how well you do at selecting the author's purpose in the
following passages. Are you remembering to read the questions first?
Are you margin marking? The margin mark to indicate the author's
purpose is an asterisk (✳).

Sample Passages and Questions: Author's Purpose

For your own safety, as well as for the safety of your family
and society, you should learn to swim. With the heavy increase in
the number of aquatic facilities and equipment, both public and
private, safety in and around water becomes a daily necessity. If
you cannot swim it is extremely unwise to participate in aquatic
activities. The ability to swim safely and the prudence to
recognize and practice safety procedures are of prime importance to you.

1. In the sentence "If you cannot swim it is extremely unwise to
   participate in aquatic activities." the author indicates that his or
   her purpose is to
   A. suggest a recreational activity.
   B. analyze the need for aquatic activities.
   C. define aquatic activities.
   D. state a problem regarding aquatic activities.

Since the beginning of the twentieth century, the world
population has more than tripled. While most of the phenomenal
growth is attributed to modern medicine, better famine relief,
and more sanitary living conditions, one factor is usually

ignored. There has been more food because, during most of the twentieth century, the farmers of the world have enjoyed a uniquely favorable warm, wet, and stable climate.

2. In the third sentence, "There has been more food because ...," the author indicates that his or her purpose is to
   A. inform the reader as to causes of increasing world population.
   B. define the causes of world hunger.
   C. describe the effects of modern medicine.
   D. compare population growth in the eighteenth and twentieth centuries.

Answers

1. (D) This isn't about aquatic activities, but about learning to swim.

2. (A) The phrase *one factor is usually ignored* is your clue.

2: IDENTIFYING THE AUTHOR'S OVERALL ORGANIZATIONAL PATTERN (P)

The "overall organizational pattern" is simply the way the author *arranges* the material in order to best accomplish what he or she wants and to make the material clear. Sometimes a writer will organize the material so that the writing employs formats such as summary, cause and effect, or even simple listing. Up to four of the questions on the CLAST will ask you to determine what the patterns are of the passages you read. These questions are always asked the same way:

—In developing the passage, the organizational pattern used by the author could be described as

The possible answer choices that you should be familiar with are limited to *ten* kinds of pattern, and you already know most of those patterns. Once you become familiar with all of these patterns, this CLAST question should be no problem to you.

Organizational Pattern Clue Words

ORGANIZATIONAL PATTERN	CLUE WORDS
1. time order	after, afterward, at that time, before, during, immediately, presently, since, shortly, thereupon, until, while, at last, now
2. simple listing	next, then, first, second, third, last
3. definition	means, can be defined as, the same as, like
4. statement and clarification	clearly, evidently, in fact, in other words, obviously, of course, too, as a matter of fact
5. classification	category, field, rank, group
6. summary	in brief, in conclusion, in short, on the whole, to sum up, to summarize
7. comparison	also, likewise, in like manner, similarly
8. contrast	although, however, but, conversely, nevertheless, yet, on the contrary, on one hand . . . on the other hand, at the same time
9. generalization and example	for example, for instance, that is, thus
10. cause and effect/condition and conclusion	accordingly, as a result, because, consequently, hence, in short, then

What To Look Out For

The only thing you have to look out for is confusing the words and patterns in the answers given. Your four answer options will simply list one correct option and three words or phrases that describe incorrect patterns of organization. For example:

A. summary.
B. time order.
C. comparison and contrast.
D. definition.

As long as you know what and how the author wrote and what each of your answer choices means, you should be able to select the correct answer easily. Note that the *summary* choice might be confusing. Often authors *employ* summary in their organizational patterns, but that does not necessarily mean that the *pattern* is summary. The author's overall intent may be, for example, to clarify.

See how well you do on determining organizational pattern on the following passages and questions. Pace yourself and margin mark. Are you reading the questions first? The margin mark to indicate purpose is a *P* (P).

Sample Passages and Questions: Organizational Pattern

If a bottle of ammonia is opened in one corner of a room, it can soon be smelled all over the room. The spaces between air molecules are large compared to the space occupied by the molecules themselves. The ammonia gas molecules will pass through the space between some air molecules and will collide with others. In time the ammonia molecules will be spread throughout the entire volume. This mixing of gases is called diffusion. Liquids also diffuse. If a lump of sugar is placed at the bottom of a vessel of water, the sugar will dissolve after a time. It will slowly diffuse throughout the water so that a sample of water taken from any part of the container will taste sweet.

1. In developing the passage, the organizational pattern used by the author could be described as
   A. simple listing.
   B. cause and effect.
   C. definition.
   D. time order

The colors of an artist's palette are referred to as warm or cool depending upon at which end of the color spectrum they fall. Reds, oranges, and yellows are said to be warm colors. Those are the colors of the sun and therefore call to mind our primary source of heat. So they carry strong implications of warmth. Colors falling on the opposite end of the spectrum—blues and greens—are cool colors because they imply shade, or lack of light and warmth. Here we have, as we will notice frequently, a stimulation that is mental but has a physical basis. Tonality and color contrast also affect our senses by creating impressions of liveliness or subdued relaxation.

2. In developing the passage, the organizational pattern used by the author could be described as
   A. comparison.
   B. contrast.
   C. statement and classification.
   D. summary.

Answers

1. (B) Cause and effect. There are two causes and two effects: ammonia is opened = smells; sugar in water = sweet taste.

2. (C) Statement and classification. There are warm colors and cool colors. The passage names specific colors that fall into these two classifications.

3: DISTINGUISHING BETWEEN STATEMENTS OF FACT AND STATEMENTS OF OPINION (O)

Occasionally students have problems distinguishing statements of fact from statements of opinion. On the CLAST Reading Test, however, these questions are fairly easy because you are given only two possible choices, fact or opinion, so what you really have is a true-false question. You will be asked to identify a specific statement as *fact* or *opinion*. The specific line in which the statement begins will be cited, and the first few words will be quoted, so there will be no confusion as to which statement is being referred to. The questions will be asked in one of two ways:

1. The statement beginning in line _____ of paragraph _____ (first few words quoted) is a statement of
   A. fact.
   B. opinion.
2. The author's statement that "_____" (in lines _____) is a statement of
   A. fact.
   B. opinion.

What To Look Out For

It is important that you recognize the difference between fact and opinion. On the simplest level—and that is a good level for the purposes of the CLAST—a fact is anything that can be validated or proved, while an opinion *cannot be validated.* An opinion is not necessarily incorrect, but it has not been proved. An opinion may seem true at times, but if it *hasn't yet been proved,* it is still an opinion. Don't be confused by a statement of fact even though it may need to be explained further. It is still a fact. *Be aware of the following guidelines:*

• Statements which deal with persons, places, objects, occurrences, or processes that actually exist or did exist and that can have their truth or falsity proved are facts.

Dr. Jean Smith spoke on the subject of penguins last night.

• Statements whose truth or falsity can be proved are statements of fact even when they could possibly be proved false.

Three hundred fifty waiters from fifty-two restaurants came to the union meeting.

This is a statement of fact even though a mistake may be made in counting the number of people or restaurants.

• Statements which deal with evaluations, attitudes, or probabilities are statements of opinion because they cannot be proved true or false.

Too few people are concerned about the number of African children who will die of starvation this year.

It may be true, but it is *opinion,* not fact, because it cannot be proved by objective means.

• Statements concerning future events are statements of opinion even when those events seem very probable.

Eventually the number of cars a family may own will be strictly regulated by the government.

It may be true eventually. It also may not be true eventually, and it is still opinion.

Try your skill at differentiating between fact and opinion with the following statements. Remember, use a margin mark only for opinion in a message (O).

Sample Questions: Fact/Opinion

1. The statement that "Fall is by far the most pleasant of the four seasons" is a statement of
   A. fact.
   B. opinion.

2. The statement that "Green is a cool color, while yellow is warm" is a statement of
   A. fact.
   B. opinion.

Answers

1. (B) Opinion. The words *most pleasant* indicate a judgment.

2. (B) Opinion. This question is not quite so obvious. You may have been told by your art teacher that green is considered "cool" and yellow "warm," but the terms are subjective and thus not strictly definable. Thus, the statement reflects an opinion (of a lot of people).

4: DETECTING BIAS IN THE PASSAGE (B)

Bias may be defined (at least for the purposes of the CLAST) as a predisposition, prejudice, or prejudgment that causes the writer to attempt to influence the reader to like or dislike, agree or disagree with, support or refute a subject. Bias is often present when the author's choice of words arouses the reader's emotions, but is always present when the author's presentation contains one or more of the following elements:

• *Stereotyping,* often characterized by overgeneralizations full of inaccuracies.

Everyone knows that women are better at housekeeping and cooking than are men.

• *False assumptions* based on weak or inaccurate information.

People from developing countries have only recently emerged from relatively primitive stages of life and will not be ready for modern technology for years to come.

• *Highly emotional statements.*

Women are supposed to fit in, keep their place, and not get out of line. They may have come a long way, but they are not yet ready to take a full share of responsibility with men.

• *Name-calling.*

The speaker was unable to continue because of a bunch of long-haired, commie troublemakers.

• *Contradiction.*

Our organization has no problems. We even have the ability to borrow a large amount of money from the bank if we can't make the mortgage payment next month because of the annual summer slump.

In short, writing that is biased is usually very interesting to read (that's not in itself a sign of bias) because it contains such strong, slanted, colorful langauge in its attempt to sway the reader.

The CLAST questions covering this skill usually take three simple forms:

—In this passage, the author shows bias in favor of (or against)
—The author expresses (reveals, shows) a biased attitude
  against _____ when he or she says that

—Which of the following statements shows (reveals, reflects) a biased attitude expressed by the author in this passage?

What To Look Out For

With this skill the CLAST question preparers get a little tricky again, so be careful. Of the four answer choices you will be given for each question, one will be the correct response and the other three may be:

• a quoted or paraphrased statement which reveals a *fair, unbiased* attitude; and/or

• a statement which reveals bias but one that was not expressed in *this* reading selection; and/or

• a statement with bias but one that wasn't biased in the reading selection. *Bias was added when it became an answer choice.*

Now, read the following selections and answer the questions to see how well you do at identifying the bias. Pace yourself and mark bias with a *B* (β).

Sample Passages and Questions: Bias

Open book exams are usually given when your teacher is interested in evaluating how well you can apply what you have learned. If you are to be given such an exam, don't waste your time memorizing facts or formulas. They are in your text or your notebook. It is much better to practice working out problems that require you to demonstrate understanding and application. Don't be misled: open book exams can be among the hardest you will take. Chances are such exams will emphasize various types of essay questions that will require you to analyze problems or situations and create an answer. Be sure you are familiar with your text and its problems. Concentrate on application, not memorization.

1. In this passage, the author shows bias against
   A. open book exams.
   B. essay questions.
   C. memorizing facts and formulas.
   D. working out problems.

The library is an intellectual time machine. It allows you to understand the past and present so you can better enter the future. The library is a silent meeting that comes to order when you ask a question of a librarian, open a book, listen to a tape cassette, or watch a filmstrip. The library is a study place. You can meet with yourself or, through multimedia resources, with thousands of other people. Each will have his or her own knowledge, allowing you the opportunity to comprehend, apply, analyze, evaluate, and synthesize. The word *college* means a group of people gathered together for a common purpose. You can find no greater gathering than that in your college library.

2. In this passage, the author shows bias in favor of
   A. libraries.
   B. college.
   C. librarians.
   D. books, cassettes, and filmstrips.

Answers

1. (C) Memorizing facts and formulas.

2. (A) Libraries. Although this passage praises all of the answer choices, it is primarily about only one of them—libraries. Thus A is the *best* choice.

5: RECOGNIZING THE AUTHOR'S TONE (T)

Tone often confuses students, and they sometimes think of it as hard to define and identify. If you think of tone as the qualities in a written passage that establish and communicate the author's *attitude* toward what he or she is writing, then it is easier to identify. The writer's mood and attitude influence word choice and emphasis. In selecting a word or phrase to describe the tone of a reading passage, think of the passage as being read *aloud* or even set to music. The same words you would use to describe a speaker's tone of voice or the mood created by a piece of music (*playful, impassioned, intimate, cheerful*) are those used to describe the tone of a reading passage. Tone questions are generally asked in one of three ways:

—The author of this passage has created a tone that could be described as

—If the author were delivering this passage orally, his or her tone of voice would probably be

—The author of this passage has created a tone (mood, feeling) that could be described as

The best way to prepare for this kind of question is to be familiar with the common "tone words" from which the four answer choices are taken. Look over this list of "tone words." Put a check next to the ones that you don't know at all or that you are unsure of, and look those up in a dictionary. Doing so will increase your retention of their meaning.

TONE WORDS				
compassionate	disapproval	frustration	awe	distressed
earnest	cruel	melancholy	wonder	sensationalism
comic	serious	formal	ridicule	ironic
bitter	vindictive	playful	intimate	gentle
absurd	amused	intense	hard	detached
tragic	malicious	reverent	impassioned	irreverent
abstruse	farcical	sympathetic	mocking	reticent
depressed	prayerful	righteous	pathetic	cynical
pessimistic	loving	solemn	outspoken	ambivalent
complex	optimistic	condescending	arrogant	indignant
ghoulish	evasive	objective	obsequious	critical
caustic	angry	apathetic	satiric	cheerful
excited	joyous	nostalgic	outraged	
condemnation	celebration	incredulous	uneasy	

What To Look Out For

There are no real pitfalls in tone questions. You will have one correct tone choice and three incorrect choices that are usually far away in meaning from the correct choice. Now see how well you do on the following readings and questions. Don't forget your tone mark as you read, a T ($\top$).

Sample Passages and Questions: Tone

Just before the Civil War, about 225,000 Indians shared the plains and mountains with the buffalo, the wild horse, the jack rabbit, and the coyote. But they would soon be overwhelmed as white Americans stormed into this area at a breathtaking pace. The speed with which prospectors, ranchers, and farmers conquered the last frontier was made possible by the transcontinental railroads that criss-crossed the region, transporting settlers and supplies and providing access to outside markets. Eager to attract settlers, the railroads made land available at low prices. The federal government also played a critical role. It proved to be as liberal in giving away land to corporations and prospective farmers as it was thorough and ruthless in moving the Indians to the less desirable places. At the same time its policies undermined Indian culture and made them the wards of government bureaucrats.

1. If the author were delivering this passage orally, his or her tone of voice would probably be
   A. ambivalent.
   B. outraged.
   C. obsequious.
   D. sympathetic.

   We see the poor fellows hobbling back from the crest or unable to do so, pale and weak, lying on the ground with the mangled stump of an arm or leg, dripping their life-blood away; or with a cheek torn open, or a shoulder mashed. And many, alas! hear not the roar as they stretch upon the ground with upturned faces and open eyes, though a shell should burst at their very ears. Their ears and their bodies this instant are only mud.

2. The author of this passage has created a tone that could be described as
   A. evasive.
   B. loving.
   C. tragic.
   D. reticent.

Answers

1. (D) Sympathy for the Indians is clearly shown. Note such words as *overwhelmed, ruthless, less desirable,* and *undermined.*

2. (C) This tone is so tragic that it is almost melodramatic.

6. RECOGNIZING RELATIONSHIPS WITHIN SENTENCES (( ))

Another reading competency that you will be expected to demonstrate on the CLAST is recognizing both explicit (stated) and implicit (implied) relationships *between* the *parts* of a sentence. This should be easy for you *if* you followed closely the explanation given previously for critical comprehension skill 2, identifying the author's overall organizational pattern. You see, what you are doing when you recognize relationships within sentences is the same thing you do when you determine *overall* organizational pattern. You even use the same words: cause and effect, comparison and contrast, statement and clarification, etc. These questions are asked in one of two ways:

—You are told to read a *sentence* carefully and then choose the word or phrase (cause and effect, comparison, etc.) which identifies the relationship between the parts of the sentence.

—You are given a passage with one or more relationship words (*and, thus, however,* etc.) deleted and told to choose the word from four choices given below the passage which best completes the passage. (In this case, you don't even need to read the whole passage. Just read the sentence with the missing word and insert each of the answer choices in the space. One will be an obvious fit. The rest of the sentences are unimportant to this question.)

If you learn the ten organizational patterns and the words which go with each pattern, you can successfully answer *three* kinds of reading questions: identifying the author's overall organizational pattern (critical comprehension skill 2), recognizing relationships within sentences (critical comprehension skill 6), and recognizing relationships between sentences (critical comprehension skill 7). Three out of twelve competencies tested (thus, 25% of CLAST reading questions) use the same information to determine correct responses on the exam. Therefore, go back and review thoroughly the material beginning on page 150, and then begin here again.

What To Look Out For

Watch out that in answering a question you don't come to conclusions too fast, especially when a blank appears in a passage.

Try *all four words* in the blank before coming to a conclusion. They may all fit *grammatically,* but only one fits in a way that makes the most sense. Test yourself on the following reading selection and questions. Mark your margins as you read (( )).

Sample Passage and Questions: Relationships Within Sentences

By itself, punishment simply inhibits responses. Ideally, punishment should be paired with reinforcement of the desired behavior. This is a more productive approach, ____1____ it teaches an alternative behavior to replace what is being punished. Children who mispronounce words while reading might learn faster if the teacher, ____2____ scolding them, also praises them for pronouncing other words correctly. The praise acts as a positive reinforcement for learning to pronounce words correctly. It also makes the children less fearful about learning in general.

1. The missing word in space 1 is
   A. finally.
   B. since.
   C. hereafter.
   D. then.

2. The missing word in space 2 is
   A. about.
   B. whereupon.
   C. besides.
   D. and.

Answers

1. (B) since

2. (C) besides

7: RECOGNIZING RELATIONSHIPS BETWEEN SENTENCES (+)

This reading competency is very similar to the one you just finished studying, except instead of concentrating on relationships *within* sentences, you concentrate on relationships *between* sentences. Once again you rely on the terms and clue words that you learned on page

150. These questions will usually be asked in one of the following ways:

1. What does the sentence beginning in line _____ (first few words quoted) do in relation to the sentence beginning in line _____ (first few words quoted)?
   A. It contradicts the sentence beginning in line _____.
   B. It draws a conclusion from the sentence beginning in line _____.
   C. It gives a specific example of what is stated in the sentence beginning in line _____.
   D. It alters the meaning of the sentence beginning in line _____.

The answer choices simply refer to the kind of relationship that exists: A = contrast; B = summary; C = generalization and example; D = clarification.

2. What is the relationship between the sentence beginning in line _____ (first few words quoted) and the sentence beginning in line _____ (first few words quoted)?
   A. cause and effect
   B. comparison and contrast
   C. statement and clarification
   D. generalization and example

Essentially you are doing the same thing for three kinds of questions—and using the same information:

1. recognizing the author's overall organizational pattern, p. 150.
2. recognizing relationships within sentences, p. 161.
3. recognizing relationships between sentences, p. 162.

See how well you do on the following reading selection and questions. Read the questions first. The margin mark for this competency is a plus sign (+).

Sample Passage and Questions: Relationships Between Sentences

The main idea is often found in the first sentence in a paragraph followed by supporting details. But this is not always the case. Some authors prefer to give the supporting details first and end with the main idea. Others give some

5 detail, the main idea, and more detail. In some paragraphs
   you must get the idea by "reading between the lines."
   Therefore, since the main idea could be found anywhere in
   the paragraph, you should have a plan to facilitate finding
   the main idea.

1. What does the sentence beginning in line 2 ("But this is . . .") do in
   relation to the sentence beginning in line 1 ("The main
   idea . . .")?
   A. It draws a conclusion from the sentence beginning in line 1.
   B. It contradicts the sentence beginning in line 1.
   C. It gives a specific example of what is stated in the sentence
      beginning in line 1.
   D. It expands what is said in the sentence beginning in line 1.

2. What is the relationship between the sentence beginning in line 7
   ("Therefore, since the main . . .") and the rest of the sentences?
   A. cause and effect
   B. comparison and contrast
   C. statement and clarification
   D. generalization and examples

Answers

1. (B) The sentence contradicts what was just said.

2. (D) Generalization and example. Don't let this fool you: the
   examples are *first*; then comes the generalization.

8: RECOGNIZING VALID ARGUMENTS (∧)

Questions that test this competency are attempting to determine if
you can recognize a valid argument (or more likely an *invalid*
argument) in a reading selection. In terms of the CLAST, a "valid
argument" refers to a statement which fits into a *logical reasoning
pattern* and which contains relevant, *verifiable* proof in support of a
conclusion. Is an argument logical? Can you prove it? That is all you
have to decide. There will probably be four questions that test your
ability to recognize valid arguments, and with just a few exceptions
all you will need is common sense to do well on them.

An important bit of advice: you will have only two options to choose
from for each question—either *valid* or *invalid*—so treat these

questions like true-false questions. And then, if you can't decide, pick the *invalid* choice because chances are it is an invalid argument that has been presented. On past exams, three out of four of this question type dealt with *invalid* arguments. The test questions are presented in a very straightforward manner with no variation:

—Is the author's argument logically valid or invalid?
  A. valid
  B. invalid

What To Look Out For

There are no "catches" in these questions; they are straightforward. Read the following summaries, with examples, of common fallacies in argument which make the argument invalid. These fallacies are suggested by Jean Wyrick's book *Steps to Writing Well* (Holt, Rinehart and Winston, 1984). This is a good source for further reading in this competency.

• *The writer bases the argument on insufficient or unrepresentative evidence* (hasty generalization). Suppose, for example, you have owned two poodles and they have both attacked you. If you declare that all poodles are vicious dogs, you are making a hasty generalization. There are, of course, thousands of poodles that have not attacked anyone. When the generalization is drawn from an unrepresentative or insufficient sample, your conclusion isn't valid.

• *The writer's conclusion is not necessarily a logical result of the facts* (*non sequitur,* "it doesn't follow"). An example of a *non sequitur* occurs when you conclude, "Professor Smith is a famous historian, so he will be a brilliant history teacher." As you may have realized by now, the fact that someone knows a subject well does not automatically mean that he or she can communicate the information clearly; hence, the conclusion is not necessarily valid.

• *The writer presents as truth what is supposed to be proven by the argument* (begging the question). For example, in the statement, "All useless laws such as Reform Bill 13 should be repealed," the writer has already assumed the bill is useless without assuming responsibility for proving that accusation. This begs the question (that is, tries like a beggar to get something for nothing from the reader) because the writer gives no evidence for what first must be argued, not merely asserted—that Reform Bill 13 is a useless law.

• *The writer introduces an irrelevant point to divert the readers' attention from the main issue* (red herring). The term *red herring* originates from the old tactic, used by escaped prisoners, of dragging a smoked herring, a strong-smelling fish, across their trail to confuse tracking dogs by making them follow the wrong scent. If a writer arguing the merits of a particular politician who is seeking reelection suddenly breaks into a description of the drinking habits of the politician's brother, such a description would be termed a red herring; the politician's brother has nothing to do with an evaluation of the incumbent's political merit.

• *Assuming that because one event follows another in time, the first event caused the second (post hoc, ergo propter hoc).* This error in logic (from the Latin phrase meaning "after this, therefore because of this") results when we mistake a temporal (time) connection for a causal (direct cause) relationship. Most of our superstitions are *post hoc* fallacies; we now realize that tripping after walking under a ladder is a matter of coincidence, not cause and effect. In any causal analysis, you must be able to prove that one event caused another, not just that it preceded it in time.

• *The writer attacks the opponent's character rather than the opponent's argument* (argument *ad hominem,* "to the man"). The statement "Professor Bloom can't be a competent philosophy teacher since he's divorced" is illogical, because Bloom's marital status has nothing to do with his ability to teach his course well.

• *The writer evades the issues by appealing to the readers' emotional reactions to certain subjects* (argument *ad populum,* "to the people"). For example, instead of arguing the facts of an issue, a writer might play upon the readers' negative response to such words as *communism* and *fascism* or their positive response to words and concepts such as *God, country,* and *liberty.* In the statement "If you are a true American, you will vote against the referendum on busing," the writer avoids any discussion of the merits or weaknesses of the referendum and merely substitutes an emotional appeal.

• *Using as proof a statement which simply repeats in different words what you are trying to prove* (circular thinking). These arguments seem to chase their own tails. "There aren't enough parking spaces for students on campus because there are too many cars."

• *The writer tries to convince the readers that there are only two sides to an issue—one right, one wrong* (either/or). The statement "If you don't go to war against Iceland, you don't love your country" is irrational because it doesn't consider the other possibilities. A classic example of this sort of oversimplification was illustrated in the 1960s bumper sticker that was popular during the debate over the Vietnam War: "America: Love It or Leave It." Obviously, there are other choices ("Change It or Lose It," for example).

• *The writer uses an abstract concept as if it were a concrete reality* (hypostatization). Always be suspicious of a writer who uses statements beginning, "History has taught us . . . ," "Science has proven . . . ," or "Medicine has discovered . . ." The implication in each case is that history or science or medicine has only one voice, one opinion. On the contrary, "history" is written by a multitude of historians who hold a variety of opinions; doctors and scientists also frequently disagree.

• *The writer tries to validate a point by intimating that "everyone else believes in this"* (bandwagon appeal). Such a tactic evades discussion of the issue itself. Advertising often uses this technique: "Discriminating women use Soft-Lips lipstick" (The ultimate in "bandwagon" humor may have appeared on a recent Colorado bumper sticker: "Eat lamb—could thousands of coyotes be wrong?")

• *The writer uses an extended comparison as proof of a point* (faulty analogy). Look closely at all extended comparisons and metaphors to see if the two things being compared are really similar. For example, in a recent editorial a woman protested the new laws requiring parents to use car seats for small children arguing that if the state could require the seats, they could just as easily require mothers to breastfeed instead of using formula. The two situations are in no way alike. Remember that even though an analogy might suggest similarities, it alone cannot *prove* anything.

Errors in reasoning come in many different forms, but these are the most common ones and should give you an idea of what to watch out for as you determine whether an argument is valid or invalid. Are the following arguments valid or invalid? Remember to use the inverted V ($\wedge$) as the margin mark for faulty reasoning.

Sample Passages and Questions: Valid Arguments

When a man destroys one of the works of man we call him a vandal. When he destroys one of the words of God we call him a sportsman.

1. In the quotation above, is the author's argument logically valid or invalid?
   A. valid
   B. invalid

Each time you drive in excess of the speed limit you jeopardize not only your own life but also the lives of others.

2. In the quotation above, is the author's argument logically valid or invalid?
   A. valid
   B. invalid

Answers

1. (B) Invalid. There is a lot wrong with this quotation, but the writer is really trying to make a point about *not* hunting.

2. (B) Invalid. This is very bad, logically, even though a good point is being made about obeying the speed limit. If I drive eleven miles per hour in a ten-mile-per-hour speed zone (yes, that's in excess of the speed limit) and there is not another person around for ten miles in any direction, how could I be jeopardizing lives?

9: DRAWING LOGICAL INFERENCES AND CONCLUSIONS

One of the things that a skillful reader is able to do is to determine the meaning of an idea when not all the meaning is clearly stated. A skillful reader is also able to put facts and information together in such a way—"reading between the lines"—as to be able to come to logical conclusions about what is being stated. In order to draw logical inferences and conclusions, you use your own past knowledge and understanding plus the new facts and ideas stated by the writer. When you combine all of this, you are able to infer or *conclude* about what you read. The CLAST questions testing drawing inferences and conclusions are asked in the following manner:

—From this passage, you could infer (conclude, predict) that
—_____ was probably the result of (caused by)
—The author implies (suggests)
—The writer of the passage probably is (feels, will, has, has never)

What To Look Out For

Watch out for two things that may throw you off:

• Logical, reasonable, or "nice" assumptions, conclusions, or inferences—but ones that cannot be drawn from the reading selection.

• A detail from the passage—but one that isn't related to the question.

Read the following passages and answer the questions to see if you understand how to draw logical inferences and conclusions.

Sample Passages and Questions: Logical Inferences and Conclusions

No sensible person would support the Equal Rights Amendment. If it passes, we'll have women in combat and then unisex bathrooms. Eventually, we won't be able to tell the sexes apart at all.

1. From this passage you could conclude that
   A. the Equal Rights Amendment is about combat and bathrooms.
   B. this issue is an emotional one.
   C. this argument has been carefully thought out.
   D. the Equal Rights Amendment is certain to pass.

The number of women earning more than $25,000 a year has doubled in the last ten years.

2. The author of this statement suggests
   A. nothing.
   B. salaries of some women have gone up.
   C. salaries of all women have gone up.
   D. salaries of all women will continue to go up.

Answers

1. (B) Emotion, not facts, is evident in this passage.

2. (B) Don't read too much "between the lines."

READING POST-TEST

Suggested Time: 60 Minutes
44 Questions

Passage 1

The jump began as a routine skydiving exercise, part of a convention of 420 parachutists sponsored by Skydive Arizona, but it quickly turned into a test of nerve, instinct, and courage, carried out within seconds. Moments after he went out the open hatch of a four-engine DC-4 airplane at 9,000 ft. near Coolidge, Arizona, sky diver Gregory Robertson, 35, could see that Debbie Williams, 31, a fellow parachutist with a modest 50 jumps to her credit, was in big trouble. Instead of "floating" in the proper stretched-out position parallel to the earth, Williams was tumbling like a rag doll. In attempting to join three other divers in a handholding ring formation, she had slammed into the backpack of another chutist, and was knocked unconscious.

From his instructor's position 40 ft. above the other divers, Robertson reacted with instincts that had been honed by 1,700 jumps during time away from his job as an A.T.&T. engineer in Phoenix. He straightened into vertical dart, arms pinned to his body, ankles crossed, head aimed at the ground in what chutists call a "no-lift" dive, and plummeted toward Williams at a speed of around 200 m.p.h. The effort was like "trying to catch a football that was flopping down the road at 40 m.p.h.," said Bill Rothe, Williams' fiance, who watched from the ground. At 3,500 ft., about ten seconds before impact, Robertson caught up with Williams, almost hitting her but slowing his own descent by assuming the open body froglike position. He angled the unconscious sky diver so her chute could open freely and, at 2,000 ft., with some six seconds left, yanked the rip cord on her emergency chute, then pulled his own rip cord. The two sky divers floated to the ground. Williams, a fifth-grade teacher from Post, Texas, landed on her back, suffering a skull fracture, nine broken ribs and a perforated kidney—but alive. In the history of recreational

173

skydiving, there has never been such a daring rescue in anyone's recollection. Several attempts have ended with both chutists crashing into the ground.

1. In the first sentence of this passage ("The jump began as a routine skydiving exercise, . . . but it quickly turned into a test of nerve, instinct, and courage, carried out within seconds.") the author indicates that his or her purpose is to
   A. describe a skydiving experience.
   B. state a problem in skydiving.
   C. define a skydiving test.
   D. analyze a skydiving problem.

2. The author's statement in the last three lines that "In the history of recreational skydiving, there has never been such a daring rescue in anyone's recollection." is a statement of
   A. fact.
   B. opinion.

3. In developing the passage, the organizational pattern used by the author could be described as
   A. statement and clarification.
   B. summary.
   C. simple listing.
   D. time order.

Passage 2

The idea that good nutrition and natural foods have a major role in health seems to be taking hold. Witness what has been happening with beta carotene: A close relative of vitamin A, this nutrient is turning out to be one of the biggest
5 natural weapons in the fight to prevent cancer and other diseases.

Sometimes called a provitamin, beta carotene is the precursor to vitamin A found in vegetables. When beta carotene is eaten, the body converts about one-sixth of this amazing
10 substance to vitamin A.

The big news is nutritional researchers have recently discovered that beta carotene has all of the health benefits of regular vitamin A, plus a few that the vitamin by itself does not have. In addition, it's absolutely safe to eat—whether in
15 vegetables or in dietary supplements. The body only converts beta carotene as it is needed, eliminating even the remote likelihood of taking too much vitamin A.

Found in most vegetables, beta carotene is the substance that gives carrots their bright yellow-orange color. After
20 decades of being considered only for its general nutritional benefits to the skin and eyes, beta carotene is now being aggressively studied for its anti-cancer properties.

Studies of beta carotene's role in cancer prevention date back to the 1930s, a time of unparalleled vitamin research.
25 Today, with renewed vigor, nine major universities and medical centers are conducting federally funded research on beta carotene's cancer-fighting role. The research programs were prompted by the positive findings of a growing number of researchers.
30 Attention turned to beta carotene in 1982 when the National Academy of Sciences issued a report, *Diet, Nutrition and Cancer,* calling for wholesale changes in American eating habits to reduce cancer risk. The report recommended a diet low in fat, red meat, and smoked foods, and high in
35 vegetables—which contain abundant beta carotene.

Meanwhile, the National Research Council conducted a comprehensive review of the scientific literature and concluded that carotene-rich vegetables and cruciferous vegetables (such as broccoli and cauliflower) were associated with a
40 reduced incidence of cancer.

4. Identify the statement below which gives the most accurate statement of the central idea of the passage.
   A. Beta carotene is found in carrots and is a useful provitamin.
   B. Beta carotene appears to have disease and cancer fighting qualities.
   C. Beta carotene has been studied for decades by researchers.
   D. Beta carotene is absolutely safe with no possibility of taking too much.

5. The example of the National Research Council review was used to illustrate
   A. the familiarity scientific organizations have with beta carotene.
   B. the need for thorough research with experimental drugs.
   C. beta carotene's cancer fighting qualities.
   D. the need for a national organization to put its stamp of approval on new products.

6. In this context, the word <u>cruciferous</u> (line 38) means
   A. hard surfaced.
   B. round shaped.
   C. single-stalk shaped.
   D. broccoli/cauliflower shaped.

7. In the sentence "Witness what has been happening with beta carotene: A close relative of vitamin A, this nutrient is turning out to be one of the biggest natural weapons in the fight to prevent cancer and other diseases." the author indicates that his or her purpose is to
   A. analyze information on beta carotene.
   B. state a problem in cancer research.
   C. define the difference between vitamin A and beta carotene.
   D. compare vitamin A and beta carotene.

8. In developing the passage, the organizational pattern used by the author could be described as
   A. comparison and contrast.
   B. cause and effect.
   C. statement and clarification.
   D. classification.

9. The author's statement "In addition, it's absolutely safe to eat—whether in vegetables or in dietary supplements." (in lines 14–15) is a statement of
   A. fact.
   B. opinion.

Passage 3

If we increase our gas mileage by 20 percent, we will spend 20 percent less on our day-to-day automobile costs.

10. Is the author's argument logically valid or invalid?
    A. valid
    B. invalid

Passage 4

Mick Jagger was married in sneakers. Woody Allen wore
canvas-tops when he escorted then First Lady Betty Ford to
the ballet. Jackie Onassis' sneakers come from Europe, but
roughly 50 percent of the sneakers the rest of us buy are
5 made in Taiwan, Korea, Japan, and Hong Kong. In a
moment of optimism, Leonardo once called the foot "a
masterpiece of engineering," but these days feet seem to have
more and more trouble doing their stuff. Everyone knows
about the explosion in footwear for maladjusted metatarsals,
10 for the fleet of foot or fat of thigh. When I hied me to my
local sports shop, though, I was dumbfounded. A young
woman jogged in, ran in place for five minutes while she had
an in-depth conversation with a salesman about some new
Nikes, then headed out with a box under her arm, still
15 jogging.

Henry VIII ordered up the earliest tennis shoes on
record—"syxe paire of shooys with feltys, to pleye in at
tennys." Today everybody knows you don't dream of playing
tennis in running shoes, or vice versa. "Jogger's knee" and
20 "tennis toe" threaten. Or worse. Nothing I'd heard, though,
quite prepared me for the sheer array of styles—one manufacturer boasted a hundred, more than 30 for joggers alone.
Or for all the heady (if that's the word) talk about the
"revolutionary midsoles," or extra room for "orthotics." I
25 began to be conscious of "higher toe boxes" and a dreadful
something called "black toenail."

Just as I was almost in danger of making an outlandish
and expensive purchase, I came toe-to-toe with something
really far-out, a fancy creation called the Micropacer. They
30 looked like all the other crazy shoes. And by then the asking
price, a mere $125, didn't faze me as much as it should have.
But yessiree! Beneath their chic second tongues (the flaps
that cover the laces on such dream-boots) Micropacers carry
a miniature battery-powered computer triggered by a sensor

35 pad sealed into the sole. Fed the right personal data the little
    gadget will tell you not only how far you've run on a
    morning's jog, but the total time elapsed, the pace in miles
    per hour and even the approximate number of calories that
    you burn. Its memory keeps a cumulative running record,
40 erased only if you take out the battery.
        Hand in my wallet I suddenly came to my senses. Was I
    really ready for hightech high-steppers? I shelled out a
    modest sum for some basic all-purpose athletic shoes. They
    can't count calories, of course, but stepping into them was
45 like stepping back into childhood.

11. From this passage, you could conclude that
    A. rich people buy European sneakers, poor people buy sneakers
       from the Orient.
    B. changes in foot structure caused the sneaker explosion.
    C. basic, old-fashioned sneakers are the best.
    D. the variety of sneakers and their uses are somewhat over-
       whelming.

12. In this passage, the author shows bias in favor of
    A. Nikes.
    B. imported sneakers.
    C. all-purpose athletic shoes.
    D. hightech high-steppers.

13. The author of this passage has created a tone that could be
    described as
    A. formal.
    B. playful.
    C. intense.
    D. uneasy.

14. As used in line 10, the word <u>hied</u> most nearly means
    A. traveled.
    B. talked.
    C. hid out.
    D. wrote.

15. All of the following were factors in the author's decision to purchase "basic all-purpose athletic shoes" except
    A. cost.
    B. many styles.
    C. comfort.
    D. hightech.

16. The main idea expressed in this passage is that
    A. modern sneakers are all hightech.
    B. sneakers are now "acceptable" everywhere.
    C. everyone wears sneakers.
    D. the variety of styles and prices of sneakers makes selection difficult.

DIRECTIONS: The following passage has several words deleted. For each blank, choose the word or phrase which best completes the passage, choices for each item are given below the passage.

Passage 5

It descended slowly, _____17_____ pollution or a wet blanket that threatened to snuff out the atmosphere around me: boredom, inertia, a terrible dullness that no number of one-man Ping-Pong games played against the outside of the plate-glass window in my living room could alleviate. I was eleven years old, _____18_____ my life lacked, entirely, any adventure. There was only one solution—to run away. By today's standards, the note I left behind was both thoughtful and cowardly. "Dear Mom and Dad, don't worry. I'm only running away for one night. Love, . . ." _____19_____, with a box of graham crackers, a Thermos of chocolate milk, and a sleeping bag, I stole out of the house after supper and made my way toward a hill covered with oak trees that was, at best, only 500 yards from our house.

It was not a particularly thrilling evening. Somebody (later on, I discovered it was my father) kept driving around honking his horn all night. My flashlight batteries died, so I couldn't read my comic books. Burrs collected on my flannel shirt and inside my sleeping bag. Taking to the hills was not, I discovered, a way out of the dullness that constricted my life. _____20_____ running away continues to be a dream that endures from one generation of children to the next, and my own children are no exception. All three of them have had a stab at it, _____21_____ each time, a knife went through my heart.

17. The missing word in space 17 is
    A. thus.
    B. because.
    C. since.
    D. like.

18. The missing word in space 18 is
    A. however.
    B. moreover.
    C. thus.
    D. and.

19. The missing word in space 19 is
    A. Similarly.
    B. Because.
    C. Then.
    D. Since.

20. The missing word or phrase in space 20 is
    A. Since.
    B. Yet.
    C. Like.
    D. Even though.

21. The missing word in space 21 is
    A. like.
    B. since.
    C. and.
    D. similarly.

Passage 6

They are technically not homeless people, but their living quarters make a mockery of the sentiment that there is no place like home. For the past two months Yolanda Gonzales, her daughter, son-in-law, and granddaughter have resided in
5 a dilapidated two-car garage in Lynwood, California. Patches of dirt blotch the linoleum floor, electrical wires

snake along bare walls, a door opens to a reeking kitchen dominated by a blackened stove. At $300 a month it is, alas, almost a bargain. "Nothing is affordable," says Gonzales, 10 42, whose daughter is on welfare and whose son-in-law lost his job as a handyman. "We had to settle for this."

So have many of Gonzales' neighbors. In Los Angeles County, which has an estimated street homeless population of more than 30,000, a growing number of the poor are the 15 not-quite-homeless, forced to live in garages, automobiles, even tool sheds and converted chicken coops. The Los Angeles *Times* estimates that as many as 200,000 stay in some 42,000 garages that rent for $200 to $600 a month. Constituting a new, anomalous demographic stratum, this 20 group is made up mostly of Hispanic working poor, many of them illegal immigrants fresh from the Mexican border. Says William Baer, associate professor of urban planning at the University of Southern California: "We've got a squatters' settlement in the backyard of the city."

25   Other cities, like New York and Detroit, face a similar problem, but it is most acute in the Los Angeles area. Steep rentals and a dearth of public housing have combined with a surging population to push people into makeshift shelters. Some feel that, given the fact that poverty is slowly increas-30 ing in the U.S. while the quantity of low-cost housing is shrinking, the L.A. trend may be the wave of the future for the nation's working poor.

In Lynwood (pop. 53,000 and 70% Hispanic), authorities have received more than 300 complaints about garage dwell-35 ing in the past eight months. In nearby South Gate, where some 4,000 garages provide shelter for 20,000 people, about 900 families have been evicted from backyards in the past three years. But a severe crackdown, officials agree, would only leave the unlucky completely homeless.

40   For others, however, a garage might seem luxurious. Jim Bird, 38, is living in his yellow 1975 Plymouth Fury in a parking lot in Studio City. A divorced former homeowner from Riverside, Bird is one of some 5,000 automobile dwellers in the San Fernando Valley. Unemployed, he could not 45 afford a home when he last worked, at $5 an hour. Says he: "There is just no way you can pay rent with that."

22. Identify the statement below which gives the most accurate statement of the central idea of this passage.
    A. Hispanic working poor make up the majority of garage dwellers.
    B. A severe crackdown on garage dwellers would only complicate the housing problem.
    C. Los Angeles County is facing a growing population of poor people who are living in such places as garages and automobiles.
    D. The L.A. trend may be the wave of the future for the nation's working poor.

23. All of the following are factors in Jim Bird's plight except
    A. alcohol.
    B. unemployment.
    C. $5 an hour wages.
    D. divorce.

24. In this context, the word dearth (line 27) most nearly means
    A. oversupply.
    B. abundance.
    C. lack.
    D. surge.

25. In the first sentence of the last paragraph ("For others, however, a garage might seem luxurious."), the author indicates that his or her purpose is to show
    A. that many people prefer garages for living.
    B. that garages can be fixed up luxuriously.
    C. that many people don't care about living conditions.
    D. how desperate for housing many people really are.

26. In developing the passage, the organizational pattern used by the author could be described as
    A. clarification.
    B. cause and effect.
    C. definition.
    D. time order.

27. The author's statement "In Los Angeles County . . . a growing
    number of the poor are the not-quite-homeless, forced to live in
    garages, automobiles, even tool sheds and converted chicken
    coops." (lines 12–16) is a statement of
    A. fact.
    B. opinion.

Passage 7

At the risk of—no, for the purpose of—inflaming the body
politic, I herewith call attention to the Supreme Court's sudden
discovery of yet another constitutional right. It is the right of a
convicted criminal in a capital case to prevent a jury, as it
considers his sentence, from receiving reports or testimony about
the suffering spread by his crime.

In a case concerning a double murder, the Court ruled 5–4
that the prohibition of "cruel and unusual punishment" is
violated if a state presents jurors with evidence of the impact of a
murder on the victim's family.

In 1983 in West Baltimore, an elderly couple was murdered
by John Booth and a friend. The victims were stabbed with a
kitchen knife.

Maryland requires a pre-sentence report that includes a
"victim-impact statement" assessing the effect of crimes on
others. In this case, the statement documented the sort of
radiating suffering that killings often cause. Relatives suffered
from sleeplessness, unfocused fear, panic when a loved one was
late arriving home. The killings were for the relatives "a
completely devastating and life-altering experience."

The Court ruled that in capital cases such information is
"irrelevant." Justice Powell (joined by Brennan, Marshall,
Blackmun and Stevens) said that an impact statement "can
serve no other purpose than to inflame the jury," is "inconsistent
with reasoned decision-making," and poses a risk that death
sentences will be imposed "arbitrarily."

The majority's rickety argument rests on a preposterous
principle: that a criminal's "personal responsibility and moral
guilt," his blameworthiness, is unrelated to the suffering his
crime causes. The Court says that because death is a sentence

unlike any other, it is impermissible to permit impact statements that might intrude "arbitrariness" into sentencing in capital cases.

• • • • • •

The majority is troubled by the fact that some relatives of murder victims will be more articulate, passionate, and moving than others, so not all murderers will be equally jeopardized by victim-impact statements. Therefore such statements impart "arbitrariness" in sentencing. For the majority, "arbitrary" describes any deviation from perfect equality of risk for defendants. But as White says, a criminal-justice system purged of such "arbitrariness" is a chimera. No two prosecutors are of equal ability, no two witnesses are of equal impact on juries.

• • • • • •

Punishment may serve several purposes. It may reform the person punished. It may deter others from following his path. But all punishment necessarily is expressive. It expresses community values. The Court, by trying to prevent juries in capital cases from being "inflamed," is trying to prevent the expression of outrage, even outrage about—no, *especially* outrage about— the most outrageous of crimes.

28. In this passage, the author shows bias in favor of which of the following?
    A. the death penalty for the crime of murder
    B. pre-sentence reports which include a "victim-impact state-ment"
    C. the Supreme Court's recent decision
    D. pre-sentence reports with no "victim-impact report"

29. The author of this passage has created a tone (mood/feeling) that could be described as
    A. amused.
    B. apathetic.
    C. detached.
    D. intense.

30. From this passage, you could conclude that the Supreme Court
    A. made the right decision.
    B. made the wrong decision.
    C. was doing its job properly.
    D. was doing its job improperly.

Passage 8

You say that gymnasts are the best all-around athletes, but you're a gymnast—what else could you say?

31. Is the argument logically valid or invalid?
    A. valid
    B. invalid

Passage 9

If Karl Linnas is guilty, this is what he did. In the early 1940s, during the German occupation of his native Estonia, he was chief of a Nazi concentration camp in a place called Tartu. Twelve thousand East Europeans were executed there
5 including 2000 Jews. Linnas ordered half-naked men, women, and children transported to a ditch and gunned down. Some of them he finished off himself.

These are the charges supported by eyewitness accounts and recovered camp documents. In 1962 a Soviet court tried
10 Linnas *in absentia* as a war criminal and sentenced him to death. But by that time he was living in Greenlawn, N.Y., having become a citizen in 1960, nine years after entering the U.S. In 1981, however, his citizenship was revoked after a court determined that he had lied about his wartime activi-
15 ties to immigration officials. The U.S. Supreme Court will shortly decide whether to block his deportation temporarily. If it refuses to do so, Linnas, 67, will probably soon be on a plane to the U.S.S.R. There his execution is very probable, though the Soviets may go through the motions of a new
20 trial.

The issue that the Supreme Court will decide is a narrow one, whether to grant him a stay in order to consider his third petition to that court. But controversy has crystallized around the larger question—as much ethical as legal—of
25 whether the U.S. is wrong to use Soviet-supplied evidence in its pursuit of Linnas and other accused Nazi war criminals. The honorable sheriff in the westerns, after all, protected even the most despicable criminal from the savage mob. In short, in its zeal to see a Nazi atrocity punished, is the U.S.
30 guilty of trimming its standards of justice?

32. Identify the statement below which gives the most accurate statement of the central idea of this passage.
    A. Karl Linnas was found guilty in 1962, *in absentia,* as a war criminal.
    B. The U.S. Supreme Court will shortly decide whether to block Linnas's deportation to Russia.
    C. Karl Linnas ordered thousands of East Europeans executed in Nazi concentration camps.
    D. In the Karl Linnas case, the U.S. may be guilty of trimming its standards of justice.

33. The example of the honorable sheriff in westerns was used to illustrate
    A. that the Linnas case has the elements of a western.
    B. that the U.S. is supposed to give equal protection to all accused.
    C. that perhaps "frontier justice" would be appropriate in the Linnas case.
    D. if Linnas is not deported soon, he may be lynched.

34. As used in line 28, the word despicable most nearly means
    A. hardened.
    B. savage.
    C. contemptible.
    D. foolish.

35. In the first sentence "If Karl Linnas is guilty, this is what he did." the author indicates that his or her purpose *in this paragraph* is to
    A. compare.
    B. classify.
    C. offer a solution.
    D. list or explain.

36. In developing the entire passage, the organizational pattern used by the author could be described as
    A. clarification.
    B. simple listing.
    C. cause and effect.
    D. comparison.

37. The author's statement "Linnas ordered half-naked men, women, and children transported to a ditch and gunned down." (in lines 5–6) is a statement of

A. fact.

B. opinion.

Passage 10

The first chapter of the Book of Genesis describes the creation of the world. The narrative is direct and simple. "In the beginning God created the heavens and the earth. . . ."

First there was light and then a division between light and darkness. Then came the firmament and the constitution of the sky and the earth. The seas were then brought together, and the dry land was made to appear.

Grass and seed-yielding herbs and trees then made their appearance upon the land. Sun, moon and stars were assigned their places in the firmament, and the seasons were established. The waters of the earth were made to swarm with living creatures, and birds were made to fly above the earth. Then came the cattle, creeping things and beasts of earth and, last of all, man.

In recent years, science has revealed how, instead of being the work of six days, creation consumed untold millions of years. Instead of the things in the world being brought into existence by a sudden fiat, they came out of the long process of a development we call evolution.

But the realization that the creation story in Genesis is not exact history or science does not destroy its worth.

Its writer, some three thousand years ago, could not know what modern science has revealed. In telling the story, he could use only the accumulated knowledge of his day. The orderly succession of creative acts that Genesis sets forth reveals an astonishing insight into the way our world did come into existence. God is at the beginning of things, the active agent in the creation of all that is. In this, scripture is not in conflict with modern science; nor is modern science in conflict with it.

Today science and religion can go hand in hand in their appreciation of the beauty and force of creation's story as recorded in Genesis.

38. In this passage, the author shows bias in favor of
    A. the unknown as creator.
    B. man as creator.
    C. science as creator.
    D. God as creator.

39. The author of this passage has created a mood that could be described as
    A. intimate.
    B. reverent.
    C. nostalgic.
    D. farcical.

40. The author's statement that "God is at the beginning of things, the active agent in the creation of all that is." is
    A. valid.
    B. invalid.

41. The writer of the passage probably feels that
    A. leaving religion out of education is wrong.
    B. leaving religion out of education is right.
    C. the story of creation of both science and Genesis should be taught to children.
    D. teaching Genesis is more important than teaching evolution.

42. What is the relationship between the sentences in the second paragraph?
    A. cause and effect
    B. time sequence
    C. statement and clarification
    D. generalization and example

DIRECTIONS: In the following sentence, a certain relationship between parts of the sentence can be identified. Read the sentence carefully; then choose the phrase which identifies the relationship between parts of the sentence.

Passage 11

They are aimless and materialistic and have no guiding principle, either aesthetic or ethical, and no stabilizing central purpose.

43. What is the phrase which identifies the relationship between parts of the sentence?
    A. time order
    B. cause and effect
    C. comparison and/or contrast
    D. statement and clarification

Passage 12

Since Dale's paintings are nontraditional and visionary, often taking advantage of quick-drying paints, they must take less time to complete.

44. Is the author's argument logically valid or invalid?
    A. valid
    B. invalid

READING POST-TEST ANSWERS, ANALYSIS, AND REVIEW GUIDE

ANSWERS AND ANALYSIS

QUESTION	ANSWER	ANALYSIS	REMINDER
1	A	author's purpose	The passage is a narrative of a specific skydiving experience.
2	B	fact/opinion	The word *daring* should suggest to you that the statement is an opinion as should the exaggerated *anyone's*. However, the statement "Rothe said that he had never seen such . . ." would be a fact—it would be *provable* that Rothe actually made the statement (whether it was true or not).
3	D	pattern	Events are described second by second, in time order.
4	B	central idea	This is a restatement of the thesis statement in the first paragraph.
5	C	details	The last sentence discusses a comprehensive review that confirms and illustrates the cancer-fighting qualities of beta carotene discussed in the passage.

QUESTION	ANSWER	ANALYSIS	REMINDER
6	D	word meaning	The answer is in parentheses in the sentence with the word.
7	A	author's purpose	*Witness what has been happening* suggests that the author is going to tell us just that.
8	C	pattern	The passage clarifies the statement made in the first paragraph.
9	A	fact/opinion	The phrase *researchers have discovered* in the previous sentence indicates something that has been proven.
10	B	valid/invalid	There are other daily costs besides gas.
11	D	conclusion	While Jackie Onassis buys European sneakers, it does not follow that *all* rich people do. Foot structure is briefly mentioned but not as having changed. Basic sneakers are mentioned as desirable but not necessarily as the best.
12	C	bias	Reread the last paragraph.
13	B	tone	The passage is light and humorous.

QUESTION	ANSWER	ANALYSIS	REMINDER
14	A	word meaning	The other options do not fit the context, which suggests movement toward the sports shop.
15	C	details	Comfort was never mentioned.
16	D	central idea	Note that all of the other choices use probable exaggerations—*all, everywhere, everyone*. That fact alone might suggest to you that they are likely incorrect answers.
17	D	relationship within sentence	The other choices fit neither grammatically nor sensibly.
18	D	relationship within sentence	You might be tempted to choose A, *however*, as an answer. But to do so, you would have to assume that being eleven *normally includes* adventure, making the contrast indicated by *however* appropriate. It is also worth noting that the punctuation given in the passage allows only choice D.
19	C	relationship between sentences	The passage obviously is telling a story chronologically, making *Then* the appropriate word.

QUESTION	ANSWER	ANALYSIS	REMINDER
20	B	relationship between sentences	Choices A, C, and D create sentence fragments. Choice B, *Yet,* appropriately signals a contrast—*was not . . . way out/continues to be a dream.*
21	C	relationship within sentence	The two parts of the sentence contain ideas of equal weight, ideas that are not logically contrasted. The conjunction *and* is the best choice.
22	C	central idea	The other choices are details.
23	A	details	Alcohol wasn't mentioned.
24	C	word meaning	The other three choices indicate *availability* of housing, which would not logically *push people into makeshift shelters.*
25	D	author's purpose	The other choices are not mentioned and are logically unlikely.
26	A	pattern	The author is explaining a problem—clarifying. While the passage does suggest poverty, high rental costs, and lack of public housing as *causes* resulting in these living conditions, the passage *pri-*

QUESTION	ANSWER	ANALYSIS	REMINDER
			marily clarifies the conditions themselves.
27	A	fact/opinion	These living conditions can be validated.
28	B	bias	The author obviously is in favor of such reports.
29	D	tone	The author has strong feelings. Note such words as *inflaming, rickety, preposterous* and *outrageous*.
30	B	conclusion	Don't confuse the correct answer with D. There is no suggestion by the author that the Supreme Court was doing its job improperly (its job being to make decisions), only that it came to the wrong decision.
31	B	valid/invalid	*What else could you say?* You could say the truth, even if you are a gymnast.
32	D	central idea	The other choices are details. In this case, the central idea is contained in the last sentence of the passage.
33	B	details	The *sheriff's* protection from the *savage mob* is an analogy for

QUESTION	ANSWER	ANALYSIS	REMINDER
			the *U.S.* protection from the possibly *savage Soviets.*
34	C	word meaning	Clearly a negative term is called for here. But in this case, knowing that is not especially helpful because all of the terms are negative to some degree. This is a case in which you must rely on your own knowledge of word meanings and on some common sense. For example, *savage* is an unlikely choice because it is used in connection with *mob,* and *foolish* is most likely too mild a negative.
35	D	author's purpose	We presume from the statement that the author will tell us *what he did.*
36	A	pattern	Many aspects of the case against Carl Linnas are explained by the passage.
37	A	fact/opinion	This is a difficult question. Note that the passage earlier states that Linnas did certain things *if* he is guilty. The guilt or innocence of the man

QUESTION	ANSWER	ANALYSIS	REMINDER
			is, at this point, an opinion—at least as far as this writer is concerned. However, it is a provable fact that the people mentioned were transported to a ditch and gunned down, and *if Linnas is guilty,* he is the one who ordered it.
38	D	bias	The author states that *God is at the beginning of things . . .*
39	B	tone	The use of the biblical passage and of words such as *beauty and force of creation's story* establishes the tone.
40	B	valid/invalid	The assertion may be true but is not provable. It is a matter of belief.
41	C	conclusion	The author suggests the value of both the story of Genesis and the scientific explanation of the creation of the world. If both are valuable, it follows that both would probably be thought appropriate to be taught to children. However, religion in its larger sense is not discussed.

QUESTION	ANSWER	ANALYSIS	REMINDER
42	B	relationship between sentences	Note the words *First, then,* etc.
43	D	relationship within sentence	Most of the sentence clarifies the terms *aimless* and *materialistic.*
44	B	valid/invalid	Other things than paint-drying time may take longer in this "nontraditional" painting.

SCORE: _____ (number of correct answers)
TIME: _____

REVIEW GUIDE

IF YOU MISSED QUESTIONS	REVIEW SECTIONS
	Literal Comprehension
4, 16, 22, 32	1. central idea (p. 139)
5, 15, 23, 33	2. details (p. 142)
6, 14, 24, 34	3. word meaning (p. 144)
	Critical Comprehension
1, 7, 25, 35	1. author's purpose (p. 148)
3, 8, 26, 36	2. organizational pattern (p. 150)
2, 9, 27, 37	3. fact/opinion (p. 153)
12, 28, 38	4. bias (p. 155)
13, 29, 39	5. tone (p. 158)
17, 18, 21, 43	6. relationship within sentence (p. 161)
19, 20, 42	7. relationship between sentences (p. 162)
10, 31, 40, 44	8. valid/invalid (p. 164)
11, 30, 41	9. conclusion (p. 168)

Part IV:
Preparing for the CLAST Essay Test
(Essay Subtest)

<table>
<tr><td colspan="1" align="center">FORMAT OF THE CLAST ESSAY TEST</td></tr>
</table>

FORMAT OF THE CLAST ESSAY TEST

One Essay
Based on One of Two Given Topics

Time: 60 Minutes

Note: If for any reason you retake the Essay Test (see page 5 for information about retakes), you will be allowed 120 minutes to write your essay on your second attempt and all subsequent attempts.

PREPARING FOR THE CLAST ESSAY TEST

INTRODUCTION

What the Essay Test Tests

The CLAST Essay Test tests your ability to write a logical, specific, and correct composition in standard written English within a limited time. You will have sixty minutes to write a complete essay on one of two topics presented on the test. You will be writing in ink, so bring two fresh pens with you.

Essay Length

The CLAST does not specify how long your essay must be. It does, however, define the standards by which essays are graded. In order to meet those standards successfully, your essay should consist of five paragraphs of from three to seven sentences each.

CLAST Essay Scoring Procedures

The essay is the only one of the four CLAST subtests that is graded by people rather than by machine. Remembering that human beings are reading what you write will make your task clearer. If you know exactly how the readers will evaluate your writing, you are more likely to earn a high score on your essay.

Your essay will be graded by two experienced readers, usually college English instructors. Each will read your essay in about two minutes, not stopping to correct errors or to puzzle out what you might be trying to say and without discussing your work with the other reader. After one reading, each grader will form an impression of your essay that is expressed in a number. These numbers range from one (1) for the worst essays to four (4) for the best.

The numbers assigned to your writing by two readers working in different areas are added to arrive at your essay score. If both independently decide that your essay is among the best, both will give you a four and your essay score will be eight, the highest essay grade on the CLAST. A grade of four from one reader and three from the second will add up to a final score of seven for your essay. If the two readers' impressions of your work disagree by more than one number, a third reader resolves the difference.

CLAST Scoring Standards

A score of five (one reader assigning a grade of two and another assigning a grade of three) is the minimum passing score. Each reader's evaluation is based on how well your essay demonstrates your skill with nine elements:

1. a definite purpose
2. a clear thesis
3. an organizational plan
4. well-developed supporting paragraphs
5. specific, relevant details
6. a variety of effective sentence patterns
7. logical transitions
8. effective word choice
9. correct standard English usage

How Part IV Teaches

The first five elements on the evaluation list have been discussed in the reading instructions in Part III of this book. Elements 6 through 9 have been fully explained in the grammar sections that make up Part II. The following pages will show you exactly how to combine these elements into a high-scoring CLAST essay.

YOU AND YOUR READERS

All successful writers are considerate of their readers. If you know how your CLAST readers work and what they expect, you will have taken an important step toward earning their highest grade.

How CLAST Readers Work

On a weekend shortly after CLAST day, your essay will be gathered with four or five thousand others at a central location in Florida. After a Friday evening practice session, readers will begin scoring those essays at 8:30 Saturday morning, and with a short break for lunch, they will continue reading until 5 P.M. They will resume reading at 8:30 Sunday morning. By the time the grading session ends late Sunday afternoon, each reader will have evaluated approximately five hundred handwritten essays.

What Readers Expect

Imagine yourself behind a reader's eyes. What sort of essay would be likely to make a good impression on you? With hundreds of unread compositions in store for you on a hot Saturday afternoon, away from your home and family while the rest of the world is at the beach, how patient would you be with sloppy handwriting, confusing organization, vague descriptions, careless sentence structure, unclear transitions, or unfunny jokes?

Readers will form a *very positive* impression of your essay if it *very obviously* demonstrates skill in the nine elements which they are evaluating. They will be able to see your abilities at work only if you write very legibly, so they expect you to put some effort into your handwriting. If you fulfill these expectations, you will have no trouble passing the CLAST Essay Test.

CONSTRUCTING A CLAST ESSAY

Writing and Time

Even if you learned enough from Parts II and III of this book to earn maximum scores on the Grammar and Reading Tests, you must—if you hope to do well on the Essay Test—learn to call up that information in a form that you can use at the moment you need it. The CLAST Essay Test is an exercise in time management as much as it is a test of your language skills. It is *not* a test of your literary originality or creativity. If you think of the essay as art you will either frighten yourself or waste time waiting for inspiration. This sort of essay is not created; it is constructed.

The instructions that follow tell you exactly what to do at every stage of the essay-writing process and how much time to spend doing it. Writing is never easy, but if you follow these step-by-step instructions you will find constructing your CLAST essay to be as straightforward as preparing Thanksgiving dinner or assembling a bike.

FIRST STAGE: Writing the Opening Paragraph—Time: 15 minutes

Step 1: Read the Two Topics Presented on the Test (30 seconds)

- *Examples:* TOPIC 1. Useful skills you have learned in college.

    TOPIC 2. Economic changes that have affected the American family.

- *What to do:* Without a moment's hesitation, underline the key words in both topics. Every topic can be simplified to a basic SVC unit (review Grammar Competencies section 1). The subject and complement will both be nouns. Therefore, underline only three words: two nouns and a verb.

- *Example:* TOPIC 1. Useful <u>skills</u> you have <u>learned</u> in <u>college</u>.

    TOPIC 2. Economic <u>changes</u> that have <u>affected</u> the American <u>family</u>.

Underlining the three words which make up the basic idea expressed by the topics makes the next very important step easier for you.

Step 2: Choose the Topic You Know the Most About (1 minute)

• *What to do:* Decide how many specific examples you could quickly provide for each topic. Do you have more detailed information in your memory about the skills you learned in college or about economic changes that affect the family? Most students would find Topic 1 easier to write about because it does not require knowledge beyond their own recent experience.

• *Tip:* Of the two topics on most CLAST Essay Tests, one will sound like a topic on a natural-science or social-science test; the other will sound like an English-essay topic. Unless you have just written a term paper on, for example, changing relationships in two-income families, the social-science-type topic would be a risky choice. The English-essay-type topic gives you more freedom to decide what examples to use. That freedom makes writing an essay much easier.

Step 3: Write Your Thesis Statement (30 seconds)

• *What to do:* Look again at the topic you have chosen. Write a sentence that combines the key words you have underlined in the printed topic with your own words. The words you add will define the main idea (thesis) of your essay. To make your thesis statement definite, which is essential, the words you add must be definite.

• *Example:* I have learned three very useful skills while at Beach-front Community College.

Write your thesis statement neatly in the answer folder in ink. Start the first word an inch to the right of the left-hand margin to indicate the beginning of a paragraph. These are the words your readers will have to understand without effort, so write legibly and skip every other line in the answer folder. Essays written in print or script are equally acceptable. If you decide to print, make clear distinctions between your capital and lower case (small) letters.

• *Tip:* When the topic you have chosen requires you to discuss a number of items (*skills*), always use the number three in your thesis statement. (The reason for this will become clear in later steps.) Some CLAST topics require you to discuss a person or place. If you choose one of those, name the person or place in your thesis statement.

Step 4: Plan Your Essay (6 minutes)

• *What to do:* On the blank page provided with the test, draw a circle and divide it into three equal wedges. Above the circle, jot down three key words of your thesis. The circle represents your thesis, and the wedges represent three divisions of that main idea. In order for your essay to be logically balanced, these three divisions must be equal in importance and concreteness. In each wedge, write a very brief name for each division. The diagram will help you see whether the divisions you come up with really are about equal and whether they relate to your thesis. Cross out divisions you reject.

• *Example:*

THREE USEFUL SKILLS

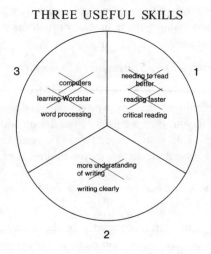

In wedge 1, *needing to read better* is rejected because it is not a skill. *Reading faster,* the next attempt to focus on a specific category, names a skill, but it does so vaguely. The final choice, *critical reading,* names a specific skill, one that you know a great deal about.

In wedge 2, *more understanding of writing* is discarded because it is not a skill. *Writing clearly* is a skill, and once again it is a subject you will have no difficulty discussing in a very detailed way.

In wedge 3, *computers* is rejected because it names a thing and not a skill. *Learning Wordstar* is a skill, but because it names the title of a computer program, it is much more specific than wedges 1 and 2. The final choice, *word processing,* names a skill that is about equal in importance and concreteness to the thesis divisions in the other two wedges.

• *Tip:* Planning is the most important single step in the essay-writing process. An error here can be terminal. If you choose to write about skills, be certain that you are not confusing skills (*critical reading*) with needs (*needing to read better*). If you do, then everything you write about that need will be irrelevant to the thesis, which promises a discussion of skills. Such irrelevance may result in a poor grade.

Use the full four minutes budgeted for this step to answer two questions very carefully: 1. Do these divisions deliver what my thesis promises? 2. Do I have some specific information about these divisions? If the answer to both questions is *yes,* your essay will take shape without any further outlining. Don't waste time writing a list of the details you plan to use for each division. If you have chosen a topic you know something about and if you have divided that topic logically, the details will spring to your mind as you need them.

Step 5: Organize Your Plan (3 minutes)

• *What to do:* Decide on the order in which you will present the three skills. Two types of organization will be easiest for you to use and your readers to follow: 1. sequence of time; 2. order of importance.

• *Example:*

Skill	Sequence in Which Skills Were Learned	Order of Importance of Skills to You
reading	first	second
writing	second	first
word processing	third	third

• *Tip:* Choose the method of organization that is most appropriate to the type of essay you write. In narrative (story-telling) essays like this one, time sequences are best; order of importance organization is most natural and effective in essays that explain or persuade (see pages 217–219).

Step 6: Complete Your Opening Paragraph (4 minutes)

• *What to do:* In the answer folder, introduce the skills you will discuss (Step 4) in the order you have chosen (Step 5). The simplest method of doing this is to name the three skills in a single sentence. Remember that standard English usage requires that similar items be listed in words of similar form (review parallelism, Grammar Competencies section 4). Keep in mind also that this sentence will be an important part of your finished essay, so write legibly and skip every other line.

• *Example:* I have learned three useful skills while at Beachfront Community College. These three skills are reading critically, writing clearly, and using a word processor.

• *Tip:* If you are feeling confident, you may want to include more information in your opening paragraph. Although the example above shows the easiest and most reliable way of getting started, readers are often favorably impressed when the opening paragraph explicitly states the writer's organizational plan.

• *Example:* I have learned three useful skills while at Beachfront Community College. After learning how to read critically, I discovered the importance and techniques of clear writing. Later, I made better use of both these skills by learning how to use a word processor.

SECOND STAGE: Writing the Body Paragraphs— Time: 27 minutes

• *What to do:* Build the body of your essay with three paragraphs, each discussing in detail one of the items introduced in the opening paragraph. Arrange the paragraphs in the order of the organizational plan.

Step 1: Write Topic Sentence 1 (2 minutes)

• *What to do:* In the answer folder, begin a new paragraph with a sentence about the skill of reading critically. Your thesis statement in the opening paragraph promises an essay about skills that are useful to you. The rest of that paragraph promises that your discussion of those skills will follow a specific order. Begin to keep those promises now with a sentence that connects the two ideas *reading critically* and *useful to me.* Introduce that sentence with a word or more indicating which order you are following.

- *Example:* In my first semester, I learned how essential critical reading skills are for a college student.

- *Tips:* The sentence that begins the body of your discussion makes a strong impression on your reader. If your first topic sentence combines two important ideas in a logical structure, that impression will be positive.

While preparing for the Essay Test, review all the types of sentence patterns available to you (see Grammar Competencies section 4). As you write the body of the essay, make a deliberate effort to use several different sentence patterns whenever appropriate in each paragraph.

In the example, a simple modifier (*In my first semester*) shows how this sentence fits into the organizational plan. The rest of the sentence uses words (*essential, college student*) that link it to the thesis.

Step 2: Complete Body Paragraph 1 (7 minutes)

- *What to do:* Write three or four sentences of varying patterns that answer the question "Why or how is this skill essential?" Pack these sentences with specific details and examples.

- *Example:* Although I had always enjoyed light reading, I soon learned that my skills could not keep up with the volume of college work. In history alone, for example, I struggled through eighty pages of facts and dates about the American Revolution every night. A course in study skills ended my struggle. By learning how to recognize main ideas and identify supporting details, I increased my reading speed by forty-five percent. Soon I was able to stay ahead of my history assignments.

- *Tips:* Use specific names and numbers even if you have to invent them. "I increased my reading speed by *forty-five percent*" will impress any reader with your use of specific detail; "I increased my reading speed *a lot"* will make no impression at all.

Concrete examples (*the American Revolution* instead of *some historical events*) are also important. When you use one, alert the reader to it with transitions (see Grammar Competencies section 2).

Step 3: Begin Body Paragraph 2 (2 minutes)

• *What to do:* Link this paragraph to both the first body paragraph and the thesis statement. Do this with an opening sentence that repeats a key word or idea from each.

• *Example:* The more I learned about reading, the more I appreciated the usefulness of clear writing.

• *Tip:* Never shift from *I* to *you.* Although "The more *you* learn about reading" may sound natural in speech and can be effective in some kinds of writing, it would be considered an error on the Essay Test. To be safe, never use the word *you* anywhere in your CLAST essay.

Step 4: Complete Body Paragraph 2 (7 minutes)

• *What to do:* Repeat the techniques used to develop body paragraph 1. Here you will be answering the question "How or why is clear writing useful to me?" For variety, you may want to place the topic sentence at the end rather than the beginning of this paragraph.

• *Example:* I saw that good writing was based on solid logic, careful word choice, and correct usage. The writing that communicated best to me was specific and detailed as well as correct. As I learned what good writers were doing, I followed their example in my own essays, and I began earning higher grades in all my courses, especially English and humanities courses. The skill of clear writing is useful to me because it enables me to communicate effectively all that I now learn from my reading.

• *Tip:* No matter where you place the topic sentence of this paragraph, make it an obvious link to both the thesis of the whole essay and the topic of body paragraph 1. The example here uses key words to refer to the overall thesis (*skill, useful*), to the content of body paragraph 2 (*clear writing*), and to the content of body paragraph 1 (*reading*).

Step 5: Write a Topic Sentence for Body Paragraph 3 (2 minutes)

• *What to do:* Write a sentence that combines references to three elements: 1. the organizational plan; 2. the third skill; 3. usefulness to me.

• *Example:* Finally, learning to use a word processor has allowed me to use my other skills more efficiently.

• *Tip:* The first word of this sentence shows that the writer is in control of this essay. *Finally* signals the end of an essay organized in a sequence of first to last. Essays constructed on a scale of importance would use a different signal.

Step 6: Complete Body Paragraph 3 (7 minutes)

• *What to do:* Repeat the process of answering the question "How or why is this skill useful to me?" Again, present many specific details and examples in a variety of sentence patterns.

• *Example:* My computer skills help me to use more of what I read in my essays without wasting time or effort. I keep notes and bibliographies in my computer's memory and use its editing capacities to reorganize my essays without rewriting the same material several times. Recently, I wrote a long research paper in less than two weeks, less time than the reading alone would have taken me in the past. The best part is that the essay was printed quickly.

• *Tip:* As you reach the end of your essay, remind yourself to write or print legibly.

THIRD STAGE: Writing the Concluding Paragraph— Time: 8 minutes

Step 1: Refresh Your Memory (1 minute)

• *What to do:* Quickly read through your first four paragraphs. Do not stop to correct any errors you might notice.

Step 2: Write Your Conclusion (7 minutes)

• *What to do:* Conclude with a general look at your topic. In a time-sequence essay, for example, you might conclude with a statement about the future applications of the skills you learned in college. An essay organized by order of importance might conclude with a brief discussion of the value of the skills in anyone's life. Only if you can't think of any other ending should you conclude with a summary of what you have just written.

> • *Example:* These three skills have made my college work both
> easier and more valuable. Now that I have learned them,
> I know that the skills of critical reading, clear writing,
> and word processing will benefit me in whatever I decide
> to do in the future.

• *Tip:* Tie this last paragraph to the first paragraph of the essay by repeating one or two key words from the thesis statement. Here *learned, skills,* and *college* give this essay a tone of completeness by closing the circle with links to the thesis.

FOURTH STAGE: Proofreading and Titling—Time: 10 minutes

Step 1: Proofread for Errors (5 minutes)

• *What to do:* Read your essay as closely as if it were a passage on the CLAST Grammar Test. Look for errors in sentence structure, punctuation, and usage. Cross out with a single line any errors you find and insert neatly written corrections in the blank spaces above the errors.

• *Tip:* Agreement errors are more likely than other types to turn up in your essay. Check all subject-verb agreement especially (review Grammar Competencies section 5). If you think you have misspelled a word and you are not sure of the correct spelling, replace it with a substitute that you can spell correctly.

Step 2: Write a Title for Your Essay (1 minute)

• *What to do:* Write a clear, simple title that combines the three key words of your thesis statement. Center the title above the opening paragraph. Capitalize the first letter of each word.

- *Example:* Three Useful College Skills

Step 3: Proofread for Improvements (4 minutes)

- *What to do:* Use all the remaining time to make small improvements in your essay. In addition to making your meaning clearer, these revisions demonstrate to your reader that you know what good writing is.

                    twenty-six-page

- *Example:* Recently, I wrote a ~~long~~ ∧ research paper in ~~less than~~

              twelve days

              ~~two-weeks~~, less time than the reading alone would have
                 ∧

                        My new word-processing skills

              taken me in the past. ~~The best part is that~~
                           ∧

              also enabled me to print the entire essay in nine

              ~~the essay was printed quickly.~~

              minutes.

- *Tip:* When proofreading for improvements, concentrate on making your language more detailed and your logical transitions smoother. The example changes approximate words (*long, less than two weeks*) to specific ones (*twenty-six-page, twelve days*). The new transition (*also*) links the last sentence to the rest of the paragraph and to the thesis. These small improvements help your reader, and anything that helps your reader helps you.

PRACTICING THE CLAST ESSAY

Format of the CLAST Essay Test

The CLAST Essay Test gives you a choice of two essay topics, each presented in the form of a single sentence. The topics are accompanied by a full page of directions which are the same on every CLAST. Get to know them now so that you will not have to spend valuable time reading them during the sixty-minute test period.

Writing a Practice Essay

Use the following sample Essay Test to practice both your writing and time-management skills. Above all, begin now to develop the habit of attacking the topics at once instead of waiting for an idea to come to you.

Improving your time-management skills now will enable you to produce your best writing on CLAST day. Time each stage of your writing in this first practice. As you finish each of the five paragraphs, make a note of how long it took you to organize and write. When you have finished writing and proofreading the practice essay, compare your actual times with the suggested timetable given in this section. Continue practicing with some of the other sample essay topics given until your actual time falls within the guidelines.

SAMPLE ESSAY TEST

DIRECTIONS FOR ESSAY

You will have 60 minutes to plan, write, and proofread an essay on one of the topics below.

TOPIC 1. A character from fiction or the movies who has a positive impact on people.

OR

TOPIC 2. A natural event which occurs periodically and which has beneficial effects.

Read the two topics again and select the one on which you wish to write your essay. In order for your essay to be scored, it *must* be on *only one* of these topics.

In your essay, you should introduce the subject and then either

---explain the subject you have chosen, or
---take a position about your subject and support it.

At least two evaluators will read your essay and assign it a score. They will pay special attention to whether you

---have a clear thesis or main idea,
---develop your thesis logically and in sufficient detail,
---use well-formed sentences and paragraphs,
---use language appropriately and effectively, and
---follow standard practices in spelling, punctuation, and grammar.

Take a few minutes to think about what you want to say before you start writing. Leave yourself a few minutes at the end of the period to proofread and make corrections.

You may cross out or add information as necessary. Although your handwriting will not affect your score, you should write as legibly as possible so the evaluators can easily read your essay.

You may use the following page to plan your essay before you begin to write in the answer folder.

Do not begin until you are told to do so.

A WRITER AND A READER AT WORK

This section will help you evaluate your own practice essay. It includes a sample essay written under CLAST conditions by a first year community college student who was trained in this book's essay-construction method. The essay was composed within sixty minutes in answer to the sample test in this section.

Each paragraph of the student essay is accompanied by a reader's response. These comments are by a reader experienced in CLAST essay-evaluation methods. By demonstrating what a trained student can actually write under CLAST conditions and how an experienced reader reacts to that writing, this section will help you measure and improve your own performance.

Background: Topic and Tone

Important choices are made before the writer begins to compose a CLAST essay. Our student writer chose Topic 2:

A natural event which occurs periodically and which has beneficial effects.

The writer decided on the natural-science-type topic only because she happened to have much information relevant to it fresh in her mind.

That decision affected more than the content of her essay, however. The science-type topics usually call for information learned in school rather than from your personal experience. As a result, science-type essays will have a different tone than English-type essays. An essay topic that draws on your personal experience ("skills *you* have learned") will include many uses of the pronouns *I* and *me,* thus creating a very personal tone. Essay topics that require you to produce more general knowledge should have a tone that is more like a textbook than like a letter. You can get that tone in your writing simply by avoiding the use of *I* and *me.* Notice how that is true in this essay.

Background: Purpose

The CLAST essay directions tell you to decide on a purpose for your essay by choosing between explaining your subject and supporting a position about it. One of the reasons for you *not* to read these directions on CLAST day is that you don't need to make this decision. The purpose of your essay will grow naturally out of the construction process detailed in this section. If your body paragraphs all answer the questions "How?" or "Why?" and are controlled by a clear thesis, your essay will have the definite purpose CLAST readers look for. As you will see in our student's essay, the writer is supporting a position about the topic. This *definite purpose* is the inevitable outcome of the writer's providing detailed answers to the *How?* and *Why?* of her thesis. Watch the purpose emerge as the essay progresses.

Sample CLAST Essay

READER'S COMMENTS	ESSAY

Wind is a Necessity of Life

The thesis is clearly relevant to the topic, and the organization shows good planning. The use of a title gives the impression that the writer is in complete control. *Periodical* is nonstandard usage, and *occurence* is a misspelling, but word choice and usage are otherwise good.

The natural, periodical occurence of wind has beneficial and necessary effects on life. Wind spreads the growth of vegetation, contributes to the survival of some animals, and helps control the climate of the earth.

This paragraph is well developed. A clear topic sentence picks up the first element of the organizational plan. Many specific details and a relevant, concrete example support the opening statement of the paragraph.

Wind assists the natural cycle of the growth of vegetation. Its occasional gusts pick up seeds and transplant them in new areas where the plants can grow and multiply. An example of this is the dandelion. The seeds of the dandelion have soft, featherlike tufts which float in the wind. When they come to rest on the soil, the seeds germinate and produce new seeds to be distributed by the wind all over the earth. Without winds that blow periodically, plant growth and diversity are sharply reduced.

A good transition in the first sentence links this clearly to the thesis statement and to the first body paragraph. The word choice here is very good: *prey* and *predators* are exactly right for the context, and *swoop* is an expressive word. More very good examples and specific details.

In addition to plants, many animals depend on the wind to survive. Using the resistance of the wind over the figure-eight motions of their wings, birds defy gravity and fly through the air. Gliding on the winds contributes to birds' survival by making them better hunters that cover great distances and swoop down quietly upon their prey. Flying squirrels are another type of animal which relies on the wind for survival. The large fold of skin under the flying squirrel's arm can be extended so that the animal can float on air currents for short periods of time. He uses this ability to move from tree to tree in search of food and to escape from predators. Like flying squirrels and birds, many animals would be extinct without the action of the winds.

The opening sentence carries out the organizational plan and shows a good control of purpose. The writer continues to vary sentence patterns and use details effectively.

Perhaps the most beneficial effect of the wind is its vital role in climate control. Wind blows evaporated water from the oceans over the land, keeping the land from drying out. Gusts of wind, for example, push water vapor from the Gulf of Mexico inland to the agricultural regions of Florida. The moisture brought in by the wind not only maintains vegetation, but also cools the air during hot summers. The moderate temperatures along Florida's coasts are also caused by the effects of the wind, which carries cooling vapor in summer and warming vapor in winter. Just as wind benefits animals and plant life, it contributes to the comfort of humans.

An effective conclusion. It makes logical general statements about the topic instead of simply repeating the thesis. Overall, this essay shows excellent control and execution.

People often take wind for granted even though it plays such a vital role in their lives. It could be described as life's transportation system. It carries life forms to areas all over the world and brings nutrients where they are needed. Without the wind, we would all perish.

Reader's Grade: 4 (maximum)

Evaluating Your Practice Essays

Unlike the three other subtests, the essay has no answer key. To evaluate your performance on this test, you will need another person's informed opinion about what you have written.

If you can, persuade an English teacher to evaluate your practice essays using the CLAST guidelines listed in this section. If an instructor is not available to you, a friend or parent who has read and understood the essay instructions can provide some useful opinions. If no suitable evaluators are close at hand, you may want to use the mail-order essay evaluation service described on page 220.

Practice Again

The more you practice constructing an essay under pressure, the better your writing will be on CLAST day. Write at least one sixty-minute essay for each of the tests in this book. Begin, if you haven't already done so, with the sample test in this section. Then take the Essay Post-Test at the end of the section. Finally, write an essay as part of your practice with all four CLAST subtests that appear at the end of the book. Following are additional sample essay topics for your use.

ADDITIONAL ESSAY TOPICS

Use these topics for further practice.

1. A character from fiction to whom people have had negative reactions.

2. Important skills for the beginning college student.

3. A political or social leader who has made a positive contribution to society.

4. The most important scientific development of this century.

5. A technological advance that has made life harder for a large number of people.

6. The influence of popular music on current moral attitudes.

7. The most serious problem facing the American family today.

8. Promising careers or jobs for today's college graduates.

COLLEGE SKILLS EVALUATION SERVICE

Two readers experienced in CLAST essay evaluation procedures will read, score, and analyze one of your essays for a fee of five dollars. Your essay will be returned to you within three weeks with a score based on two independent readers' grades, an analysis of your essay's strengths and weaknesses, and a review guide for use with this book.

Since a different set of readers will grade your actual CLAST essay, which will be written under different conditions and on a different topic, the score given to your practice essay will not necessarily predict your actual CLAST score. The response to your practice essay will, however, let you know how informed, experienced readers react to your essay and what they think you could do to improve your writing.

College Skills Evaluation Service is an independent organization and is not affiliated with the College Level Academic Skills Program or the state of Florida. The service is limited to providing an informed assessment of writing skills and guidance in the improvement of those skills.

• To Use the Service:

1. Write an essay in sixty minutes on any one of the sample topics in this book. Write the essay in pen by hand; do *not* type it.

2. Mail your essay in a standard business envelope ($9\frac{1}{2}'' \times 4\frac{1}{4}''$) along with a *check or money order for $5 made payable to:* College Skills Evaluation Service. DO NOT SEND CASH. Be sure to *print your name and return address legibly on your practice essay.* Mail your essay and check or money order to:

    College Skills Evaluation Service
    Post Office Box 10709
    57th Avenue Branch
    Bradenton, FL 34282

3. When your essay is returned, make good use of the analysis and review guide included with it. The guide will tell you which sections of this book contain information that can improve your essay-writing skills. All the improvements you make in your practice writing will increase your confidence and competence on CLAST day.

ESSAY POST-TEST

DIRECTIONS FOR ESSAY

You will have 60 minutes to plan, write, and proofread an essay on one of the topics below.

TOPIC 1. A book written more than fifty years ago that has had a positive impact on people.

OR

TOPIC 2. A natural object that should be preserved.

Read the two topics again and select the one on which you wish to write your essay. In order for your essay to be scored, it *must* be on *only one* of these topics.

In your essay, you should introduce the subject and then either

---explain the subject you have chosen, or
---take a position about your subject and support it.

At least two evaluators will read your essay and assign it a score. They will pay special attention to whether you

---have a clear thesis or main idea,
---develop your thesis logically and in sufficient detail,
---use well-formed sentences and paragraphs,
---use language appropriately and effectively, and
---follow standard practices in spelling, punctuation, and grammar.

Take a few minutes to think about what you want to say before you start writing. Leave yourself a few minutes at the end of the period to proofread and make corrections.

You may cross out or add information as necessary. Although your handwriting will not affect your score, you should write as legibly as possible so the evaluators can easily read your essay.

You may use the following page to plan your essay before you begin to write in the answer folder.

Do not begin until you are told to do so.

Part V:
Preparing for the CLAST Mathematics Test

FORMAT OF THE CLAST MATHEMATICS TEST

Approximately 56 Questions
Time: 90 Minutes

One Question for Each of 56 Competencies
(5 competencies commonly left untested)

Note: On some occasions in the past, a few experimental questions have been added. Experimental questions *are not counted* in scoring your exam.

PREPARING FOR THE CLAST
MATHEMATICS TEST

INTRODUCTION

What the Mathematics Test Tests

The CLAST Mathematics Test includes multiple-choice questions that test for competency in five broad areas:

- arithmetic
- geometry and measurement
- algebra
- statistics, including probability
- logical reasoning

Test questions will be presented in ways that will require that you understand the following:

- algorithms—procedures for getting answers to problems
- concepts—understanding how to use algorithms
- generalizations—using formulas or laws
- problem solving—principles and procedures of problem solving

In each case, the correct answer will be given along with incorrect answers. For many questions, approximating can be a valuable tool. There is no value in completely working out a solution to each question if you don't need to in order to determine the correct answer. You should work out a problem only until you are *certain* (beyond a reasonable doubt) of the correct answer. When you know enough to select the correct answer, stop working the problem and move on. In math classes this was frowned upon, but *not* in taking standardized tests in math.

The CLAST Mathematics Test contains a minimum of fifty questions. Commonly, fifty-six questions are asked. These questions are to be completed in ninety minutes. Each question represents one *specific math competency* within the five broad math areas. For instance, there are at least thirteen arithmetic questions, each one testing a different competency. For example, one arithmetic question tests competency in adding and subtracting rational numbers, while another arithmetic question tests competency in calculating percent increase and decrease. This section identifies each of these math competencies and reviews each. In addition, these competencies and their sample problems are presented in the same order that they are likely to appear on the CLAST. A familiarity with the CLAST content and the pattern of the exam will help you eliminate a good bit of CLAST-phobia.

The number of mathematics competencies (and possible test questions) for each of the five broad areas are listed below.

- arithmetic: 15
- geometry and measurement: 12
- algebra: 17
- statistics, including probability: 9
- logical reasoning: 8

Notice that there are *sixty-one* mathematics competencies in these five areas, but you probably will have only *fifty-six* questions on the test. Five competencies (possibly one from each of the five areas) may not be tested. Unfortunately, you don't know which five, so you will have to review all sixty-one. In addition, there may be a few experimental questions, which *are not counted* in scoring your exam.

Reviewing Your Math

This book is not intended to be a text that will teach you general math. If you don't know basic college math already, you may have to do some intensive self-study, take a college math course, or be tutored in math. You will find that *Cliffs Math Review for Standardized Tests* is an extremely helpful book for those who need intensive review for the basics in standardized test math. You can purchase the book at your bookstore.

What you will find following is a brief description of each math competency that the CLAST tests, very helpful summaries of possible question content, sample problems which illustrate different methods of testing the competency, a listing of common errors that people often make when they work the problems, and in many cases an explanation of how the problem should (or could) be worked. These solutions frequently explain why other answer choices are incorrect. In addition, this book includes three complete CLAST-like exams and their answers: a Pre-Test to enable you to see how well you might do on the CLAST at this moment, a Post-Test to take after you have studied this CLAST math review, and a third math exam included as part of the complete, full-length, CLAST-like exam. You will get a good idea of your weak areas after reviewing the following materials and taking the exams, and you'll be able to selectively brush up your skills in those areas.

BASIC TERMINOLOGY, FORMULAS, AND MATHEMATICAL INFORMATION YOU SHOULD KNOW

As a refresher for all those basic (but often forgotten) math terms, formulas, rules, and general information that is used, referred to, or implied on the CLAST Mathematics Test, the following basic expressions are presented for your review. Before you take the Pre-Test, take a few minutes to look over these basics to reacquaint yourself with them. The more familiar you are with this material, the more efficient you will be in taking the CLAST Mathematics Test.

Common Math Symbol References

$=$ is equal to	$\geq$ is greater than or equal to
$\neq$ is not equal to	$\leq$ is less than or equal to
$>$ is greater than	$<$ is less than

Natural numbers: 1, 2, 3, . . .
Whole numbers: 0, 1, 2, 3, . . .
Integers: $-3, -2, -1, 0, 1, 2, \ldots$
Rational numbers: $-\frac{1}{2}, -\frac{3}{4}, 5, .6, .777 \ldots, \sqrt{25} = 5$
Irrational numbers: numbers whose decimal numerals do not end and do not have a repeating pattern—(.12031 . . .), $\sqrt{3}$
Prime number: number divisible by only 1 and itself—2, 3, 5, 7, 11, 13, . . .

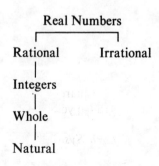

Math Formulas

Triangle	Perimeter $= s_1 + s_2 + s_3$
	Area $= \frac{1}{2}bh$

| Square | Perimeter = $4s$ |
| | Area = $s \cdot s$, or s^2 |

| Rectangle | Perimeter $2(l + w)$ or $2l + 2w$ |
| | Area = bh, or lw |

| Parallelogram | Perimeter = $2(l + w)$, or $2l + 2w$ |
| | Area = bh |

| Trapezoid | Perimeter = $b_1 + b_2 + s_1 + s_2$ |
| | Area = $\frac{1}{2}h(b_1 + b_2)$ |

| Circle | Circumference = $2\pi r$, or πd |
| | Area = πr^2 |

Pythagorean theorem (for right triangles) $a^2 + b^2 = c^2$

The sum of the squares of the legs of a right triangle equals the square of the hypotenuse.

| Cube | Volume = $s \cdot s \cdot s = s^3$ |

| Rectangular solid | Volume = $l \cdot w \cdot h$ |
| | Surface area = $2(lw) + 2(lh) + 2(wh)$ |

| Right Circular Cylinder | Volume = $\pi r^2 h$ |
| | Surface area = $2\pi r^2 + 2\pi r$ |

| Right Circular Cone | Volume = $\frac{1}{3}\pi r^2 h$ |

Measures

Length
5,280 feet = 1 mile

Area
144 square inches (sq in) = 1 square foot (sq ft)
9 square feet = 1 square yard (sq yd)

Metric System

Length—meter
Kilometer (km) = 1000 meters (m)
Hectometer (hm) = 100 meters
Dekameter (dam) = 10 meters
10 decimeters (dm) = 1 meter

100 centimeters (cm) = 1 meter
1000 millimeters (mm) = 1 meter

Volume—liter
1000 milliliters (ml, or mL) = 1 liter (l, or L)
1000 liters = 1 kiloliter (kl, or kL)

Some Approximations
Meter is a little more than a yard ✓
Kilometer is about .6 mile ⬚
Kilogram is about 2.2 pounds ✓
Liter is slightly more than a quart ✓

Math Words and Phrases

Addition	Multiplication
Sum	Of
Total	Product
More than	Times
Greater than	Total (sometimes)
Increase	At (sometimes)
Plus	Twice

Subtraction	Division
Difference	Quotient
Less	Divided by
Fewer	Divided into
Reduced	
Decreased	
Have left	

Properties of Real Numbers Under Addition and Multiplication

Commutative means that the *order* does not make any difference.

$$a + b = b + a \qquad a \times b = b \times a$$

(Commutative does *not* hold for subtraction or division)

Associative means that the *grouping* does not make any difference.

$$(a + b) + c = a + (b + c) \qquad (a \times b) \times c = a \times (b \times c)$$

(Associative does *not* hold for subtraction or division)

The *distributive property* is the process of distributing the number on the outside of the parenthesis to each number on the inside.

$$a(b + c) = a(b) + a(c)$$

(You *cannot* use the distributive property with only *one* operation.)

$$4(3 \times 6 \times 7) \neq 4(3) \times 4(6) \times 4(7)$$

The *identity element* for addition is 0. A number added to 0 gives the original number.

$$a + 0 = a$$

The *identity element* for multiplication is 1. A number multiplied by 1 gives the original number.

$$a \times 1 = a$$

Order of Operations

Working from left to right:
1. do all operations in the *grouping* symbols.
2. do all *exponents* (powers)
3. do all *multiplication* and *division*
4. do all *addition* and *subtraction*

Basic Properties of Exponents

$$x^a \cdot x^b = x^{a+b}$$

$$\frac{x^a}{x^b} = x^{a-b}$$

$$(x^a)^b = x^{ab}$$

$$(xy)^a = x^a y^a$$

$$\left(\frac{x}{y}\right)^a = \frac{x^a}{y^a}$$

Quadratic Equation

$$ax^2 + bx + c = 0$$

Quadratic Formula

$$x = \frac{-b \pm \sqrt{b^2 - 4ac}}{2a}$$

Probability

$$P(A) = \frac{\text{number of favorable outcomes (elements in A)}}{\text{number of possible outcomes (elements in S)}}$$

P(A or B) = P(A) + P(B) − P(A and B occur simultaneously)
P(A and B) = P(A) · P(B)

Odds in Favor of an Event

$$\frac{\text{probability the event will occur}}{\text{probability the event will not occur}}$$

Odds Against an Event

$$\frac{\text{probability the event will not occur}}{\text{probability the event will occur}}$$

Geometry Terms and Basic Information

Supplementary angles: two angles whose total is 180 degrees
Complementary angles: two angles whose total is 90 degrees
Angle bisector: divides an angle into two equal angles
Straight angle, or line: measures 180 degrees
Vertical angle: formed by two intersecting lines, across from each other, always equal
Adjacent angles: next to each other, share a common side and vertex
Right angle: measures 90 degrees
Obtuse angle: greater than 90 degrees
Acute angle: less than 90 degrees

Parallel Lines

Transversal—Line which intersects the pair of parallel lines
   8 pairs of congruent (equal) angles

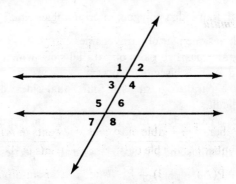

Corresponding pair
    (a) on same side of transversal (left or right)
    (b) same relative position (above or below)
       ∠1 and ∠5, ∠2 and ∠6, ∠3 and ∠7, ∠4 and ∠8

Alternate interior
    (a) on opposite sides of transversal
    (b) between the parallel lines
       ∠3 and ∠6, ∠4 and ∠5

Alternate exterior
    (a) on opposite sides of transversal
    (b) outside the parallel lines
       ∠1 and ∠8, ∠2 and ∠7

Polygons

Polygon: a many-sided (more than two sides) closed figure
Regular polygon: all sides and all angles equal

Triangle: interior angles total 180 degrees

    Right triangle: containing a right angle
    Equilateral triangle: all sides equal
    Isosceles triangle: two sides equal
    Scalene triangle: all sides of different lengths
    Similar triangle: corresponding congruent angles or corresponding
       sides are proportional

In a triangle: angles opposite equal sides are equal
    An exterior angle is equal to the sum of the remote two angles

Quadrilateral: four-sided polygon; interior angles equal 360 degrees

Trapezoid: has one pair of parallel sides

Parallelogram: has two pairs of parallel sides which are equal in length; diagonals bisect each other

Rhombus: a parallelogram with four equal sides: diagonals are perpendicular

Rectangle: a parallelogram with four right angles; diagonals are equal

Square: a rhombus and a rectangle with all properties of both

Pentagon: a five-sided polygon

Hexagon: a six-sided polygon

Octagon: an eight-sided polygon

Sum of the interior angles in any polygon = $(n - 2) 180°$, where n is the number of sides in the polygon.

Example: The pentagon (5 sides) $(n - 2)180° =$
$(5 - 2)180° =$
$(3) 180° = 540°$

Graphing

$Ax + By = C$ has a straight line graph when A and B are not both zero

$x = C$ has a vertical line as its graph

$x = 0$ graphs as the y axis

$y = C$ has a horizontal line as its graph

$y = 0$ graphs as the x axis

Statistics

Measures of Central Tendency

Mean: $\dfrac{\text{sum of scores}}{\text{number of scores}}$

Median: middle score or the average of the two scores in the middle when data are arranged in order

Mode: most frequent score or scores

Connectives of Symbolic Logic

Name	Symbol	Meaning	Translation
Conjunction	$\wedge$	and	$p \wedge q$; p and q
Disjunction	$\vee$	or	$p \vee q$; p or q
Implication	$\rightarrow$	if . . . then	$p \rightarrow q$; if p, then q q if p
Equivalence	$\leftrightarrow$	if and only if	$p \leftrightarrow q$; p if and only if q p is equivalent to q

Major Tautologies of Symbolic Logic

"not (not p)" is equivalent to p. $\sim(\sim p) \equiv p$ ✓

"p, or not p." $p \vee \sim p$

"not (p and q)" is equivalent to "not p, or not q."
   $\sim(p \wedge q) \equiv (\sim p \vee \sim q)$

"not (p or q)" is equivalent to "not p, and not q."
   $\sim(p \vee q) \equiv (\sim p \wedge \sim q)$

"if p, then q" is equivalent to "(not p) or q." $(p \rightarrow q) \equiv (\sim p \vee q)$

"if p, then q" is equivalent to "if not q, then not p."
   $(p \rightarrow q) \equiv (\sim q \rightarrow \sim p)$

Equivalence Statements

Original Statement	Equivalence
All are p	None are not p
Some are not p	Not all are p
None are p	All are not p

HOW TO BEGIN

Take the Mathematics Pre-Test that starts on page 239. Don't be concerned about time, but do note how long you take to complete the test. Use the answers immediately following the test to add up the number of questions you answered correctly. Record that number and your time on page 9. Use the Answer Key and Analysis sections to help you determine your areas of weakness. The Analysis includes an identification of the specific competency (by number) that is tested by each problem, enabling you to refer to the Mathematics Competencies Tested section to review a specific skill in which you are having difficulty.

MATHEMATICS PRE-TEST

1. $-3 + 1\frac{1}{3} =$
   (A) $1\frac{2}{3}$ (B) $-2\frac{2}{3}$ (C) $-1\frac{2}{3}$ (D) $-1\frac{1}{3}$

2. $(-\frac{2}{5}) \div (-\frac{2}{3}) =$
   (A) $\frac{3}{5}$ (B) $-\frac{3}{5}$ (C) $-\frac{5}{3}$ (D) $\frac{5}{3}$

3. $-5.304 + 2.19 =$
   (A) 3.285 (B) 3.114 (C) -5.085 (D) -3.114

4. $3.41 \times 2.8 =$
   (A) 95.48 (B) 9.548 (C) 8.548 (D) 3.410

5. If 50 is increased to 60, what is the percentage rise?
   (A) 5% (B) 10% (C) 15% (D) 20%

6. Round the measurement 36.47 cm to the nearest centimeter.
   (A) 36 cm   (B) 37 cm   (C) 36.5 cm   (D) 365 cm

7. What is the distance around a circular doghouse that has a 6 ft diameter?
   (A) 6π sq ft   (B) 6π ft   (C) 12π ft   (D) 36π ft

8. What is the area of a circular region whose diameter is 14 cm?
   (A) 14π sq cm   (B) 49π sq cm
   (C) 28π sq cm   (D) 196π sq cm

9. $11\pi - 7\pi + 2 =$
   (A) $4\pi^2 + 2$ (B) $4\pi + 2$ (C) $6\pi + 13$ (D) 6π

10. $\sqrt{2} \times \sqrt{6} =$
    (A) 144 (B) $4\sqrt{3}$ (C) $2\sqrt{3}$ (D) 8

11. $\frac{2}{3} - 8(\frac{1}{2} + 1) =$
    (A) $-11\frac{1}{3}$ (B) $-7\frac{1}{3}$ (C) -11 (D) $11\frac{1}{3}$

239

12. $6,420,000 \div .00214 =$
    (A) 3.00×10^9 (B) 3.00×10^{-2}
    (C) 3.00×10^3 (D) 3.00×10^{-9}

13. What is the volume of a right circular cone with a diameter of
    10 m and a height of 20 m?
    (A) 513.33 cu m   (B) 523.33 cu m
    (C) 523.33 sq m   (D) 423.33 sq m

14. If $3(a + 1) = 4[a - (2 + 3a)]$, then
    (A) $a = -\frac{11}{3}$ (B) $a = -1$ (C) $a = 1$ (D) $a = \frac{11}{13}$

15. Given $a = 2(b + 4)^2$, if $b = 2$, then $a =$
    (A) 12   (B) 40   (C) 36   (D) 72

16. Find $f(-3)$ given: $f(x) = 2x^2 - 4x - 2$
    (A) -5 (B) 1   (C) 22   (D) 28

17. Find a linear factor of the following expression: $3x^2 - 4x - 4$
    (A) $x + 1$ (B) $3x + 2$ (C) $x + 2$ (D) $3x - 4$

18. Find the real roots of this equation: $x^2 - x - 3 = 0$

    (A) $\dfrac{-1 - \sqrt{11}}{2}$ and $\dfrac{-1 + \sqrt{11}}{2}$

    (B) $\dfrac{1 - \sqrt{11}}{2}$ and $\dfrac{1 + \sqrt{11}}{2}$

    (C) $\dfrac{-1 - \sqrt{13}}{2}$ and $\dfrac{-1 + \sqrt{13}}{2}$

    (D) $\dfrac{1 - \sqrt{13}}{2}$ and $\dfrac{1 + \sqrt{13}}{2}$

19. The graph on the following page represents the monthly average
    air conditioning costs for 6 months of the year. How much lower
    is the average cost in March than it is in June?
    (A) $8   (B) $10   (C) $15   (D) $20

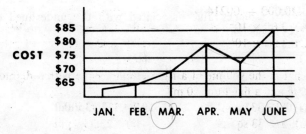

20. What is the *mode* of the data in the following sample? 4, 7, 3, 2, 3, 4, 6, 3
    (A) 32   (B) 3   (C) 3.5   (D) 4

21. From a group of 3 flowers and 3 ribbons, each different from the other, a flower and a ribbon will be selected to make a corsage. How many possible ways can the selection be made?
    (A) 6   (B) 9   (C) 12   (D) 36

22. Sets D, E, F, and U are related as shown in the diagram.

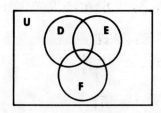

Which of the following statements is true, assuming none of the eight regions is empty?
    (A) Any element which is a member of sets D and E is also a member of set F.
    (B) Any element which is a member of set U is also a member of sets D, E, and F.
    (C) No element is a member of all three sets, D, E, and F.
    (D) None of the above statements is true.

23. $(4^3)^2 =$
    (A) 4^5 (B) 4^9 (C) $(4 \times 3)^2$ (D) $4^3 \times 4^3$

24. Select the place value associated with the underlined digit.
    2.0243 (base ten)

    (A) $\dfrac{1}{10^4}$ (B) $\dfrac{1}{10^3}$ (C) $\dfrac{1}{10^2}$ (D) $\dfrac{1}{10^0}$

25. 350 % =
    (A) 0.350   (B) 3.50   (C) 350.0   (D) 3500.0

26. Identify the symbol that should be placed in the box to form a
    true statement.

    $$\frac{10}{16} \ \Box \ \frac{5}{8}$$

    (A) =   (B) <   (C) >

27. A man is shopping for a television and looks at over 25 sets
    ranging in price from over $400 to under $1800. Which of the
    following values is a reasonable estimate of the average price of
    the TV sets?
    (A) $2300   (B) $700   (C) $350   (D) $250

28. Which of the statements below is true for the figure shown?

    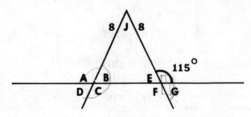

    (A) m ∠D = m ∠J   (B) ∠A is a supplement of ∠C
    (C) m ∠C = 115°   (D) m ∠B ≠ m ∠G

29. Select the geometric figure that possesses *all* of the following
    characteristics:

    i.   two pairs of parallel sides
    ii. congruent opposite angles
    iii. diagonals of equal length

    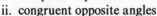

    (A) parallelogram   (B) trapezoid
    (C) rhombus   (D) rectangle

30. Which of the statements A–D is true for the pictured triangles?

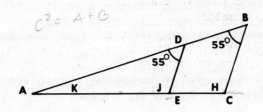

(A) $\dfrac{DE}{BC} = \dfrac{AD}{AB}$ (B) $m\angle H \neq m\angle J$ (C) $\dfrac{DE}{BC} = \dfrac{AC}{AE}$

(D) None of the above statements is true.

31. What type of measure is needed to express the volume of the cylinder shown below?

(A) square
(B) linear
(C) cubic
(D) equilateral

32. Identify the property of operation which is illustrated:
$(x \cdot 6) + y = (6 \cdot x) + y$
(A) associative property of multiplication
(B) associative property of addition
(C) commutative property of multiplication
(D) distributive property of multiplication over addition

33. For each of the three statements below, determine whether (-2) is a solution.

  i. $|2a - 4| = 0$
  ii. $(a - 4)(a + 4) \leq 9$
  iii. $a^2 + 4a - 12 = 16$

Which option below identifies *every* statement that has (-2) as a solution and *only* that (those) statements(s)?
(A) i only   (B) ii only   (C) iii only   (D) i and ii only

34. Two machines can complete 9 parts in 4 minutes. Let p represent the number of parts these machines can complete in 60 minutes. Select the correct statement of the given condition.

    (A) $\dfrac{4}{9} = \dfrac{p}{60}$ (B) $\dfrac{p}{9} = \dfrac{4}{30}$ (C) $\dfrac{9}{4} = \dfrac{p}{60}$ (D) $\dfrac{p}{4} = \dfrac{60}{18}$

35. Which option gives the condition(s) that corresponds to the shaded region of the plane shown below?

    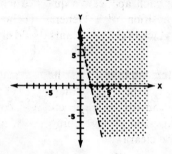

    (A) $4x + y < 8$
    (B) $4x + y > 8$
    (C) $y \geq 8$ and $x \geq 2$
    (D) $y > 8$ and $x > 2$

36. In a legal documents seminar, half the legal secretaries scored 75 on an efficiency test. Most of the remaining secretaries scored 65 except for a few who scored 15. Which of the following statements is true about the distributions of scores?
    (A) The mean and the mode are the same.
    (B) The mean is less than the median.
    (C) The median is less than the mean.
    (D) The mean is greater than the mode.

37. A bag contains 3 red, 4 green, and 5 yellow marbles. Two marbles are drawn from the bag at random without replacement. What is the probability that neither is red?

    (A) $\dfrac{81}{132}$ (B) $\dfrac{9}{12} \times \dfrac{3}{12}$ (C) $\dfrac{9}{12} \times \dfrac{8}{11}$ (D) $\dfrac{9}{12} \times \dfrac{2}{12}$

38. Select the statement which is the negation of the statement "Smith is an engineer and Royce is an accountant."
    (A) Smith is not an engineer, and Royce is not an accountant.
    (B) Smith is not an engineer, or Royce is not an accountant.
    (C) Smith is not an engineer, and Royce is an accountant.
    (D) Smith is an engineer, and Royce is not an accountant.

39. Select the statement below which is logically equivalent to "It is not true that both Jackie and Susan are teachers."
    (A) If Susan is not a teacher, Jackie is not a teacher.
    (B) Susan is not a teacher, or Jackie is not a teacher.
    (C) Susan is not a teacher, and Jackie is not a teacher.
    (D) If Jackie is not a teacher, Susan is not a teacher.

40. Read the requirements *and* each applicant's qualifications for obtaining a management position with General Technology Corporation. Then identify which of the applicants would qualify for the position.

    To qualify for the position an applicant must have a master's degree in a science, seven years experience managing 20 or more employees, a superior on-the-job attendance record, high competency in computer languages and programming skills, and a top-secret federal government clearance.

    Mr. Prickett just completed an M.S. in computer science. He has a superior work and attendance record at National Aviation, where he has supervised 20 employees for nearly 10 years. He comes highly recommended.

    Mrs. Adams worked at the Pentagon for 20 years, where she supervised 25 employees. Her clearance was top secret. She is proficient in several computer languages and is comfortable programming. She has a superior attendance on the job.

    Ms. Fish taught computer sciences and programming at the university where she received a Ph.D. in chemistry. She had a staff of over 50 while working at NASA for 12 years, where she was never absent from the job. She has a top-secret federal government clearance.
    (A) Mr. Prickett
    (B) Mrs. Adams
    (C) Ms. Fish
    (D) No one is eligible for the position.

41. All of the following arguments A–D have true conclusions, but one of the arguments is not valid. Select the argument that is *not* valid.

    (A) All birds have wings, and all parrots are birds. Therefore, all parrots have wings. $P + Q \rightarrow 1$

    (B) All flies have six legs, and all insects have six legs. Therefore, all flies are insects.

    (C) All birds have beaks, and all parrots are birds. Therefore, all parrots have beaks.

    (D) Every city in Lake County is in Florida. Mt. Dora is a city in Lake County. Therefore, Mt. Dora is in Florida.

42. Look for a common linear relationship between the numbers in each pair, then identify the missing term.

$$(6, 2), (.9, .3), (-3, -1), \left(\frac{1}{5}, \frac{1}{15}\right), (33, 11), \left(\frac{1}{6}, \frac{1}{18}\right)$$

    (A) $\frac{1}{3}$ (B) $\frac{1}{18}$ (C) 18   (D) $\frac{2}{3}$

43. Select the property or properties of operation(s) illustrated in this equation.

$$(4 \times 5) \times 7 = 4 \times (5 \times 7)$$

    (A) distributive property and associative property of multiplication

    (B) distributive property and commutative property of multiplication

    (C) distributive property only

    (D) associative property of multiplication only

44. Select the property used to justify the following statement:

    If $2 < x + 4 < 9$, then $-1 < x + 1 < 6$

    (A) If $a > b$ and $b > c$, then $a > c$

    (B) If $a + c > b + c$, then $a > b$

    (C) If $ac > bc$ and $c > 0$, then $a > b$

    (D) If $ac < bc$ and $c < 0$, then $a > b$

45. Study the outcomes for tossing 1, 2, or 3 coins simultaneously.

1 coin	2 coins	3 coins
H	HH	HHH
T	HT	HHT
	TH	HTH
	TT	HTT
		THH
		THT
		TTH
		TTT

If 7 coins were tossed simultaneously, how many possible arrangements of heads and tails would there be?
(A) 32   (B) 64   (C) 98   (D) 128

46. Read each of the following valid arguments, then select the symbolic form of the reasoning pattern illustrated by both arguments.

If you like candy, then you like cake. If you like cake, then you like pies. Therefore, if you like candy, then you like pies.

Mary dislikes liver if she doesn't eat liver. If Mary dislikes liver, then she doesn't eat liver burgers. Therefore, if Mary doesn't eat liver, then she doesn't eat liverburgers.

(A) $p \rightarrow q$
$\underline{p \rightarrow r}$
$\therefore q \rightarrow r$

(B) $q \rightarrow p$
$\underline{p \rightarrow r}$
$\therefore q \rightarrow r$

(C) $p \rightarrow q$
$\underline{q \rightarrow r}$
$\therefore p \rightarrow r$

(D) $p \rightarrow q$
$\underline{q \rightarrow r}$
$\therefore \sim p \rightarrow \sim r$

47. Select the rule of logical equivalence which *directly* (in one step) *transforms* statement i into statement ii.

i. If 3x is odd, then x is odd.
ii. 3x is not odd, or x is odd.

(A) "If p, then q" is equivalent to "if not q, then not p."
(B) "Not (p and q)" is equivalent to "not p, or not q."
(C) "If p, then q" is equivalent to "(not p) or q."
(D) The correct equivalence rule is not given.

48. A bookstore ordered 30 books for a class of 29 students. Each book, which cost $20, was to be sold for $25. The bookstore must pay a $2 service charge for each unsold book returned. If the bookstore had to return 3 books, how much profit did the bookstore make?
(A) $135   (B) $129   (C) $139   (D) $119

49. In a high school there are 350 students. 76% do not sign up for drama. How many students sign up for drama?
(A) 82 students   (B) 84 students
(C) 236 students   (D) 266 students

50. Find the smallest positive multiple of 4 which leaves a remainder of 1 when divided by 3 and a remainder of 1 when divided by 5.
(A) 36   (B) 52   (C) 16   (D) 28

51. A rectangular yard measures 45 ft by 60 ft and has a pool in the center that measures 18 ft by 30 ft. What will it cost to sod the yard around the pool if sod costs $1.35 a sq yd plus $100 to lay it?
(A) $240   (B) $324   (C) $424   (D) $505

52. A park wants to construct a path connecting Flower Path and Cactus Path as shown in the diagram below. Construction costs have been estimated at $50 per linear foot. What is the estimated cost for contructing the new path?
(A) $1,315,000
(B) $1,320,000
(C) $2,630,000
(D) $6,600,000

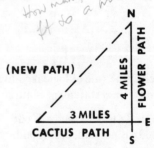

53. In 4 years a woman paints 96 pictures. If she works at the same speed, how many pictures can she produce in 12 years?
(A) 336   (B) 384   (C) 288   (D) 312

$x - (2x - 5) = 3$

54. The difference between a number and five less than twice the number is three. What equation could be used to find x, the number?

(A) $x - 2x - 5 = 3$ (B) $x - (2x - 5) = 3$
(C) $x - (2x + 5) = 3$ (D) $x - (5x - 2) = 3$

55. The probability that an event will occur is 3/5. What are the odds against the event?
(A) 2/3   (B) 3/2   (C) 5/3   (D) 6/25

$\frac{2}{5} \cdot \frac{\cdot 3}{\cdot 3}$

56. Study the information given below. If a logical conclusion is given, select that conclusion. If none of the conclusions given is warranted, select the option expressing this condition.

All intelligent people are boring. All boring people like to read. Harriet likes to read.

(A) Harriet is intelligent.
(B) Harriet is unattractive.
(C) Harriet gets straight A's.
(D) None of the above is warranted.

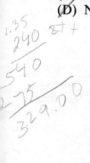

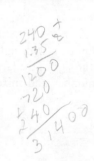

MATHEMATICS PRE-TEST ANSWER KEY AND ANALYSIS

ANSWER KEY

1. (C)	13. (B)	24. (C)	35. (B)	46. (C)
2. (A)	14. (B)	25. (B)	36. (B)	47. (C)
3. (D)	15. (D)	26. (A)	37. (C)	48. (B)
4. (B)	16. (D)	27. (B)	38. (B)	49. (B)
5. (D)	17. (B)	28. (C)	39. (B)	50. (C)
6. (A)	18. (D)	29. (D)	40. (C)	51. (C)
7. (B)	19. (C)	30. (A)	41. (B)	52. (B)
8. (B)	20. (B)	31. (C)	42. (B)	53. (C)
9. (B)	21. (B)	32. (C)	43. (D)	54. (B)
10. (C)	22. (D)	33. (B)	44. (B)	55. (A)
11. (A)	23. (D)	34. (C)	45. (D)	56. (D)
12. (A)				

SCORE: _____38_____ (number of correct answers)

TIME: _____75 mm_____ .

ANALYSIS

1. (C) Competency 1. To add two numbers with different signs, subtract the two numbers and keep the sign of the larger number. Remember to convert the whole number and mixed fractions before working the problem.

$$-\frac{9}{3}(-) + \frac{4}{3} = -\frac{5}{3} = -1\frac{2}{3}$$

2. (A) Competency 2. To divide fractions, turn the second fraction upside down (invert) and then multiply. Reduce, if necessary. Remember that a $- \div - = +$.

$$-\frac{2}{5} \times -\frac{3}{2} = \frac{6}{10} = \frac{3}{5}$$

3. (D) Competency 3. Remember, to add two numbers with different signs, subtract the two numbers and keep the sign of the larger.

$$-5.304$$
$$(-)+2.190$$
$$-3.114$$

4. **(B)** Competency 4.

   $$3.41 \quad \text{2 digits to right of decimal, and}$$
   $$\times 2.8 \quad \underline{1 \text{ digit to right of decimal, equals}}$$
   $$9.548 \quad \text{3 total digits to right of decimal}$$

5. **(D)** Competency 5. Percent rise is the same as percent change. The formula for percent increase/decrease is

   $$\frac{\text{change}}{\text{starting point}} = \text{percent change}$$

   change = 60 − 50 = 10
   starting point = 50

   $$\frac{10}{50} = \frac{1}{5} = \frac{2}{10} = 20\%$$

6. **(A)** Competency 6. The problem asks for the nearest centimeter, so the answer will be either 36 cm or 37 cm. To determine which, look at the two numbers to the right of the decimal. Since .47 is closer to 0 than it is to 100, you round down to 36.

7. **(B)** Competency 7. The distance around a circle is the circumference, C. The circumference is found by multiplying the diameter, d, by π. C = πd. In this problem, the diameter, d, is 6 feet. Therefore, C = π6 or 6π.

8. **(B)** Competency 8. The formula for the area of a circle is A = πr^2. The radius, r, is ½ the diameter, d. Since the diameter given is 14 cm, the radius, r, is 7 cm. Therefore, A = $\pi 7^2 = \pi 49$ sq cm or 49π sq cm.

9. **(B)** Competency 9. You can subtract only like terms (11π, 7π).

   $$(11\pi - 7\pi) + 2 = 4\pi + 2$$

10. **(C)** Competency 10. To multiply square roots, multiply the numbers under the signs and simplify.

$$\sqrt{2} \times \sqrt{6} = \sqrt{2 \times 6} = \sqrt{12} = \sqrt{4 \times 3} = \sqrt{4} \times \sqrt{3} = 2\sqrt{3}$$

11. (A) Competency 11. The rules for order of operations are, working from *left* to *right*: (1) do all operations in the *grouping symbols,* (2) do all *exponents (powers)*, (3) do all *multiplication* and *division*, (4) do all *addition* and *subtraction*.

$$\frac{2}{3} - 8\left(\frac{1}{2} + 1\right) = \frac{2}{3} - \frac{\cancel{8}^4}{1}\left(\frac{3}{\cancel{2}_1}\right) = \frac{2}{3} - 12 = -11\frac{1}{3}$$

12. (A) Competency 12.

   6,420,000 = 6.42 (moved 6 digits to left)
   .00214 = 2.14 (moved 3 digits to right)
   $6.42 \times 10^6 \div 2.14 \times 10^{-3}$ (whole numbers [6,420,000] have positive powers and fractions [.00214] have negative)

   To solve

   $6.42 \div 2.14 = 3.00$ (first figure)

   Subtract the powers.

   $6 - (-3) = 9$ (final power of 10)
   $6,420,000 \div .00214 = 3.00 \times 10^9$

13. (B) Competency 13. The formula for the volume of a right circular cone is $V = \frac{1}{3}\pi r^2 h$. The problem gives the diameter, and the radius is needed for the formula.

   $$r = \frac{1}{2}d = \frac{1}{2}(10) = 5$$

   $$V = \frac{1}{3}\pi r^2 h = \frac{1}{3}\pi(5)^2(20) = \frac{1}{3}\pi(25)(20) =$$

   $$\frac{1}{3}(3.14)(500) = \frac{1570}{3} = 523.33 \text{ cu m}$$

14. (B) Competency 14.

   $3(a + 1) = 4[a - (2 + 3a)]$
   $3a + 3 = 4[a - 2 - 3a]$
   $3a + 3 = 4a - 8 - 12a$
   $3a + 3 = -8a - 8$
   $3a + 8a = -8 - 3$
   $11a = -11$
   $a = -1$

15. **(D)** Competency 15. Replace b with 2 and simplify.

$a = 2(2 + 4)^2$

$a = 2(6)^2$

$a = 2(36)$

$a = 72$

16. **(D)** Competency 16. Replace x in the problem with -3 and simplify.

$f(-3) = 2(-3)^2 - 4(-3) - 2 = 2(9) + 12 - 2 = 18 + 10 = 28$

17. **(B)** Competency 17. The factors for $3x^2 - 4x - 4$ are $(3x + 2)(x - 2)$. Check by multiplying out.

$(3x + 2)(x - 2)$ first term = $(3x)(x) = 3x^2$

middle term = the sum of $(3x)(-2) = -6x$

$(2)(x) = \underline{2x}$

$-4x$

last term = $(2)(-2) = -4$

first	*middle*	*last*
$3x^2$	$-4x$	-4

18. **(D)** Competency 18. Given $x^2 - x - 3$; $a = 1$, $b = -1$, $c = -3$. Substitute the numbers for a, b, and c into:

$$x = \frac{-b \pm \sqrt{b^2 - 4ac}}{2a} \quad \text{(quadratic formula)}$$

$$x = \frac{-(-1) \pm \sqrt{(-1)^2 - 4(1)(-3)}}{(2)(1)}$$

$$x = \frac{1 \pm \sqrt{1 + 12}}{2} = \frac{1 - \sqrt{13}}{2} \quad \text{and} \quad \frac{1 + \sqrt{13}}{2}$$

19. **(C)** Competency 19.

cost June $85

cost March $\underline{-70}$

$15

20. (B) Competency 20. The mode is the most frequent number in the data. 2, <u>3, 3, 3</u>, 4, 4, 6, 7

21. (B) Competency 21.

$$
\begin{array}{lll}
\underline{F_1F_2F_3} & \underline{R_1R_2R_3} & \\
F_1R_1 & F_2R_1 & F_3R_1 \\
F_1R_2 & F_2R_2 & F_3R_2 = 9 \text{ ways} \\
F_1R_3 & F_2R_3 & F_3R_3
\end{array}
$$

22. (D) Competency 22.

A is false:

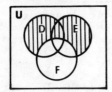

The shaded area shows elements of sets D and E that are not in set F.

B is false:

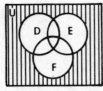

The shaded area shows elements of set U which are not in sets D, E, and F.

C is false:

The small shaded area shows elements that are members of all three sets D, E, and F.

23. (D) Competency 23. Remember, when an exponential expression is raised to a power, multiply the exponents.

$$(4^3)^2 = 4^{3 \times 2} = 4^6$$

4^6 is the same as $4^3 \times 4^3$

24. (C) Competency 24. In a base ten number, the place values are as shown.

base ten   2.   0   <u>2</u>   4   3

place value 10^0. 10^{-1} $\underline{10^{-2}}$ 10^{-3} 10^{-4}

or

1. $\dfrac{1}{10^1}$ $\underline{\dfrac{1}{10^2}}$ $\dfrac{1}{10^3}$ $\dfrac{1}{10^4}$

The underlined digit's place value is 10^{-2} or $\dfrac{1}{10^2}$

25. (B) Competency 25. To change percent to a decimal, place the decimal point two places to the left of the last digit. 350% = 3.50

26. (A) Competency 26. To compare fractions, write them with a common denominator.

$$\frac{2}{2} \times \frac{5}{8} = \frac{10}{16}$$

27. (B) Competency 27. The average price has to be *between* $400 and $1800. $700 is the only answer which qualifies.

28. (C) Competency 28.

∠F = 115° (vertical angles are equal)
∠E = 65° (∠E and ∠F are supplementary angles)
∠B = ∠E = 65° (isosceles triangle)
∠C = 115° (∠B and ∠C are supplementary angles)

29. (D) Competency 29. A, B, and C do not have diagonals of equal length. Also, for B, opposite angles are not congruent.

30. (A) Competency 30. The two triangles AED and ACB are similar because they each have two angles of equal measure. ∠D = ∠B = 55° and they have ∠K in common. A is true because the matching sides of similar triangles are proportional.

$$\frac{\text{small } \triangle}{\text{large } \triangle} \qquad \frac{\text{DE}}{\text{BC}} = \frac{\text{AD}}{\text{AB}}$$

31. (C) Competency 31. Volume is measured in cubic units.

32. (C) Competency 32. The commutative property changes order. $(x \cdot 6)$ is the same as $(6 \cdot x)$.

33. (B) Competency 33. To find the answer, replace the letter in each statement with -2.

  i. $|2(-2) - 4| = 0, |-4 - 4| = 0, |-8| = 0$, false.
  ii. $(-2 - 4)(-2 + 4) \le 9, (-6)(2) \le 9, -12 \le 9$, true.
  iii. $-2^2 + 4(-2) - 12 = 16, 4 - 8 - 12 = 16, -16 = 16$, false.

34. (C) Competency 34. Be sure to keep the comparisons in the proportions the same.

$$\frac{\text{parts}}{\text{minutes}} \qquad \frac{9 \text{ parts}}{4 \text{ minutes}} = \frac{p \text{ parts}}{60 \text{ minutes}}$$

35. (B) Competency 35. A would be the opposite of B. C and D would show a horizontal area across the graph.

36. (B) Competency 36. 50% of the scores are 75. The other 50% are 65 and 15, so *75* is the most frequent (greatest number of) score, the *mode*. The *mean* is the average of the scores. Choice A could be true only if there were scores higher than 75 to offset the lower scores. The *median* is the score in the middle, but you are not dealing with only three scores of 75, 65, and 15. You have

So the *median* is between 75 and 65, or *70*. You cannot find the exact *mean* (the average), so you have to estimate, noting that 50% of the scores are 75, *most* of the rest are 65, and *a few* are 15.

Example: 100 legal secretaries--50%, 75; 40%, 65; 10%, 15

$$
\begin{array}{r}
50 \times 75 = 3750 \\
40 \times 65 = 2600 \\
\underline{10 \times 15 = 150} \\
100 \qquad\qquad 6500
\end{array}
$$

$$6500 \div 100 = 65 \text{ (estimated mean)}$$

You can see that choice B is correct.

37. (C) Competency 38. The probability that the first ball drawn is not red is 9/12 because there are 9 balls that are not red and 12 balls total. After the first ball is drawn, there are 8 balls out of 11 balls left, a probability of 8/11. The probability that both balls are not red is (9/12)(8/11).

38. (B) Competency 39. The sentence is in the form "p and q," which has a negation "not p, or not q."

39. (B) Competency 40. This sentence is in the form "not both p and q," which is equivalent to "not p, or not q," "If p, then not q," and "if q, then not p." Choice B is the first form ("not p, or not q").

40. (C) Competency 41. Ms. Fish meets all the requirements.

41. (B) Competency 42. When you are given several arguments, as in the format for problem 41, and asked to pick the one that is valid or not valid, check the arguments for a pattern.

    A   B   C   B

All flies have six legs and all insects have six legs.

                A   C

Therefore, all flies are insects. (AB, CB, AC)

The pattern of the invalid argument will be different from the other three.

42. (B) Competency 43. The first term in each pair is multiplied by 1/3 to find the second term.

$$6 \times \frac{1}{3} = 2 \quad (6, 2)$$

$$\frac{1}{6} \times \frac{1}{3} = \frac{1}{18} \quad \left(\frac{1}{6}, \frac{1}{18}\right)$$

1/18 is the missing term.

43. **(D)** Competency 44. $(a \times b) \times c = a \times (b \times c)$

44. **(B)** Competency 48. Choice B gives the additive property of inequalities which allows the -3 to be added to each component in the first statement to obtain the second statement.

$$2 + (-3) < x + 4 + (-3) < 9 + (-3) = -1 < x + 1 < 6$$

45. **(D)** Competency 49. 1 coin tossed has 2^1 outcomes. 2 coins tossed have 2^2 outcomes or 4 outcomes. 3 coins tossed have 2^3 or 8 outcomes. 7 coins tossed have 2^7 or 128 outcomes.

46. **(C)** Competency 50. Answer C is in the format

$$
\begin{array}{c}
p \to q \\
q \to r \\
\hline
\therefore p \to r
\end{array}
$$

If you like candy, then you like cake.	$= p \to q$
If you like cake, then you like pies.	$= q \to r$
Therefore, if you like candy, then you like pies	$\therefore p \to r$

47. **(C)** Competency 51. Let *3x is odd* $= p$ and *x is odd* $= q$. Statement i would then read "If p, then q." In statement ii, *3x is not odd* $=$ *not p* and *x is odd* $= q$. The statement then reads, "(not p) or q." Choice C is in the format $p \to q \equiv p \lor q$.

48. **(B)** Competency 52. $30 - 3 = 27$ books sold. $27 \times \$5 = \$135$ total income. $\$135 - \$6$ (service charge for returned books) $= \$129$ profit.

49. **(B)** Competency 53. The problem asks for how many students *signed* up for drama. 76% *didn't* sign up, so 24% did. $350 \times .24 = 84$ students.

50. **(C)** Competency 54. The number 16 fulfills all the requirements.

$4 \times 4 = 16$
$16 \div 3 = 5$ (remainder 1)
$16 \div 5 = 3$ (remainder 1)

51. (C) Competency 55.

$$45 \text{ ft} \times 60 \text{ ft} = 15 \text{ yds} \times 20 \text{ yds} = 300 \text{ sq yds}$$

less $18 \text{ ft} \times 30 \text{ ft} = 6 \text{ yds} \times 10 \text{ yds} = \underline{-60 \text{ sq yds}}$

$$240 \text{ sq yds}$$

$240 \text{ sq yds} \times \$1.35 = \$324$ *Couldn't get this rt*

$\$324 + \$100 = \$424$

52. (B) Competency 56. Let c equal the length of the new path. You can assume that the triangle is a right triangle because of the directions (north, south, and east) given in the diagram. Therefore, you can use the Pythagorean theorem to solve the problem.

$a^2 + b^2 = c^2$
$4^2 + 3^2 = c^2$
$16 + 9 = 25$
$c^2 = 25$
$c = 5$

Part I didn't know

$5 \times 5280 \text{ (feet in a mile)} \times \$50 = \$1,320,000$

53. (C) Competency 57.

$\dfrac{\text{pictures}}{\text{total yrs}}$ $\dfrac{x}{12} = \dfrac{96}{4}$

$4x = 12(96)$
$x = 288$

54. (B) Competency 58. x = the number. 2x = twice the number. $(2x - 5) = 5$ less than twice the number. *Difference* means *subtract*, and *is* becomes =. $x - (2x - 5) = 3$

55. (A) Competency 60. To change a probability to odds:

odds in favor of an event $\dfrac{\text{probability event will occur}}{\text{probability event will not occur}}$

odds against an event $\dfrac{\text{probability event will not occur}}{\text{probability event will occur}}$

The probability that this event will occur is 3/5. The probability that the event will not occur is $1 - (3/5) = 2/5$. Therefore, the odds against are

$$\frac{2/5}{3/5} = \frac{2}{3}$$

56. (D) Competency 61. Choice D is correct because A, B, or C cannot be logically concluded from the premise. A is invalid because many people who are not intelligent may be boring. Choices B and C are invalid because nothing in the premise warrants these conclusions.

MATHEMATICS COMPETENCIES TESTED

There are sixty-one specific mathematics competencies tested by the CLAST. For each competency tested, the following section provides a list of basics you'll need to know to master each competency, sample problems to give you practice in each skill, and solutions and explanations to help you strengthen your weak areas. Work carefully through this review section before you take the Mathematics Post-Test that follows and the full-length, complete CLAST exam. Give special emphasis to any skill areas with which you had difficulty in the Mathematics Pre-Test.

1: ADD AND SUBTRACT RATIONAL NUMBERS

Basics You'll Need to Know to Master This Competency

Converting mixed numbers to improper fractions
Converting improper fractions to mixed numbers $\Big\}$ regrouping
Converting like and unlike denominators
Finding equivalent fractions
Working with negative quantities

Sample Problems

$$\frac{4}{3} + \frac{1}{5} = \frac{20 + 3}{15} = \frac{23}{15} = 1\,{}^8/_{15}$$

1. $1\frac{1}{3} + \frac{1}{5} =$
   (A) $1\frac{2}{8}$ (B) $1\frac{1}{15}$ (C) $1\frac{8}{15}$ (D) $\frac{8}{15}$

2. $5 - 2\frac{1}{3} =$
   (A) $3\frac{1}{3}$ (B) 3 (C) $3\frac{2}{3}$ (D) $2\frac{2}{3}$

Sample Problem Solutions

1. (C) To add the fractions, first convert the mixed fraction $(1\frac{1}{3})$ to an improper fraction $(\frac{4}{3})$. Then convert both fractions to a common denominator.

$$1\frac{1}{3} = \frac{4}{3}$$

$$\frac{4}{3} \times \frac{5}{5} = \frac{20}{15} \quad \text{and}$$

261

$$\frac{1}{5} \times \frac{3}{3} = \frac{3}{15}$$

$$\frac{20}{15} + \frac{3}{15} = \frac{23}{15} = 1\,^8/_{15}$$

2. (D) The rules for subtracting fractions are the same as for adding fractions except you subtract the numerators.

$$5 \times \frac{3}{3} \times \frac{15}{3}$$

$$2\frac{1}{3} = \frac{7}{3}$$

$$\frac{15}{3} - \frac{7}{3} = \frac{8}{3} = 2\,^2/_3$$

If You Were Wrong, Here's Why

Adding or subtracting denominators as well as numerators

Failing to convert or making an error in converting to common denominator

Failing to regroup or making an error in regrouping

Adding or subtracting fractions correctly but failing to include whole numbers

Getting common denominators correctly but failing to change numerators

Making an addition or subtraction fact error

Not recognizing that subtracting a negative quantity is the same as adding the positive amount

Not recognizing that adding a negative quantity is the same as subtracting the positive amount

Concluding that two negative quantities yield a positive result

Using the incorrect sign

√ 2: MULTIPLY AND DIVIDE RATIONAL NUMBERS

Basics You'll Need to Know to Master This Competency

Multiplying and dividing unlike denominators; mixed fractions

Changing a mixed number to an improper fraction in order to multiply

Changing an improper fraction to a mixed number in the product
Working with negative quantities

Sample Problems

$$1\frac{1}{3} \cdot \left(-\frac{5}{12}\right) = \frac{4}{3} \cdot \frac{-5}{12} = \frac{-20}{36} = \frac{5}{9}$$

1. $1\frac{1}{3} \div (-2\frac{2}{5}) =$
   (A) $-3\frac{1}{5}$ (B) $\frac{5}{9}$ (C) $3\frac{1}{5}$ (D) $-\frac{5}{9}$

2. $(-2\frac{1}{5}) \times (-1\frac{2}{3}) =$
   (A) $-2\frac{2}{15}$ (B) $-3\frac{2}{3}$ (C) $3\frac{2}{3}$ (D) $2\frac{2}{15}$

Sample Problem Solutions

1. (D) To divide fractions, turn the second fraction upside down (invert) and then multiply. Reduce, if necessary. Remember to change mixed numbers to improper fractions and that a $+ \div - = -$.

$$\frac{4}{3} \div \left(-\frac{12}{5}\right) = \frac{4}{3} \times \left(-\frac{5}{12}\right) = -\frac{20}{36} = -\frac{5}{9}$$

2. (C) To multiply fractions, just multiply the numerators, then multiply the denominators. Remember to convert mixed numbers to improper fractions and that a $- \times - = +$.

$$-\frac{11}{5} \times \left(-\frac{5}{3}\right) = \frac{55}{15} = \frac{11}{3} = 3\frac{2}{3}$$

If You Were Wrong, Here's Why

Getting common denominator and multiplying numerators only
Multiplying whole numbers and fractions separately
Making an error in regrouping
Making an error in cancelling
Multiplying denominators only when numerators cancel to 1
Making a multiplication fact error
Failing to invert in division
Inverting the dividend rather than the divisor
Failing to regroup before inverting
Inverting both dividend and divisor
Not recognizing that the product, or quotient, of a *negative and positive* quantity is negative
Not recognizing that the product, or quotient, of *two negative* quantities is positive

3: ADD AND SUBTRACT RATIONAL NUMBERS IN DECIMAL FORM

Basics You'll Need to Know to Master This Competency

Working with an unequal number of decimal places
Regrouping
Working with negative quantities

Sample Problems

1. $-14.63 - 3.042 =$
    (A) 17.672   (B) -11.588 (C) -17.672 (D) -18.050

2. $.2850 + (-.089) =$
    (A) $-.2761$ (B) .1960   (C) $-.1960$ (D) .2761

Sample Problem Solutions

1. To add or subtract decimals, line up the decimal points and then add or subtract just as you would add or subtract non-decimal numbers. You may need to add zeros to help work some problems. Remember, to subtract *negative* and/or positive numbers, change the sign of the number being subtracted and then add.

$$\begin{array}{r} -14.630 \\ (+) \underline{-\ 3.042} \\ -17.672 \end{array}$$

2. (B) Remember, to add two numbers with different signs, subtract the two numbers and keep the sign of the larger number.

$$\begin{array}{r} .2850 \\ (-) \underline{-.0890} \\ .1960 \end{array}$$

If You Were Wrong, Here's Why

Misplacing a decimal point
Aligning a place value improperly
Making an addition or subtraction fact error (with correct or incorrect decimal placement)
Making an error in regrouping

"Bringing down" members of the subtrahend that are not located directly under members of the minuend

Not recognizing that subtracting a negative quantity is the same as adding the positive amount

Not recognizing that adding a negative quantity is the same as subtracting the positive amount

Concluding that two negative quantities yield a positive result *or* that two quantities of opposite sign always yield a negative result

Using the positive quantity as a minuend when it has the smaller absolute value

4: MULTIPLY AND DIVIDE RATIONAL NUMBERS IN DECIMAL FORM

Basics You'll Need to Know to Master This Competency

Working with problems that include an embedded zero in the product, quotient, divisor, or the dividend

Working with problems that may contain elements with unequal numbers of decimal places

Working with problems that may require regrouping

Working with negative quantities

Sample Problems

1. $(-.02901) \div (-.03) =$
   (A) -9.67 (B) $.967$ (C) $-.0967$ (D) $.00967$

2. $(-.03) \times (-1.8) =$
   (A) -5.4 (B) 5.4 (C) $-.054$ (D) $.054$

Sample Problem Solutions

1. (B) When the divisor has a decimal, move the decimal to the right as many places as necessary until it is a whole number. Then move the decimal point of the dividend the same number of places to the right. It may be necessary to add zeros to the dividend.

$$-.03\overline{)-.02901} \stackrel{+\ .967}{= -3\overline{)-2.901}}$$

Remember that a $- \div - = +$.

2. (D) There is a *total* of 3 digits to the right of the decimal in the top
   portion of the problem ($-.03$ has two, -1.8 has one). Therefore,
   there must be 3 digits to the right of the decimal in the answer.

$$
\begin{array}{r}
-.03 \\
\times\ -1.8 \\
\hline
.054
\end{array}
$$

Remember that $- \times - = +$.

If You Were Wrong, Here's Why

Misplacing a decimal point

Making an error from improper alignment with place value

Making multiplication or division fact error

Making an error in regrouping

Not recognizing that the product, or quotient, of a negative and
positive quantity is negative

Not recognizing that the product, or quotient, of two negative
quantities is positive

5: CALCULATE PERCENT INCREASE
AND PERCENT DECREASE

Basics You'll Need to Know to Master This Competency

Using the formula for figuring percent increase/decrease

Sample Problems

1. If 20 is decreased to 15, what is the percent decrease?
   (A) 5%   (B) 15%   (C) 25%   (D) 33%

2. If you increase 36 by 25% of itself, what is the result?
   (A) 40   (B) 45   (C) 9   (D) 27

Sample Problem Solutions

1. (C) The formula for percent increase/decrease:

$$
\frac{\text{change}}{\text{starting point}} = \text{percent change}
$$

In this problem, change $= 20 - 15 = 5$, and starting point $= 20$.

$$\frac{5}{20} = \frac{1}{4} = \frac{25}{100} = 25\%$$

2. (B) First find 25% of 36: $36 \times .25 = 9$. To increase 36 by 25% or 9, simply add. $36 + 9 = 45$

If You Were Wrong, Here's Why

Calculating decrease (increase) when increase (decrease) is required

Misplacing decimal point in answer

Multiplying (dividing) quantities when you should divide (multiply)

Not converting percent to decimal form before performing computations

Computing percentage change but failing to add or subtract from the original amount

Performing an arithmetic operation other than the one indicated

Using an incorrect base

6: ROUND MEASUREMENTS TO THE NEAREST GIVEN UNIT OF THE MEASURING DEVICE

Basics You'll Need to Know to Master This Competency

Measuring devices of both English and metric units of length, area, volume, mass, weight, and time are used, and sometimes you must convert from one to the other

Rounding involving both decimals and fractions

The rule for rounding off is

1. If the digit to the right of the desired place is 5 or greater, add one to the digit in the desired place and drop the other digits on the right (for example, $35.5 = 36$)

2. If the digit to the right of the desired place is less than 5, drop the digits on the right and leave the digit in the desired place as it was ($35.4 = 35$).

3. If given a number like 456 and asked to round to the nearest *hundred*, both the digits to the right of the desired place must be considered. First, go back to rules (1) and (2) and round off 56 to 60. The adjusted number (460) is subjected to rules (1) and (2) and rounded off to 500 ($456 = 500$, $451 = 500$, $426 = 400$).

Sample Problems

1. Round the measurement of the length of the
    pictured rectangle to the nearest ¼ inch.

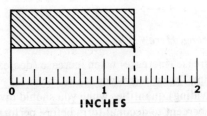

INCHES

    (A) 1 in   (B) 1¼ in   (C) 1½ in   (D) 2 in

2. Round the measurement 35.51 feet to the nearest foot.
        (A) 35 ft   (B) 35.50 ft   (C) 35.55 ft   (D) 36 ft

Sample Problem Solutions

1. (B) The problem asks for the nearest ¼ inch. The pictured
    rectangle measures 1⁵⁄₁₆ inch, which is closer to 1¼ than it is to 1½
    inch.

2. (D) The problem asks for the nearest foot, so the answer will be 35
    ft or 36 ft. To determine which, look at the two numbers to right of
    the decimal. Since .51 is closer to 100 than it is to 0, you round up
    to 36.

If You Were Wrong, Here's Why

Applying rounding principles improperly
Failing to make correct conversions between units within the same
   system
Failing to round to the specified unit
Incorrectly reading a diagram

7: CALCULATE DISTANCES

Basics You'll Need to Know to Master This Competency

Working with geometric figures presented pictorially
Finding perimeters of any given polygon or the circumference of any
   given circle

Knowing the Pythagorean theorem and how to use it

Understanding metric-metric conversions or English-English conversions that may be included without formulas or conversion factors

Sample Problems

1. What is the distance around a circular carousel that has a 9 foot radius?

    (A) 18π sq ft   (B) 81π ft   (C) 9π ft   (D) 18π ft

2. What is the distance around this polygon, in kilometers?

    (A) 1.6 km   (B) 16 km   (C) 160 km   (4) 1600 km

Sample Problem Solutions

1. (D) $C = 2\pi r$ or $2r\pi$ (commutative property of multiplication).
    $C = 2(9)\pi = 18\pi$ ft

2. (A) Distance around is the same as perimeter. The perimeter of any polygon is found by adding up the lengths of all the sides. $350 + 450 + 300 + 500 = 1600$ meters. The problem asks for kilometers. 1000 meters = 1 kilometer. $1600 \div 1000 = 1.6$ km.

If You Were Wrong, Here's Why

Using a wrong formula

Applying a formula or conversion incorrectly

Making a computational error

Using an incorrect unit of measurement with a correct value

8. CALCULATE AREAS

Basics You'll Need to Know to Master This Competency

Calculating the area of a circular region

Calculating the area of a square region

Calculating the area of a rectangular region

Calculating the area of a triangular region
Calculating the surface area of a rectangular solid
Understanding metric-metric conversions or English-English conver-
sions that may be included without formulas or conversion factors

Sample Problems

1. What is the surface area of a rectangular solid that is 9 inches
   long, 7 inches wide, and 5 inches high?
   (A) 315 cu in   (B) 286 sq in   (C) 286 in   (D) 336 sq in

2. What is the area of a circular region whose diameter is 12 cm?
   (A) 12π sq cm   (B) 36π sq cm
   (C) 24π sq cm   (D) 144π sq cm

Sample Problem Solutions

1. (B) To find the surface area of a rectangular solid, first find the
   area of side 1 ($5 \times 7 = 35$ sq in), next of side 2 ($7 \times 9 = 63$ sq in),
   and then of side 3 ($5 \times 9 = 45$ sq in). Since there are two of each of
   the sides, the surface area = $2(35) + 2(63) + 2(45) = 70 + 126$
   $+ 90 = 286$ <u>sq</u> in

2. (B) $A = \pi r^2$. Since $r = \frac{1}{2}d$ and $d = 12$ cm, then $r = \frac{1}{2} \times 12 = 6$ cm.
   Therefore, $A = \pi\ 6^2$ or $A = 36\pi$ sq cm. Remember, area is in
   square measures.

If You Were Wrong, Here's Why

Using a wrong formula
Applying a formula or conversion incorrectly
Making a computational error
Using an incorrect unit of measurement with a correct value

9: ADD AND SUBTRACT REAL NUMBERS

Basics You'll Need to Know to Master This Competency

Working with items or factors which involve irrational numbers (no
   fractions)
Working with square roots

Sample Problems

1. $5\pi + 7\pi - 4 =$
   (A) $12\pi^2 - 4$ (B) $12\pi - 4$ (C) $8 + 4\pi$ (D) 8π

2. $\sqrt{3} + \sqrt{27} =$
   (A) $\sqrt{30}$ (B) $4\sqrt{3}$ (C) 9 (D) 729

Sample Problem Solutions

1. (B) $5\pi + 7\pi - 4 = 12\pi - 4$. Note: You can add or subtract only like terms $(5\pi, 7\pi)$.

2. (B) $\sqrt{3} + \sqrt{27} = \sqrt{3} + \sqrt{3 \times 9} = \sqrt{3} + \sqrt{3}\,\sqrt{9} =$ $\sqrt{3} + 3\sqrt{3}$ (1 radical 3 plus 3 radical 3) $= 4\sqrt{3}$.

If You Were Wrong, Here's Why

Incorrectly combining irrational numbers—such as adding or subtracting two radicands
Incorrectly combining a rational and an irrational number
Simplifying radicals incorrectly
Performing an arithmetic operation other than the one indicated
Squaring when taking the square root is indicated

10: MULTIPLY AND DIVIDE REAL NUMBERS

Basics You'll Need to Know to Master This Competency

Working with factors which involve irrational numbers
Rationalizing denominators
Working with square roots

Sample Problems

1. $\sqrt{3} \times \sqrt{8} =$
   (A) 9×64 (B) $4\sqrt{6}$ (C) $2\sqrt{6}$ (D) 11

2. $\dfrac{2}{2\sqrt{5}} =$
   (A) $\dfrac{\sqrt{2}}{5}$ (B) $\dfrac{\sqrt{5}}{25}$ (C) $\dfrac{\sqrt{5}}{5}$ (D) $2\sqrt{5}$

Sample Problem Solutions

1. (C) $\sqrt{3} \times \sqrt{8} = \sqrt{3 \times 8} = \sqrt{24} = \sqrt{4 \times 6} = \sqrt{4} \times \sqrt{6} = 2\sqrt{6}$
   To multiply square roots, multiply the numbers under the signs and simplify.

2. (C) To divide by a radical, use the following steps to eliminate the radical from the denominator.

$$\frac{2}{2\sqrt{5}} = \frac{2}{2\sqrt{5}} \times \frac{\sqrt{5}}{\sqrt{5}} = \frac{2\sqrt{5}}{2\sqrt{25}} = \frac{\overset{1}{\cancel{2}}\sqrt{5}}{\underset{1}{\cancel{2}}(5)} = \frac{\sqrt{5}}{5}$$

If You Were Wrong, Here's Why

Incorrectly combining irrational numbers—such as adding or sub-
tracting radicands
Incorrectly combining a rational and an irrational number
Simplifying radicals incorrectly
Performing an arithmetic operation other than the one indicated,
such as adding when multiplication is indicated
Squaring when taking the square root is indicated

11: APPPLY THE ORDER-OF-OPERATIONS AGREEMENT TO COMPUTATIONS INVOLVING NUMBERS AND VARIABLES

Basics You'll Need to Know to Master This Competency

Applying the order-of-operations agreement to find the reduced or
simplified form
Working with computations of three to six positive rational numbers
(whole numbers, mixed numbers, fractions, or combinations)
Working with a computation that will require at least one addition or
subtraction *and* at least one multiplication, division, or use of
exponents.

Sample Problems

1. $\frac{1}{3} - 4(\frac{1}{2} + 2) =$
   (A) $-9\frac{2}{3}$ (B) $-9\frac{1}{6}$ (C) $-5\frac{2}{3}$ (D) $9\frac{2}{3}$

2. $6t - 2t \times 2 + 16t^2 \div 8 \times 2 =$
   (A) $4t^2 + 8t$ (B) $4t^2 + 2t$ (C) $t^2 + 8t$ (D) $t^2 + 2t$

Sample Problem Solutions

1. (A) Working from *left to right:* (1) do all operations in the *grouping symbols,* (2) do all *exponents (powers),* (3) do all multiplication and division, (4) do all addition and subtraction.

$$\frac{1}{3} - 4(\frac{1}{2} + 2) = \frac{1}{3} - 4(\frac{5}{2}) = \frac{1}{3} - 10 = -9\frac{2}{3}$$

2. (B) Remember, you work left to right and work the multiplication and division before the addition and subtraction.

$$6t - (2t \times 2) + (16t^2 \div 8) \times 2 = 6t - 4t + 2t^2 \times 2 =$$
$$6t - 4t + 4t^2 = 4t^2 + 2t$$

If You Were Wrong, Here's Why

Failing to read from left to right

Failing to perform multiplication and division before addition and subtraction

Failing to perform multiplication and division in order of their appearance (when reading from left to right)

Failing to observe grouping symbols

12: USE SCIENTIFIC NOTATION IN CALCULATIONS INVOLVING VERY LARGE OR VERY SMALL MEASUREMENTS

Basics You'll Need to Know to Master This Competency

Identifying the product or quotient in scientific notation when given an expression involving multiplication of numbers in scientific or decimal notation

Identifying the product or quotient in decimal notation when given a calculation in scientific notation

Sample Problems

1. $.000792 \div 396,000,000 =$
   (A) 2.00×10^{-12} (B) 2.00×10^{-2}
   (C) 2.00×10^{4} (D) 2.00×10^{12}

2. $(2.3 \times 10^4) \times (3.1 \times 10^{-5}) =$
   (A) -7.13 (B) 7.13 (C) $.713$ (D) 71.3

Sample Problem Solutions

1. (A) A number written in scientific notation is simply a number between 1 and 10 multiplied by a power. In this problem, place the decimal point to get a number between 1 and 10 and either: (1) count the digits to the right of the decimal to get the power of 10

$$.000792 = 7.92 \times 10^{-4}$$

or (2) count the digits from the original decimal point to the new one.

$$396,000,000. = 3.96 \times 10^{8}$$

(Whole numbers—396,000,000—have positive powers, and fractions—.000792—have negative.)

$$7.92 \times 10^{-4} \div 3.96 \times 10^{8} =$$

To solve:
Divide the numbers to get the first figure.

$$7.92 \div 3.96 = 2.00$$

Subtract the powers of ten to get the final power of 10.

$$-4 - (+8) = -12$$

Thus

$$.000792 \div 396,000,000 = 2.00 \times 10^{-12}$$

2. (C) Multiply the numbers together to get the first figure.

$$2.3 \times 3.1 = 7.13$$

Add the powers of 10.

$$4 + (-5) = -1$$
$$(2.3 \times 10^{4}) \times (3.1 \times 10^{-5}) = 7.13 \times 10^{-1} = .713$$

If You Were Wrong, Here's Why

Moving decimal in wrong direction
Failing to perform the appropriate operation on either the coefficient or the power or both
Moving decimal a wrong number of places
Interpreting a negative exponent as a negative number

13: CALCULATE VOLUME

Basics You'll Need to Know to Master This Competency

Calculating volumes of the following three dimensional figures:
Rectangular solid
Right circular cylinder
Circular cone
Sphere
Understanding metric-metric conversions or English-metric conversions (metric-English will not be required)

Sample Problems

1. What is the volume of a rectangular solid that is 12 inches long, 10 inches wide, and 8 inches high?
   (A) 960 cu in   (B) 840 cu in   (C) 960 sq in   (D) 592 sq in

2. What is the volume in liters (l) of a flask that will hold 1275 milliliters (ml)?
   (A) 1.275 l   (B) 12.75 l   (C) 127.5 l   (D) 12,750 l

Sample Problem Solutions

1. (A) V = *lwh*. V = (12)(10)(8) = 960 cu in. Remember, volume is in cubic units.

2. (A) 1 liter = 1000 milliliters. 1275 ÷ 1000 ml = 1.275 liter

If You Were Wrong, Here's Why

Using a wrong formula
Applying a formula or conversion incorrectly
Making a computational error
Using an incorrect unit of measurement with a correct value

14: SOLVE LINEAR EQUATIONS AND INEQUALITIES

Basics You'll Need to Know to Master This Competency

Calculating solutions which take three to six steps
Grouping symbols

Working with as many as three unknowns in the equation or
  inequality
Working with unknowns that may be in the left and/or the right
  sides
Calculating solutions involving rational numbers

Sample Problems

1. If $2(a + 2) = 2[a - (3 - a)]$, then:
   (A) $a = -4$ (B) $a = 5$ (C) $a = -5$ (D) $a = 7$

2. If $4b - 8 \leq 5b + 2$, then:
   (A) $b \leq -10$ (B) $b \geq -10$ (C) $b \leq 10$ (D) $b = 10$

Sample Problem Solutions

1. **(B)** To solve or simplify equations and inequalities: (1) add
   opposites to eliminate terms that are added or subtracted, (2)
   divide each side by the coefficient of the variable.

$$2(a + 2) = 2[a - (3 - a)]$$
$$2a + 4 = 2[a - 3 + a]$$
$$2a + 4 = 2a - 6 + 2a$$

$$\left.\begin{array}{rl} 2a + 4 = & 4a - 6 \\ -4 & -4 \end{array}\right\} \text{step 1}$$

$$\left.\begin{array}{rl} 2a = & 4a - 10 \\ -4a & -4a \end{array}\right\} \text{step 1}$$

$$-2a = -10$$

$$\frac{-2a}{-2} = \frac{-10}{-2} \quad \text{step 2}$$

$$a = 5$$

2. **(B)** To work with an inequality, treat it exactly like an equation,
   except if you multiply or divide *both* sides by a negative number,
   you must *reverse* the direction of the sign.

$$\begin{array}{rcl} 4b - 8 \leq & 5b + & 2 \\ + 8 & & + 8 \\ \hline 4b \leq & 5b + & 10 \\ -5b \leq & -5b & \\ \hline -b \leq & & 10 \end{array}$$

$$\frac{-1b}{-1} \leq \frac{10}{-1}$$
$$b \geq -10$$

If You Were Wrong, Here's Why

Applying properties of equality and inequality incorrectly
Applying properties of operations (and grouping rules) incorrectly

15: USE GIVEN FORMULAS TO COMPUTE RESULTS WHEN GEOMETRIC MEASUREMENTS ARE NOT INVOLVED

Basics You'll Need to Know to Master This Competency

Calculating answers from a given formula or relationship that will contain a dependent variable and one to three independent variables

Working with formulas limited to first and second degree expressions involving positive rational numbers

Sample Problems

1. Given $a = 2(b + 3)^2$, if $b = 4$, then $a =$
   (A) 14   (B) 28   (C) 50   (D) 98

2. The formula for converting a Fahrenheit temperature to Celsius is $C = \frac{5}{9}(F - 32°)$. What is the temperature on the Celsius scale when the Fahrenheit temperature is 95°?
   (A) 20.5°   (B) 35°   (C) 40°   (D) 75°

Sample Problem Solutions

1. (D) Replace b with 4 and simplify: $a = 2(4 + 3)^2 = 2(7)^2 = 2(49) = 98$.

2. (B) Replace F in the Fahrenheit formula with 95° and simplify.

$$C = \frac{5}{9}(95° - 32°), \quad C = \frac{5}{9}(63°), \quad C = 35°$$

If You Were Wrong, Here's Why

Making an order-of-operations error

Using the formula incorrectly
Substituting wrong numbers for variables

16: FIND PARTICULAR VALUES OF A FUNCTION

Basics You'll Need to Know to Master This Competency

Working with f(x) notation (replacing a given value for "x" in the
  formula for the function "f"
Working with a domain value that is a rational number

Sample Problems

1. Find $f(-2)$ given: $f(x) = 3x^2 - 2x - 1$
   (A) -9 (B) 7   (C) 15   (D) 21

2. Given the following function, find $f(-3)$.

$$f(x) = x^3 - 2x^2 - 4x$$

   (A) -51 (B) -33 (C) -3 (D) 21

Sample Problem Solutions

1. (C) $f(x) = 3x^2 - 2x - 1$
      $f(-2) = 3(-2)^2 - 2(-2) - 1 = 3(4) + 4 - 1 =$
      $12 + 3 = 15$

2. (B) $f(x) = x^3 - 2x^2 - 4x$
      $f(-3) = (-3)^3 - 2(-3)^2 - 4(-3) = -27 - 2(9) + 12 =$
      $-27 - 18 + 12 = -27 - 6 = -33$

If You Were Wrong, Here's Why

Making an incomplete or incorrect substitution of the domain value
  into the polynomial expression
Incorrectly raising the domain value to a power
Incorrectly combining values of different terms of the polynomial
  into a single value
Incorrectly computing the value of one or more terms of the polynomial

17: FACTOR A QUADRATIC EXPRESSION

Basics You'll Need to Know to Master This Competency

Factoring the general quadratic expression $ax^2 + bx + c$

Sample Problems

1. Which is a linear factor of the following expression?
   $4x^2 - 4x - 3$
   (A) $x + 1$ (B) $2x - 1$ (C) $2x - 3$ (D) $x - 1$

2. Find a linear factor of the following expression: $6x^2 - 7x + 2$
   (A) $x - 2$ (B) $6x - 2$ (C) $2x + 1$ (D) $2x - 1$

Sample Problem Solutions

1. (C) The factors for $4x^2 - 4x - 3$ are: $(2x - 3)(2x + 1)$. Check by multiplying out:

$$4x^2 + 2x - 6x - 3 =$$

$$(2x - 3) \quad (2x + 1)$$

first term $= (2x)(2x) = 4x^2$

middle term $=$ *the sum of* $(2x)(1) = \quad 2x$
$$(-3)(2x) = \underline{-6x}$$
$$-4x$$

last term $= (-3)(1) = -3$

$$4x^2 - 4x - 3$$

2. (D) The factors for $6x^2 - 7x + 2$ are: $(2x - 1)(3x - 2)$.
   Check by multiplying out

$$(2x - 1) \quad (3x - 2)$$

$$6x^2 - 4x - 3x + 2 = 6x^2 - 7x + 2$$

If You Were Wrong, Here's Why

Finding factors for the coefficients of the leading and ending terms of the quadratic equation but which are not factors for the entire quadratic equation

18: FIND THE ROOTS OF A QUADRATIC EQUATION

Basics You'll Need to Know to Master This Competency

Finding real roots which are *not integers*
Calculations involving factoring or the quadratic formula

$$\frac{-b \pm \sqrt{b^2 - 4ac}}{2a}$$

Sample Problems

1. Find the real roots of this equation: $2x^2 - x - 2 = 0$

   (A) $\dfrac{-1 - \sqrt{15}}{4}$ and $\dfrac{-1 + \sqrt{15}}{4}$ (B) $\dfrac{1 - \sqrt{15}}{4}$ and $\dfrac{1 + \sqrt{15}}{4}$

   (C) $\dfrac{-1 - \sqrt{17}}{4}$ and $\dfrac{-1 + \sqrt{17}}{4}$ (D) $\dfrac{1 - \sqrt{17}}{4}$ and $\dfrac{1 + \sqrt{17}}{4}$

2. What are the real roots of this equation? $6x^2 - 4 = 5x$
   (A) $4/3$ and $-(1/2)$ (B) $-(4/3)$ and $-(1/2)$

   (C) $1/3$ and $-(1/2)$ (D) $\dfrac{5 - 3\sqrt{6}}{6}$ and $\dfrac{5 + 3\sqrt{6}}{6}$

Sample Problem Solutions

1. (D) $ax^2 + bx + c = 0$ (standard form of a quadratic equation).
   Given $2x^2 - x - 2$; $a = 2, b = -1, c = -2$. Substitute the numbers for a, b, and c into:

   $$x = \frac{-b \pm \sqrt{b^2 - 4ac}}{2a} \text{ (quadratic formula)}$$

   $$x = \frac{-(-1) \pm \sqrt{(-1)^2 - 4(2)(-2)}}{2(2)} = \frac{1 \pm \sqrt{1 + 16}}{4} =$$

   $$\frac{1 \pm \sqrt{17}}{4} = \frac{1 + \sqrt{17}}{4} \text{ and } \frac{1 - \sqrt{17}}{4}$$

2. (A) Write the equation as $6x^2 - 5x - 4 = 0$.
   Factor and rewrite the equation as $(3x - 4)(2x + 1) = 0$.

Solve the equations that result from setting each of the factors equal to zero.

$$3x - 4 = 0 \quad \text{or} \quad 2x + 1 = 0$$
$$3x = 4 \quad \text{or} \quad 2x = -1$$
$$x = \tfrac{4}{3} \quad \text{or} \quad x = -\tfrac{1}{2}$$

If You Were Wrong, Here's Why

Factoring incorrectly
Failing to set each factor equal to zero
Substituting incorrectly into the quadratic formula
Using an incorrect version of the quadratic formula

19: IDENTIFY INFORMATION CONTAINED IN BAR, LINE, AND CIRCLE GRAPHS

Basics You'll Need to Know to Master This Competency

Determining specific frequencies or proportions indicated by or computed from, identified categories
Determining specific categories from identified frequencies
Obtaining sums and differences of frequencies
Obtaining a percent of the whole
Obtaining a frequency from a percent

Sample Problems

1. The graph below represents the monthly average temperatures for 6 months of the year. How much higher is the average temperature in August than it is in May?

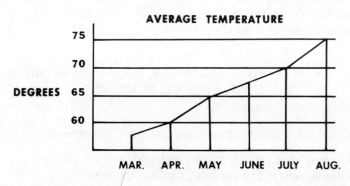

AVERAGE TEMPERATURE

(A) 3° (B) 5° (C) 10° (D) 15°

2. On the circle graph below of money contributed to five TV evangelists, what per cent of total money contributed is contributed to evangelists 2, 3, and 5 combined?

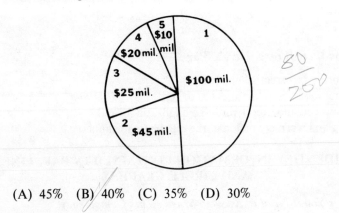

(A) 45%   (B) 40%   (C) 35%   (D) 30%

Sample Problem Solutions

1. (C) Subtract the average May temperature from the average August temperature. 65° from 75° = 10°

2. (B) Add the money contributed to evangelists 2, 3, and 5, and divide by the total money contributed. (45 + 25 + 10) ÷ 200 = .4 = 40%

If You Were Wrong, Here's Why

Obtaining wrong data
Reading a frequency or category adjacent to the correct one
Making a computational error

20: DETERMINE THE MEAN, MEDIAN, AND MODE OF A SET OF NUMBERS

Basics You'll Need to Know to Master This Competency

Knowing what a mean, median, and mode are
Knowing how to find the mean, median, and mode

Sample Problems

1. What is the *median* of the data in the following sample? 7, 5, 3, 7, 5, 6, 7, 8

   3 5 5 6 7 7 8

   (A) 5.5   (B) 6   (C) 6.5   (D) 7

2. What is the *mean* of the data in the following sample? 8, 6, 4, 6, 12, 14, 6, 8

   (A) 6   (B) 7   (C) 8   (D) 9

Sample Problem Solutions

1. (C) The *median* for a set of data is found by arranging the data in order of size. If there is an odd number of scores, the median is the score in the middle. If there is an even number of scores, it is the average of the two scores in the middle.

$$3, 5, 5, \underline{6, 7}, 7, 7, 8$$

$$(6 + 7) \div 2 = 6.5$$

2. (C) The mean is the average of all the scores.

$$\text{mean (average)} = \frac{\text{sum of scores}}{\text{number of scores}}$$

$$\text{mean} = \frac{64}{8} = 8$$

If You Were Wrong, Here's Why

Finding the mean when it is not the value specified
Finding the median when it is not the value specified
Finding the mode when it is not the value specified
Finding some other value (not the mean, median, or mode) which is within the range of the sample

21: COUNT SUBSETS OF A GIVEN SET

Basics You'll Need to Know to Master This Competency

Identifying (by listing or by calculating) the number of subsets of a specific size and stated criteria

Working with problems that may involve permutations or combinations

Sample Problems

1. From a group of two men and two women, a man and a woman will be selected to attend a conference. How many possible ways can the selection be made?
   (A) 2 (B) 4 (C) 8 (D) 12

2. A cereal company decides to test five different brands of cereal. The different brands of cereal have been labeled A, B, C, D, and E. The company decides to compare each brand with the other brands by pairing together different brands. How many different pairs will result by selecting two different brands at a time?
   (A) 25 (B) 20 (C) 10 (D) 5

Sample Problem Solutions

1. (B) Let two men = m_1 and m_2. Let two women = w_1 and w_2. The pairs possible from m_1, m_2, w_1, and w_2 are

$$m_1, w_1; m_1, w_2; m_2, w_1; m_2, w_2 = 4 \text{ ways}$$

2. (C) Note that the question asks for *different pairs;* therefore, AB and BA are not different and are counted as one pair. C(n, r) denotes this situation and is read "the number of combinations of n things taken r at a time." The formula used is

$$C(n, r) = \frac{n!}{r!(n - r)!}$$

where n = 5 and r = 2 (5 brands of cereal taken 2 at a time). Therefore, the equation is

$$\frac{5!}{2!(5 - 2)!} = \frac{5!}{2!3!} = \frac{5 \cdot 4 \cdot 3 \cdot 2 \cdot 1}{2 \cdot 1 \cdot 3 \cdot 2 \cdot 1} = \frac{20}{2} = 10$$

If You Were Wrong, Here's Why

Counting combinations when combinations are not the appropriate arrangements

Counting permutations when permutations are not the appropriate arrangements

Using the wrong size for the subsets

Using the wrong size for the original set

Multiplying number of elements in set by the number of elements in one of the defined subsets

22: DEDUCE FACTS OF SET-INCLUSION OR NON-SET-INCLUSION FROM A DIAGRAM

Basics You'll Need to Know to Master This Competency

Understanding relationships among sets and set membership using a Venn diagram

Sample Problems

1. Sets D, E, F, and U are related as shown in the diagram

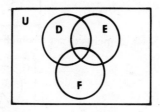

Which of the following statements is true, assuming none of the eight regions is empty?

(A) Any element which is a member of set E is also a member of set D.

(B) No element is a member of all three sets, D, E, and F.

(C) Any element which is a member of set U is also a member of set D.

(D) None of the above statements is true.

2. Sets J, K, L, and U are related as shown in the diagram.

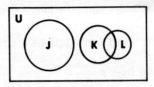

Which of the following statements is true, assuming none of the eight regions is empty?

(A) No element is a member of both sets K and L.

(B) Any element which is a member of set U is a member of set J.

√(C) No element is a member of both J and K.

(D) None of the above statements is true.

Sample Problem Solutions

1. (D) D is the correct answer.

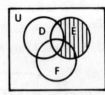

A is false.

The shaded area shows elements of set E which are not in set D.

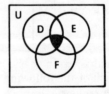

B is false.

The small shaded area shows elements that are members of all 3 sets, D, E, and F.

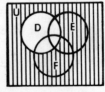

C is false.

The shaded area shows elements of set U that are not in set D.

2. (C) C is true. Sets J and K do not have any region in common; therefore, no element is a member of both sets.

A is false.

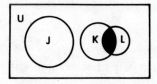

The shaded area shows elements which are members of sets K and L.

B is false.

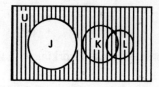

The shaded area shows elements of set U that are not in set J.

If You Were Wrong, Here's Why

Failing to "shade" your illustrations (remember to mark on the test materials as you are reading the equations and the choices)

23: RECOGNIZE THE MEANING OF EXPONENTS

Basics You'll Need to Know to Master This Competency

Changing an expression in exponential form to an equivalent expanded expression ($2^3 = 2 \cdot 2 \cdot 2$)
Understanding the basic properties of exponents

Sample Problems

1. $(6^3)(3^2) =$
   (A) $(6 + 6 + 6)(3 + 3)$ (B) $(6 \times 6 \times 6)(3 \times 3)$
   (C) $(6 \times 3)(3 \times 2)$ (D) $(6 \times 3)^5$

2. $5^3 \div 3^2 =$
   (A) $(5)(3) \div (3)(2)$ (B) $(5)(5)(5) \div (3)(3)$
   (C) $(5 \div 3)^5$ (D) $5^1 \div 3^0$

Sample Problem Solutions

1. (B) Remember, the rule for multiplying with exponents

$$(x^a)\underbrace{(x^b)} = x^{a+b}$$
$$\text{same base}$$

applies only when working with the same base. For example:

$$(6^3)(6^2) = 6^5$$

2. (B) Remember, the rule for dividing with exponents,

$$\text{same} \begin{cases} \dfrac{x^a}{x^b} = x^{a-b} \\ \text{base} \end{cases}$$

applies only when working with the same base. For example:

$$\frac{5^6}{5^2} = 5^4$$

If You Were Wrong, Here's Why

Multiplying bases by the exponents
Adding bases rather than multiplying
Using an incorrect order of operation
Multiplying exponents when adding them is the correct operation, or
   vice versa
Applying laws of exponents that require like bases to expressions
   having unlike bases
Using other incorrect applications of laws of exponents

24: RECOGNIZE THE ROLE OF THE BASE NUMBER IN DETERMINING PLACE VALUE IN THE BASE-TEN NUMERATION SYSTEM AND IN SYSTEMS THAT ARE PATTERNED AFTER IT

Basics You'll Need to Know to Master This Competency

Determining the place value of any specified digit
Determining the base-ten equivalent of a given number

Sample Problems

1. Select the place value associated with the underlined digit.
    3.0<u>6</u>21

(A) $\dfrac{1}{10^2}$ (B) $\dfrac{1}{10^3}$ (C) $\dfrac{1}{10^1}$ (D) $\dfrac{1}{10^0}$

2. Select the base-ten equivalent of the given base-five numeral.
   2034 (base five)
   (A) 269   (B) 290   (C) 1269   (D) 1345

Sample Problem Solutions

1. (B)   3.   0   6   <u>2</u>   1   (base ten)
   $10^0.$ 10^{-1} 10^{-2} $\underline{10^{-3}}$ 10^{-4} (place values)

   or

   1. $\dfrac{1}{10^1}$ $\dfrac{1}{10^2}$ $\underline{\dfrac{1}{10^3}}$ $\dfrac{1}{10^4}$

2. (A) To find the equivalent in base ten:

   5^3 5^2 5^1 5^0 (place values)
   2   0   3   4   (base five) =
   $2 \cdot 5^3 + 0 \cdot 5^2 + 3 \cdot 5^1 + 4 \cdot 5^0 =$
   $2 \cdot 125 + 0 \cdot 25 + 3 \cdot 5 + 4 \cdot 1 =$
   $250 + 0 + 15 + 4 =$
   269 (base ten)

If You Were Wrong, Here's Why

Associating the incorrect power of the base with the specified digit
Using the relationship between digits and powers of the base incorrectly in converting to base ten

25: IDENTIFY EQUIVALENT FORMS OF POSITIVE RATIONAL NUMBERS INVOLVING DECIMALS, PERCENTS, AND FRACTIONS

Basics You'll Need to Know to Master This Competency

Converting decimal to percent, percent to decimal
Converting decimal to fraction, fraction to decimal
Converting percent to fraction, fraction to percent

Sample Problems

1. $1.74 =$
   (A) 1.74%   (B) 17.4%   (C) 174%   (D) .174%

2. $\dfrac{17}{25} =$
   (A) 0.68   (B) 0.068   (C) 6.8%   (D) 0.68%

Sample Problem Solutions

1. (C) To change decimals to percents, move the decimal point 2 places to the right and add a percent sign. $1.74 = 174.\%$

2. (A) To change a fraction to a decimal, just do what the operation says.

$$25\overline{)17.00}\,^{.68}$$

If You Were Wrong, Here's Why

Essentially, incorrect answers result from incorrect conversions of decimals, percents, or fractions

26: DETERMINE THE ORDER RELATION BETWEEN MAGNITUDES

Basics You'll Need to Know to Master This Competency

Understanding the correct order relation between
> Positive fractions and mixed numbers
> Positive decimal numbers
> Negative fractions

Understanding inequality signs

Sample Problems

1. Identify the symbol that should be placed in the box to form a true statement.
   ¼ □ .20
   (A) =   (B) <   (C) >

2. Identify the symbol that should be placed in the box to form a true statement.

   4.1$\overline{3}$ □ 4.$\overline{13}$ 4.1333   4.131313

   (A) =   (B) <   (C) >

Sample Problem Solutions

1. (C) To compare, convert ¼ to a decimal by dividing 1 by 4.

$$4\overline{)1.00} \quad .25$$

$$.25 > .20$$

2. (C) 4.1$\overline{3}$ is greater than 4.$\overline{13}$ because there is a 3 in the thousandths place of 4.1333 . . . and only a 1 in the corresponding place of 4.1313. Note: the mark above the number(s) means to repeat what is below.

If You Were Wrong, Here's Why

Not understanding inequality signs
Using the wrong equivalence or order relation

27: IDENTIFY A REASONABLE ESTIMATE OF A SUM, AVERAGE, OR PRODUCT OF NUMBERS

Basics You'll Need to Know to Master This Competency

Estimating a sum, average, or product of numbers when given a word problem

Sample Problems

1. 100 policemen take an achievement test. All of the policemen scored less than 92 but more than 63. Which of the following values is a reasonable estimate of the average score of the policemen?
   (A) 95   (B) 71   (C) 63   (D) 52

2. Thirty people work for a chemical plant. The lowest paid person earns $75 per week and the highest paid person earns $250 per week. Which of the following values could be a reasonable estimate of the total weekly payroll for the company?
   (A) $9750   (B) $5400   (C) $1500   (D) $325

Sample Problem Solutions

1. **(B)** The average score has to be *between* 92 and 63. 71 is the only score that qualifies.

2. **(B)** Don't forget to multiply each amount per week by thirty. Then look for an answer in between your two numbers. $30 \times 250 = 7500$; $30 \times 75 = 2250$. 5400 is the only choice that falls between these amounts.

If You Were Wrong, Here's Why

Using a value that is less than the smallest value in the set
Using a value that is greater than the largest value in the set
Making an obvious error in place value
Using the smallest (largest) value when the largest (smallest) should have been used

28: IDENTIFY RELATIONSHIPS BETWEEN ANGLE MEASURES

Basics You'll Need to Know to Master This Competency

Understanding relationships between angle measures involving
    Parallel line properties
    Properties of plane figures, including isosceles and equilateral triangles and parallelograms
    Properties of vertical, supplementary, and complementary angles

Sample Problems

1. Which of the statements below is true for the figure shown?

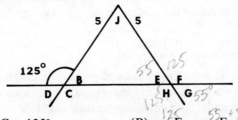

   (A) m∠G = 125°   (B) m∠F = m∠E + m∠B
   (C) m∠C ≠ m∠H   √ (D) ∠E is a supplement of ∠F

2. Which of the statements below is true for the figure shown, given that L_1 and L_2 are parallel lines?

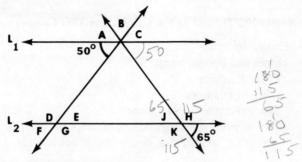

(A) Since m∠ F = 50°, m∠ K = 130°
(B) Since m∠ E = 50°, m∠ B = 65°
(C) m∠ H = m∠ C
(D) None of the above statements is true.

Sample Problem Solutions

1. **(D)** Supplementary angles are two adjacent angles that form a straight line. Their sum is 180°. A is false: ∠B is the supplementary angle of ∠ 125°, so ∠ B = 55°. Since BJE is an isosceles triangle, ∠E = ∠B = 55°. ∠E and ∠G are vertical angles, so ∠G = ∠E = 55°. B is false: the exterior angle of a triangle has a measure equal to the sum of the measures of its two remote interior angles. ∠F = ∠J + ∠B. C is false: ∠C = 125° (vertical angles are equal). ∠B = 55° since ∠C and ∠B are supplementary angles. ∠B = ∠E = 55° (isosceles triangle). ∠E and ∠H are supplementary angles.

2. **(B)** ∠C = 50° (vertical angles). ∠E = ∠C = 50° (corresponding angles are equal). ∠A = 65° (alternate exterior angles are equal). 180° − (∠A + ∠C) = ∠B = 65°. A is false: ∠K is a supplement of ∠65°, ∠K = 115°. C is false: ∠H = ∠C + ∠B (corresponding angles).

If You Were Wrong, Here's Why

Not knowing parallel line properties
Not knowing properties of plane figures, including isosceles and equilateral triangles and parallelograms
Not knowing properties of vertical, supplementary, and complementary angles

29: CLASSIFY SIMPLE PLANE FIGURES BY RECOGNIZING THEIR PROPERTIES

Basics You'll Need to Know to Master This Competency

Identifying
  Lines and line segments
  Types of angles
  Types of triangles
  Types of convex quadrilaterals
  Convex pentagons, regular and nonregular, when given a
    diagram, description, or characteristics of a plane figure

Sample Problems

1. Select the geometric figure that possesses *all* of the following characteristics

    i. quadrilateral
    ii. two pairs of parallel sides
    iii. perpendicular diagonals

  (A) parallelogram   (B) rectangle
  (C) rhombus   (D) trapezoid

2. Identify the type of triangle pictured below:

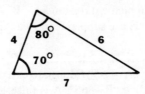

  (A) scalene; obtuse   (B) scalene; acute
  (C) isosceles; acute   (D) isoceles; obtuse

Sample Problem Solutions

1. (C) A, B, and D do not have perpendicular diagonals.

2. (B) A scalene triangle has no equal sides. An acute triangle has all angles less than 90°.

If You Were Wrong, Here's Why

Not knowing the plane figures specified

30: RECOGNIZE SIMILAR TRIANGLES AND THEIR PROPERTIES

Basics You'll Need to Know to Master This Competency

Determining specific angle measures and side lengths from knowledge of

The sum of the measures of a triangle's interior angles

The relationships among angles formed when parallel lines are cut by a transversal

The Pythagorean theorem

The relationship between congruent angles of a triangle and the lengths of sides opposite these angles

The properties of corresponding angles and sides of similar triangles

Sample Problems

1. Which of the statements A–D is true for the pictured triangles?

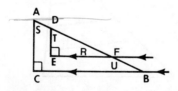

(A) m∠S = m∠U

(B) m∠S = m∠T

(C) DE/AC = AB/DF

(D) None of the above statements is true.

2. Study the figures A, B, C, D. Then select the figure in which all triangles are similar.

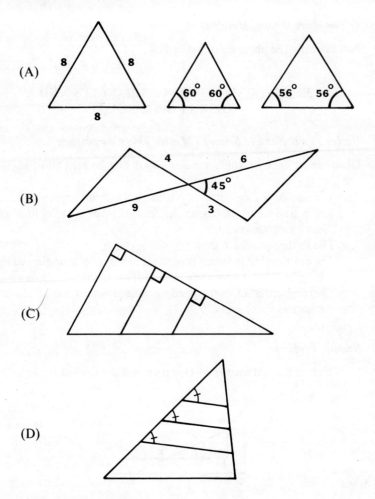

(A)

(B)

(C)

(D)

Sample Problem Solutions

1. **(B)** B is true. In the two triangles, ACB and DEF:

   ∠C = ∠E because they are both marked as right angles. Sides EF and CB are parallel; therefore, ∠R and ∠U are equal because they are corresponding angles.

Triangles are similar if two angles of one have equal measures to two angles of the other.

2. (C) Triangles are similar when their corresponding sides are proportional or when they have equal measures for their three angles. In choice C, all three triangles have a 90° angle and corresponding angles are equal. In choice A, the first two are equilateral triangles, but the third is an isosceles triangle. In choice B the sides are not proportionate. In choice D the triangles do not have equal measures for their three angles.

If You Were Wrong, Here's Why

Choosing an incorrect relation or statement

31: IDENTIFY APPROPRIATE TYPES OF MEASUREMENT OF GEOMETRIC OBJECTS

Basics You'll Need to Know to Master This Competency

Understanding the appropriate type of measure for a specified characteristic of the object
Understanding when linear (length), square (area), or cubic (volume) measurement is appropriate

Sample Problems

1. What type of measure is needed to express the length of line segment EF shown below?

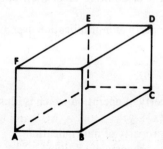

(A) linear   (B) square   (C) cubic   (D) surface

2. What type of measure is needed
to express the area of the triangle
ABD?

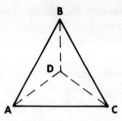

(A) surface   (B) square   (C) cubic   (D) linear

Sample Problem Solutions

1. (A) Length measure is linear.
2. (B) Area is always measured in square units.

If You Were Wrong, Here's Why

Choosing the wrong type of measure

32: RECOGNIZE AND USE PROPERTIES OF OPERATIONS

Basics You'll Need to Know to Master This Competency

Identifying the following properties when given an algebraic statement:
    Commutative property of addition: $a + b = b + a$
    Associative property of addition: $(a + b) + c = a + (b + c)$
    Commutative property of multiplication: $ab = ba$
    Associative property of multiplication: $(ab)c = a(bc)$
    Identity property of addition or of multiplication: $a + 0 = a$,
    $a \times 1 = a$
    Distributive property of multiplication over addition: $a(b + c) =$
    $ab + ac$

Sample Problems

1. Identify the property of operation which is illustrated:
   $4(x) + 4(y) = 4(x + y)$
   (A) associative property of multiplication
   (B) commutative property of addition
   (C) commutative property of multiplication
   (D) distributive property of multiplication over addition

2. Choose the expression equivalent to the following: $2(5) + 2(a) =$
   (A) $(2)(2) + (5)(a)$ (B) $(2 + 2)(5 + a)$
   (C) $4(5)(a)$ (D) $2(5 + a)$

Sample Problem Solutions

1. (D) $ab + ac = a(b + c)$

2. (D) The distributive property.

If You Were Wrong, Here's Why

Using properties of operations not illustrated by the statement
Using statements that do not illustrate the specified property
Using expressions which result from incorrect application of the
  property

33: DETERMINE WHETHER A PARTICULAR NUMBER IS AMONG THE SOLUTIONS OF A GIVEN EQUATION OR INEQUALITY

Basics You'll Need to Know to Master This Competency

Determining whether a given number is a solution for each of the
  given equations and inequalities:
      The number to be tested as a solution will be an integer between
      -10 and 10 or a common fraction
      Equations or inequalities will be of the first or second degree

Sample Problems

1. For each of the three statements below, determine whether (-3)
   is a solution.

   i. $|a - 3| = 0$
   ii. $(a + 7)(a - 2) \leq 8$
   iii. $a^2 + 2a + 11 = 14$

   Which option below identifies *every* statement that has (-3) as a
   solution and *only* that (those) statement(s)?
   (A) i only   (B) ii only   (C) iii only   (D) ii and iii only

2. For each of the statements below, determine whether ($\frac{1}{4}$) is a solution.

   i. $3x - \frac{5}{4} < 0$
  ii. $(4y - 1)(2y - 3) = 0$
 iii. $4t - 2 = -4t$

Which option below identifies *every* statement that has ($\frac{1}{4}$) as a solution and *only* that (those) statement(s)?
(A) i only   (B) ii only
(C) ii and iii only   (D) all of the statements

Sample Problem Solutions

1. (D) To find the answer, replace the letter in each statement with -3.

   i. $|-3 - 3| = 0$, $|-6| = 0$,   false
  ii. $(-3 + 7)(-3 - 2) \le 8$, $(4)(-5) \le 8$, $-20 \le 8$,   true
 iii. $-3^2 + 2(-3) + 11 = 14$, $9 - 6 + 11 = 14$,
     $14 = 14$,   true

2. (D) i. $3(\frac{1}{4}) - \frac{5}{4} < 0$, $\frac{3}{4} - \frac{5}{4} < 0$, $-\frac{2}{4} < 0$,   true
      ii. $(4 \cdot \frac{1}{4} - 1)(2 \cdot \frac{1}{4} - 3) = 0$, $0(-2\frac{1}{2}) = 0$,   true
     iii. $4(\frac{1}{4}) - 2 = -4(\frac{1}{4})$, $-1 = -1$,   true

If You Were Wrong, Here's Why

Identifying equation(s) or inequalities that do not have the given
    number as a solution
Not identifying *all* the equations or inequalities that have the given
    number as the solution

34: RECOGNIZE STATEMENTS AND CONDITIONS OF PROPORTIONALITY AND VARIATION

Basics You'll Need to Know to Master This Competency

Setting up proportions or variations (direct/inverse) from a word
problem
Using the constant of variation

Sample Problems

1. Two people can paint 5 rooms in 3 days. Let P represent the number of rooms these people can paint in a 30-day month. Select the correct statement of the given condition.

(A) $\dfrac{3}{5} = \dfrac{P}{30}$ (B) $\dfrac{5}{3} = \dfrac{P}{30}$ (C) $\dfrac{P}{5} = \dfrac{3}{30}$ (D) $\dfrac{P}{3} = \dfrac{30}{10}$

2. The area of two rectangular billboards is held constant while the length and width change. If the length is 10 when the width is 4, select the statement of the condition when the width is 5.

(A) $\dfrac{L}{5} = \dfrac{4}{10}$ (B) $\dfrac{10}{4} = \dfrac{L}{5}$ (C) $\dfrac{L}{10} = \dfrac{5}{4}$ (D) $\dfrac{L}{10} = \dfrac{4}{5}$

Sample Problem Solutions

1. (B) Be sure to keep the comparisons in the proportions the same.

$$\frac{5 \text{ rooms}}{3 \text{ days}} = \frac{P \text{ rooms}}{30 \text{ days}}$$

2. (D) The area of both billboards is the same, 40. 4(10) = 5L. The only ratios that will cross multiply correctly are D.

$$\frac{L}{10} = \frac{4}{5}$$

$$5L = 40$$

If You Were Wrong, Here's Why

Mistaking inverse variation for direct variation, or vice versa
Selecting an incorrect constant of variation
Improperly holding a variable constant
Mistaking solution(s) to a different but similar problem for solutions to the given problem

35: RECOGNIZE REGIONS OF THE COORDINATE PLANE WHICH CORRESPOND TO SPECIFIC CONDITIONS

Basics You'll Need to Know to Master This Competency

Identifying the linear conditions that correspond to a given graph
Identifying the graph that corresponds to the given linear conditions

Sample Problems

1. Which option gives the condition(s) that corresponds to the shaded region of the plane shown below?

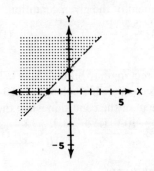

(A) x < 5 and y > 2   (B) y = −x
(C) x < 5, y > 2, and y > x   (D) x < y − 2

2. Which shaded region identifies the portion of the plane in which x ≥ 2 and y ≤ 0?

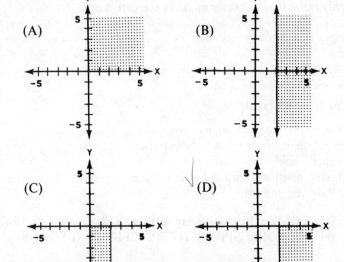

Sample Problem Solutions

1. (D) A and C would show a horizontal area across the graph. B would show a straight line.

2. (D) A shows $x \geq 2$ and $y \geq 0$. B shows only $x \geq 2$ and does not satisfy the y requirement. C shows $x \geq 0$, $x \leq 2$, and $y \leq 0$.

If You Were Wrong, Here's Why

Thinking that graphs show regions which do not correspond to the conditions

Assuming conditions which do not correspond to the region shown in the graph

36: RECOGNIZE PROPERTIES AND INTERRELATIONSHIPS AMONG THE MEAN, MEDIAN, AND MODE IN A VARIETY OF DISTRIBUTIONS

Basics You'll Need to Know to Master This Competency

Identifying the relationship that is true about the mean, median, and mode from a given diagram and/or description of a distribution of data

Sample Problems

1. In an English class, half the students scored 80 on a grammar test. Most of the remaining students scored 70 except for a few students who scored 15. Which of the following statements is true about the distributions of scores?
   (A) The mean is greater than the median.
   (B) The mode and the mean are the same.
   (C) The mean is less than the median.
   (D) The mean and the median are the same.

2. The graph below represents the distribution of ratings, for the manager at Emerson Electric on a popularity poll. Select the statement that is true about the distribution of ratings.

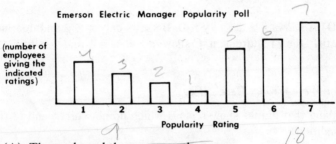

Emerson Electric Manager Popularity Poll

(number of employees giving the indicated ratings)

Popularity Rating

(A) The mode and the mean are the same.
(B) The median is greater than the mean.
✓(C) The mode is greater than the median.
(D) The mean is less than the median.

Sample Problem Solutions

1. (C) 50% of the scores are 80. The other 50% of the scores are 70 and 15, so 80 is the most frequent (greatest number of) score, the *mode.* Look at answer B. It could only be true if there were some scores higher than 80 to offset the scores lower than 80. The *median* is the score in the middle, but, you are not dealing with just three scores of 80, 70 and 15.
   you have:

$$\underbrace{}_{50\%} \quad \underbrace{}_{50\%}$$

80   70   15

So the *median* is between 80 and 70, or *75.* You cannot find the exact *mean* (the average) so you have to estimate, noting that 50% of the scores are 80, *most* of the rest are 70, and *a few* are 15. For example: 100 students, 50%, 80; 40%, 70; 10%, 15.

$$
\begin{array}{r}
50 \times 80 = 4000 \\
40 \times 70 = 2800 \\
\underline{10} \times 15 = \underline{150} \\
100 \qquad\qquad 6950
\end{array}
$$

$$6950 \div 100 = \underline{69.5}$$

You can see that C is the correct answer.

2. (C) The *mode* is the most frequent (greatest number) score. In the above graph the manager received the rating of *7* the most times. The *median* is the score in the middle and the graph shows that *1* is in the middle of the ratings. The *mean* is the average of the scores. In the above graph the mode happens to be the highest rating 7 and the median happens to be the lowest rating so the mean (average) has to be *between the mode and the median*. Summary: mode 7, mean between, median 1. You can see from this summary that the following answers are false:

(A) The mode and mean are the same.
(B) The median is greater than the mean.
(C) The mean is less than the median.

If You Were Wrong, Here's Why

Not knowing what the mean, median, and mode are and how to find them

37: CHOOSE THE MOST APPROPRIATE PROCEDURE FOR SELECTING AN UNBIASED SAMPLE FROM A TARGET POPULATION

Basics You'll Need to Know to Master This Competency

Identifying appropriate surveying methods
Identifying the difference between statistically biased and unbiased samples

Sample Problems

1. A clothing store wants to find out which newspaper ads for their store have been most effective with its customers. The clothing store decides to conduct a survey of a sample of its readers. Which of the following procedures would be most appropriate for obtaining a statistically unbiased sample of the store's customers?
   (A) having customers voluntarily mail in their preferences
   (B) surveying the first hundred customers from an alphabetical listing of customers
   (C) surveying a random sample of customers from a list of all customers
   (D) surveying a random sample of people from the telephone directory

2. A family counseling center needs to estimate the average number of people per family in its city. To do so, the counseling center decides to conduct a survey. Which of the following procedures would be most appropriate for selecting a statistically unbiased sample?

   (A) surveying all the residents of the largest subdivision in the city
   (B) surveying a random sample of people at a certain shopping mall in the city
   (C) selecting the largest employer in the city and surveying a random sample of its employees
   (D) randomly selecting geographic regions of the city and then surveying a random sample of people within the regions

Sample Problem Solutions

1. (C) D can be eliminated because they are not necessarily customers. A leaves it to chance that *all* customers surveyed will mail in their preferences. Logically, we can assume many won't. B biases the sample by "choosing" customers. C is the only choice that doesn't have obvious problems.

2. (D) is the only choice that keeps *everything* randomly selected.

If You Were Wrong, Here's Why

Randomly selecting from a population other than the target population

Using a selection process that is not random

Using a process that is not random and also does not select from the target population

38: IDENTIFY THE PROBABILITY OF A SPECIFIC OUTCOME IN AN EXPERIMENT

Basics You'll Need to Know to Master This Competency

Identifying the
    Probability of a simple event:
        $P(A) = m/n$
    Probability that a simple event does not occur:
        $P(\text{not } A) = 1 - P(A)$

Probability of the disjunction of two events which may or may not be mutually exclusive:

$$P(A \text{ or } B) = P(A) + P(B) - P(A \text{ and } B)$$

Probability of the conjunction of two or three events which may or may not be independent:

$$P(A \text{ and } B) = P(A) \times P(B)$$

Sample Problems

1. A box contains 2 green, 3 red, and 4 blue balls. Two balls are drawn from the box at random without replacement. What is the probability that neither is green?
   (A) $\frac{7}{9} \times \frac{2}{9}$ (B) $\frac{7}{9} \times \frac{6}{8}$ (C) $\frac{7}{9} \times \frac{7}{9}$ (D) $\frac{56}{72}$

2. A box contains 3 green and 5 red balls. If one ball is drawn, what is the probability that a green or red ball is drawn?
   (A) 100   (B) .50   (C) 1   (D) .60

Sample Problem Solutions

1. (B) The probability that the first ball drawn is not green is $\frac{7}{9}$ because there are 7 balls that are not green (elements in A) and 9 balls altogether. After the first ball is drawn there are 6 balls out of 8 balls left, a probability of $\frac{6}{8}$. The probability that both balls drawn are not green is $(\frac{7}{9})(\frac{6}{8})$.

2. (C) You will always draw either a green or red ball. Remember, the probability of an event is a fraction. Zero means the event cannot possibly occur. One means the event must occur.

If You Were Wrong, Here's Why

Computing the size of the sample space incorrectly
Choosing an incorrect probability formula
Incorrectly evaluating the correct formula
Making an arithmetic error

39: IDENTIFY SIMPLE AND COMPOUND STATEMENTS AND THEIR NEGATIONS

Basics You'll Need to Know to Master This Competency

Identifying simple quantified statements, conjunctions, disjunctions, and conditionals and *negations* of these four forms (statements limited to two variables)

Sample Problems

1. Select the statement which is the negation of the statement "Johnson is a teacher, or Dennis is a banker."
   (A) Johnson is not a teacher, and Dennis is not a banker.
   (B) Johnson is not a teacher, or Dennis is not a banker.
   (C) Johnson is not a teacher, and Dennis is a banker.
   (D) Johnson is a teacher, and Dennis is not a banker.

2. Select the negation of the statement "If Mary goes shopping, she will buy a dress."
   (A) If Mary goes shopping, she will not buy a dress.
   (B) If Mary does not go shopping, she will not buy a dress.
   (C) Mary goes shopping, and she does not buy a dress.
   (D) Mary does not go shopping, and she does not buy a dress.

Sample Problem Solutions

1. (A) The sentence is in the form "p, or q," which has a negation "not p, and not q."

2. (C) The sentence is in the form "if p, then q" which has a negation "p, and not q."

If You Were Wrong, Here's Why

Applying variables which are not equivalent to the negation of the stimulus statement

40: DETERMINE EQUIVALENCE OR NON-EQUIVALENCE OF STATEMENTS

Basics You'll Need to Know to Master This Competency

Identifying conjunctions, disjunctions, conditionals, and negations of these three forms
Determining statements of equivalence

Sample Problems

1. Select the statement below which is logically equivalent to "If I live in Miami, then I live in Florida."
   - (A) If I do not live in Florida, then I do not live in Miami.
   - (B) I live in Miami, or I live in Florida.
   - (C) If I live in Florida, then I live in Miami.
   - (D) If I do not live in Miami, then I do not live in Florida.

2. Select the statement below which is logically equivalent to "It is not true that both Bill and Tom are students."
   - (A) If Bill is not a student, then Tom is not a student.
   - (B) Bill is not a student, and Tom is not a student.
   - (C) Bill is not a student, or Tom is not a student.
   - (D) If Tom is not a student, then Bill is not a student.

Sample Problem Solutions

1. (A) The sentence is in the form "if p, then q," which is equivalent to the contrapositive, "if not q, then not p."

   $$p \longrightarrow q \qquad p \longrightarrow q$$
   If I live in Miami, then I live in Florida. (if p, then q)

   $$\sim q \longrightarrow \sim p$$
   If I do not live in Florida, then I do not live in Miami.

   $$\sim q \longrightarrow \sim p$$
   (if not q, then not p)

   $$p \rightarrow q \equiv q \rightarrow p.$$

   Note: The symbol for "if, then" is $\rightarrow$. The symbol for equivalent is $\equiv$.

2. (C) This sentence is in the form "not both p and q," which is equivalent to "not p, or not q," "if p, then not q," or "if q, then not p."

   $$p \qquad\qquad q$$
   Bill is not a student, or Tom is not a student.

If You Were Wrong, Here's Why

Not being familiar with conjunctions, disjunctions, and conditionals

41: DRAW LOGICAL CONCLUSIONS FROM DATA

Basics You'll Need to Know to Master This Competency

Identifying logical conclusions from statements of conditions formed
  through quantifications, negation, conjunction, disjunction, and
  implication

Analyzing data through computations, comparisons, or transforma-
  tions in order to determine conclusions

Sample Problems

1. Read the requirements *and* each applicant's qualifications for
   obtaining an $80,000 mortgage. Then identify which of the
   applicants would qualify for the loan. To qualify for a mortgage of
   $80,000 an applicant must have a gross income of $70,000 if single
   ($90,000 combined income if married) and assets of at least
   $40,000.

   Mr. Thomas is a bachelor and works at two jobs. He makes
   $50,000 on one job and $23,000 on the other; he also owns a
   $36,000 condo.

   Mr. Briggs is married with five children, makes $70,000, owns a
   $45,000 house, and his wife does not work.

   Mrs. Gray and her husband have assets of $60,000. One makes
   $35,000 and the other makes $45,000.

   (A) Mr. Thomas   (B) Mr. Briggs
   (C) Mrs. Gray   (D) No one is eligible.

2. Given that:

   i. No dogs that growl are lovable.   ii. All mongrels growl.

   determine which conclusion can be logically deduced.
   (A) All mongrels are lovable.   (B) Some mongrels are lovable.
   (C) No mongrels are lovable.   (D) none of the above

Sample Problem Solutions

1. (D) A, B, and C lack at least one of the qualifications.

2. (C) C is the only answer which can be deduced.

If You Were Wrong, Here's Why

Not identifying options which express conclusions not supported by the data

42: RECOGNIZE THAT AN ARGUMENT MAY NOT BE VALID EVEN THOUGH ITS CONCLUSION IS TRUE

Basics You'll Need to Know to Master This Competency

Being able to recognize an argument the conclusion of which is true but not justified by the premise(s)

Sample Problems

1. All of the following arguments A–D have true conclusions, but one of the arguments is not valid. Select the argument that is *not* valid.
   - (A) All beagles have eyes, and all dogs have eyes. Therefore, all beagles are dogs.
   - (B) All dogs have four legs, and all collies are dogs. Therefore, all collies have four legs.
   - (C) Every city in Orange County is in Florida. Orlando is a city in Orange County. Therefore, Orlando is in Florida.
   - (D) All fish live in water, and all trout are fish. Therefore, all trout live in water.

2. All of the following arguments A–D have true conclusions, but one of the arguments is not valid. Select the argument that is *not* valid.
   - (A) If you cut yourself, then you will bleed. You are not bleeding. Therefore, you have not cut yourself.
   - (B) If a dog is blind, then it cannot see. The dog can see. Therefore, it is not blind.
   - (C) If you are deaf, then you cannot hear. You are not deaf. Therefore, you can hear.
   - (D) If you overeat, then you are fat. You are not fat. Therefore you do not overeat.

Sample Problem Solutions

1. (A) When you are given several arguments, as in the format for this problem, and asked to pick the one that is valid or not valid, check the arguments for a pattern. For example:

    A   B   C   B

All beagles have eyes and all dogs have eyes.

                  A   C

Therefore, all beagles are dogs.   (AB, CB, AC)

The pattern of the invalid argument will be different from the other three (AB, CA, CB).

2. (C) Choice C is an invalid argument in the form

$$p \rightarrow q$$
$$\underline{\sim p}$$
$$\therefore \sim q$$

A, B, and D are all valid forms of

$$p \rightarrow q$$
$$\underline{\sim q}$$
$$\therefore \sim p$$

If You Were Wrong, Here's Why

Not differentiating between invalid and valid arguments even though the conclusions are true.

43: INFER RELATIONS BETWEEN NUMBERS IN GENERAL BY EXAMINING PARTICULAR NUMBER PAIRS

Basics You'll Need to Know to Master This Competency

Identifying the missing term in arithmetic, geometric, or harmonic progressions

Identifying a common linear or quadratic relationship between numbers in pairs

Sample Problems

1. Look for a common linear relationship between the numbers in each pair; then identify the missing term.

   (4, 1), (.8, .2), ($-12, -3$), (1/10, 1/40), (44, 11), (1/5, ____)

   (A) 1/20   (B) 2/5   (C) 5/2   (D) 5

2. Identify the missing term in the following geometric progression.

   $$8, -2, 1/2, -(1/8), 1/16, \text{____}$$

   (A) $-(1/32)$ (B) $-(1/64)$ (C) 1/64   (D) 1/8

Sample Problems Solutions

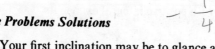

1. (A) Your first inclination may be to glance at the first three pairs and think that the second number in each pair is found by dividing the first number by 4. However, the fourth pair should alert you to the fact that a fraction with 1 as the numerator is needed. In this case, 1/4 is the multiplier. To find 1/4:

$$(4, 1)$$

$$4n = 1$$

$$n = 1/4$$

Then multiply each term by 1/4 to find the next term.

2. (B) Note: In a geometric progression, r = common ratio.

$$r = \frac{a_{i+1}}{a_i} \quad \text{and} \quad \begin{array}{l} a_i = \text{1st term} \\ a_{i+1} = \text{2nd term} \end{array}$$

For example:

$$a_i = 8, \quad a_{i+1} = -2, \quad r = \frac{a_{i+1}}{a_i} = \frac{-2}{8} = -\frac{1}{4}$$

Each term is then multiplied by $-(1/4)$ to find the next term. In a geometric progression when you see the $+ - + -$ pattern the common ratio will be negative.

If You Were Wrong, Here's Why

Using an incorrect operation or relationship

44: SELECT APPLICABLE PROPERTIES FOR PERFORMING ARITHMETIC CALCULATIONS

Basics You'll Need to Know to Master This Competency

Selecting the property or properties illustrated in an equation or used to simplify a given numerical expression:

    Associative property of addition or multiplication
    Commutative property of addition or multiplication
    Distributive property
    Exponentiation with positive integral exponents

Sample Problems

1. Select the property or properties of operation(s) illustrated in this equation: $4(5 + 2^2) = 4 \times 5 + 4(2)^2$
   - (A) distributive property and associative property of multiplication
   - (B) distributive property and commutative property of multiplication
   - (C) distributive property only
   - (D) associative property of multiplication only

2. Select the property or properties of operation(s) illustrated in this equation: $2(4 + 5) = 2 \times 5 + 2 \times 4$
   - (A) $a(b + c) = ab + ac$ (B) $a(b + c) = ac + ab$
   - (C) $a(bc) = (ba)c$ (D) $a(b + c) = ba + ca$

Sample Problem Solutions

1. (C) The distributive property is $a(b + c) = ab + ac$. Let $a = 4$, $b = 5$, and $c = 2^2$. Then $4(5 + 2^2) = 4(5) + 4(2^2)$.

2. (B) Let $a = 2$, $b = 4$, and $c = 5$.
$$2(4 + 5) = 2 \times 5 + 2 \times 4$$
$$a(b + c) = ac + ab$$

If You Were Wrong, Here's Why

Using one but not both properties, if two are involved
Using additional similar properties when only one property should be used
Using a single wrong property

45: INFER FORMULAS FOR MEASURING GEOMETRIC FIGURES

Basics You'll Need to Know to Master This Competency

Calculating or specifying the entity to be measured by measurement generalization when given several geometric figures for which a specific measurement has been computed

Understanding measurements of areas, volumes, surface areas, angle measures, perimeters, or circumferences between different, related figures

Sample Problems

1. Study the given information. For each figure, S represents the sum of the measure of the interior angles.

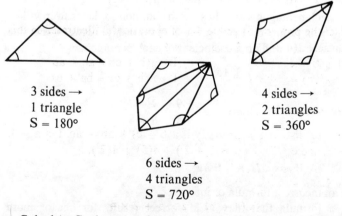

3 sides →
1 triangle
S = 180°

6 sides →
4 triangles
S = 720°

4 sides →
2 triangles
S = 360°

Calculate S, the sum of the measure of the interior angles of a ten-sided convex polygon.
(A) 1260°   (B) 1800°   (C) 1440°   (D) 2880°

2. Study the information with the regular pentagons.

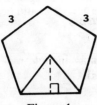

Figure 1
Area $= 15\sqrt{3}$

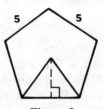

Figure 2
Area $= 30\sqrt{3}$

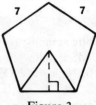

Figure 3
Area $= 49\sqrt{3}$

Calculate the area of a regular pentagon with a side equal to 9.
(A) $56\sqrt{3}$ (B) $72\sqrt{3}$ (C) $81\sqrt{3}$ (D) $98\sqrt{3}$

Sample Problem Solutions

1. **(C)** Note: Each figure has 2 sides more than the number of triangles. For example: 3 sides, 1 triangle; 4 sides, 2 triangles; 6 sides, 4 triangles; 10 sides, 8 triangles. To find S: Number of triangles times 180°. For example: $1 \times 180° = 180°$, $2 \times 180° = 360°$, $4 \times 180° = 720°$, $8 \times 180° = 1440°$.

2. **(B)** Each pentagon's area has $\sqrt{3}$ in common so the answer will be $x\sqrt{3}$. x is found by looking for a relationship between the side measurement and area coefficient of each pentagon.

$$
\begin{array}{ll}
3, 15 & 15 \div 3 = 5 \\
5, 30 & 30 \div 5 = 6 \\
7, 49 & 49 \div 7 = 7 \\
9, x & x \div 9 = 8 \\
 & x = 72
\end{array}
$$

If You Were Wrong, Here's Why

Using an incorrect formula or inference
Using a formula that may yield correct results for one or more figures, but not all of the figures
Using an incorrect estimation

46: IDENTIFY APPLICABLE FORMULAS FOR COMPUTING MEASURES OF GEOMETRIC FIGURES

Basics You'll Need to Know to Master This Competency

Understanding two-dimensional figures
Understanding three-dimensional figures (figures may include rectangular solids, cylinders, and right circular cones)

Sample Problems

1. Study the figure showing a regular octagon; then select the formula for computing the total area of the octagon.

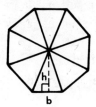

 (A) Area = $4bh$
(B) Area = $8bh$
(C) Area = $4b + h$
(D) Area = $8(b + h)$

2. Study the figure showing a pyramid with a square base and triangles of equal size; then select the formula for calculating the total surface area (SA) of the pyramid.

(A) SA = $\frac{1}{3}bh$
(B) SA = $2bh + b^2$
(C) SA = $4bh + 4b$
(D) SA = $2bh + 4b$

Sample Problem Solutions

1. (A) "Regular" means all sides have equal length and all angles have the same measure. There are 8 triangles so Area = $8(\frac{1}{2}bh)$ = $4bh$.

2. (B) Surface area is the sum of the area of the figure's faces. Area of a square is s^2 or in this case, b^2. Area $\triangle$ = $\frac{1}{2}bh$. There are 4 triangles. $4(\frac{1}{2}bh) = 2bh$. SA = $2bh + b^2$.

If You Were Wrong, Here's Why

Using a formula similar to the correct formula but with a conspicuous error

Confusing formulas for area, volume, and perimeter

47: INFER SIMPLE RELATIONS AMONG VARIABLES

Basics You'll Need to Know to Master This Competency

Understanding relationships involving fundamental principles and/or properties of algebra (such as the laws of exponents, properties of the number system, order of operations, operations with signed numbers)

Sample Problems

1. Study the examples:

   $a^2 * a^4 = a^{10}, \quad a^2 * a^3 = a^8, \quad a^5 * a^2 = a^9$

   Select the equation which is compatible with the data.

   (A) $a^x * a^y = a^{xy+2}$
   (B) $a^x * a^y = a^{3x+y}$
   (C) $a^x * a^y = a^{x+y+2}$
   (D) $a^x * a^y = a^{x+2y}$

2. Study the examples:

   $a^4 * a^2 = a^6, \quad a^5 * a^2 = a^8, a^6 * a^3 = a^9$

   Select the equation which is compatible with the data

(A) $a^x * a^y = a^{x+2y}$
(B) $a^x * a^y = a^{xy-2}$
(C) $a^x * a^y = a^{x+y}$
(D) $a^x * a^y = a^{2x-y}$

Sample Problem Solutions

1. (D) $a^x * a^y = a^{x+2y}$, $a^2 * a^4 = a^{2+2(4)} = a^{10}$, $a^2 * a^3 = a^{2+2(3)} = a^8$, $a^5 * a^2 = a^{5+2(2)} = a^9$

2. (D) $a^x * a^y = a^{2x-y}$, $a^4 * a^2 = a^{2(4)-2} = a^6$, $a^5 * a^2 = a^{2(5)-2} = a^8$, $a^6 * a^3 = a^{2(6)-3} = a^9$

If You Were Wrong, Here's Why

Seeing a pattern which illustrated one or two of the patterns, but not all

48: SELECT APPLICABLE PROPERTIES FOR SOLVING EQUATIONS AND INEQUALITIES

Basics You'll Need to Know to Master this Competency

Understanding how the following algebraic properties can be used to solve an equation or inequality:

$a = b$ if and only if $a + c = b + c$
$a = b$ if and only if $ac = bc$, $c \neq 0$
$a > b$ if and only if $a + c > b + c$
$a > b$ if and only if $ac > bc$ and $c > 0$
$a > b$ if and only if $ac < bc$ and $c < 0$
If $a > b$ and $b > c$, then $a > c$
If $a = b$ and $b = c$ then $a = c$
$a = b$ if and only if $b = a$

If you're completely puzzled as to the answer for a question, look for an answer with the same operation of arithmetic. Note: the statement may contain more elements than does the correct property.

Sample Problems

1. Select the property used to justify the following statement:

$$\text{If } 3 < x + 5 < 14, \text{ then } -2 < x < 9$$

   (A) If $a + c > b + c$, then $a > b$
   (B) If $a > b$ and $b > c$, then $a > c$
   (C) If $ac > bc$ and $c > 0$, then $a > b$
   (D) If $ac < bc$ and $c < 0$, then $a > b$

2. Select the property used to justify the following statement:

$$\text{If } -2x > 7, \text{ then } x < -(7\!/\!2)$$

   (A) If $a > b$, then $a + c > b + c$
   (B) If $a > b$ and $b > c$, then $a > c$
   (C) If $ac > bc$ and $c > 0$, then $a > b$
   (D) If $ac < bc$ and $c < 0$, then $a > b$

Sample Problem Solutions

1. **(A)** A gives the additive property of inequalities which allows the -5 to be added to each component in the first statement to obtain the second statement.

$$3 + (-5) < x + 5 + (-5) < 14 + (-5) = -2 < x < 9$$

2. **(D)** D gives the multiplicative property of inequalities when $C < 0$ (negative). This allows both sides of the first statement to be multiplied by $-(1/2)$ to obtain the second statement. Because C is negative, the direction of the inequality sign changes.

$$-\tfrac{1}{2}(-2x) > -\tfrac{1}{2}(7) = x < 7\!/\!_{-2}$$

If You Were Wrong, Here's Why

Using a property of relations or operations which is inapplicable to the situation shown in the stimulus

49: INFER RELATIONS AND MAKE ACCURATE PREDICTIONS FROM STUDYING PARTICULAR CASES IN PROBABILITY AND STATISTICS

Basics You'll Need to Know to Master This Competency

Knowing laws of concepts (the counting principles, combinatorial formulas, and arithmetic or algebraic formulas which include the mean, median, and mode)

Sample Problems

1. Study the outcomes of tossing 1, 2, or 3 coins simultaneously.

1 coin	2 coins	3 coins
H	HH	HHH
T	HT	HHT
	TT	HTH
	TH	HTT
		THH
		THT
		TTH
		TTT

If 6 coins were tossed simultaneously, how many possible arrangements of heads and tails would there be?
(A) 16   (B) 32   (C) 48   (D) 64

2. Study the examples illustrating ways of combining objects two at a time.

3 objects	4 objects	5 objects
{a, b, c}	{p, q, r, s}	{e, f, g, h, i}
(a, b)	(p, q)	(e, f) (f, h)
(a, c)	(p, r)	(e, g) (f, i)
(b, c)	(p, s)	(e, h) (g, h)
	(q, r)	(e, i) (g, i)
	(q, s)	(f, g) (h, i)
	(r, s)	

How many two member combinations can be formed from a set containing 8 objects.
(A) 21   (B) 28   (C) 36   (D) 56

Sample Problem Solutions

1. (D) Note: 2 coins $= 2^2$, 3 coins $= 2^3$, 4 coins $= 2^4$. Thus, $2^6 = 64$.

2. (B) $C = \dfrac{n!}{r!(n-r)!} = \dfrac{8!}{2!(8-2)!} = \dfrac{8!}{2!6!} =$

$$\frac{8 \cdot 7 \cdot \cancel{6} \cdot \cancel{5} \cdot \cancel{4} \cdot \cancel{3} \cdot \cancel{2} \cdot \cancel{1}}{2 \cdot 1 \cdot \cancel{6} \cdot \cancel{5} \cdot \cancel{4} \cdot \cancel{3} \cdot \cancel{2} \cdot \cancel{1}} = \frac{8 \cdot 7}{2} = \frac{56}{2} = 28$$

If You Were Wrong, Here's Why

Using the wrong formula (such as combinations rather than permutations)

Failing to distinguish between measures such as the mean, median, and mode

Making an incorrect estimation

50: INFER VALID REASONING PATTERNS AND EXPRESS THEM WITH VARIABLES

Basics You'll Need to Know to Master This Competency

Recognizing reasoning patterns possibly used:

modus ponens
$p \rightarrow q$
p
$\overline{}$
$\therefore q$

modus tollens
$p \rightarrow q$
$\sim q$
$\overline{}$
$\therefore \sim q$

disjunctive syllogism
$p \vee q$
$\sim p$
$\overline{}$
$\therefore q$

hypothetical syllogism
$p \rightarrow q$
$q \rightarrow r$
$\overline{}$
$\therefore p \rightarrow r$

Identifying the symbolic form of the reasoning pattern (rules of logic) expressed in words.

Sample Problems

1. Read each of the following valid arguments, then select the symbolic form of the reasoning pattern illustrated by both arguments.

If Joe is to get the trophy, then he must win three races before June 15. Joe does not win three races before June 15. Thus, Joe does not get the trophy.

Sue enjoys painting if she likes the subject matter. She is not enjoying painting. Therefore, Sue does not like the subject matter.

(A) $p \rightarrow q$ (B) $p \rightarrow q$ (C) $p \rightarrow q$ (D) $p \rightarrow q$
$$\frac{\sim p}{\therefore \sim q} \qquad \frac{\sim q}{\therefore \sim q} \qquad \frac{\sim q}{\therefore \sim p} \qquad \frac{q}{\therefore p}$$

2. Read each of the following valid arguments, then select the symbolic form of the reasoning pattern illustrated by both arguments.

   Frank will walk to school, or he will ride the bus. Frank will not walk to school. Therefore, he will ride the bus.

   Gail likes to play tennis, or she likes to read books. Gail doesn't like to play tennis. Therefore, she likes to read books.

   (A) $p \vee q$ (B) $p \vee q$ (C) $p \vee q$ (D) $p \vee q$
$$\frac{q}{\therefore p} \qquad \frac{\sim q}{\therefore \sim p} \qquad \frac{p}{\therefore \sim q} \qquad \frac{\sim p}{\therefore q}$$

Sample Problem Solutions

1. (C)

   If Joe is to get the trophy then he must win three races
   (p)   (→)   (q)
   before June 15.

   Joe does not win three races before June 15.
        (~) (q)

   Thus, Joe does not get the trophy.
   (∴)   (~) (p)

$$\frac{\begin{array}{l} p \rightarrow q \\ \sim q \end{array}}{\therefore \sim p}$$

Note: "If Sue likes the subject matter, then she enjoys painting" is the same as "Sue enjoys painting if she likes the subject matter." "if, then" is symbolized by $\rightarrow$.

2. **(D)**

$$\overset{p}{\underline{\text{walk to school}}} \overset{\vee}{} \text{ or he will } \overset{q}{\underline{\text{ride the bus}}}.$$

Frank will $\underline{\text{walk to school}}$ or he will $\underline{\text{ride the bus}}$.

Frank will $\underset{\sim}{\text{not}} \underline{\text{walk to school}}^{p}$.

$\therefore$ Therefore, he will $\underline{\text{ride the bus}}^{q}$.

$$p \vee q$$
$$\underline{\sim p}$$
$$\therefore q$$

If You Were Wrong, Here's Why

Reasoning from the inverse or converse
Using correct premise(s) with an incorrect conclusion

51: SELECT APPLICABLE RULES FOR TRANSFORMING STATEMENTS WITHOUT AFFECTING THEIR MEANING

Basics You'll Need to Know to Master This Competency

Knowing rules for transformation, expressed in words rather than symbols, which include the following:

$$\sim(\sim p) \equiv p$$
$$\sim(p \wedge q) \equiv (\sim p) \vee \sim q$$
$$\sim(p \vee q) \equiv (\sim p) \wedge \sim q$$
$$p \rightarrow q \equiv (\sim p) \vee q$$
$$\sim(p \rightarrow q) \equiv p \wedge \sim q$$
$$p \rightarrow q \equiv \sim q \rightarrow \sim p$$

Sample Problems

1. Select the rule of logical equivalence which *directly* (in one step) *transforms* statement i into statement ii.

   i. If 3x is even, then x is even.
   ii. If x is not even, then 3x is not even.

   (A) "If p, then q" is equivalent to "(not p) or q."
   (B) "If p, then q" is equivalent to "if not q, then not p."
   (C) "Not (p and q)" is equivalent to "not p, or not q."
   (D) The correct equivalence rule is not given.

2. Select the rule of logical equivalence which *directly* (in one step) *transforms* statement i into statement ii.

i. Not all of the men and women are intelligent.
ii. Some man or woman is not intelligent.

(A) "All are not p" is equivalent to "none are p."
(B) "Not (not p)" is equivalent to "p."
(C) "Not all are p" is equivalent to "some are not p."
(D) "If p, then q" is equivalent to "if not q, then not p."

Sample Problem Solutions

1. (B)

i. If $\underline{3x \text{ is even}}$, then $\underline{x \text{ is even}}$. (If p, then q.)
$\qquad\quad p \qquad\longrightarrow\qquad q$

ii. If $\underline{x \text{ is not even}}$, then $\underline{3x \text{ is not even}}$. (If not q, then not p.)
$\qquad\quad \sim q \qquad\longrightarrow\qquad \sim p$

$p \rightarrow q \equiv \sim q \rightarrow \sim p$ ($\equiv$ is the symbol for "equivalent")

2. (C)

i. $\underline{\text{Not all}}$ of the men and women $\underline{\underline{\text{are intelligent}}}$. (Not all are p.)
$\qquad\qquad\qquad\qquad\qquad\qquad\qquad p$

ii. $\underline{\text{Some}}$ man or woman $\underline{\text{is}\ \underline{\underline{\text{not intelligent}}}}$. (Some are not p.)
$\qquad\qquad\qquad\qquad\qquad\qquad p$

If You Were Wrong, Here's Why

Using correct rules of logic that don't aid in the stimulus transformation
Using incorrect rules of logic similar to the correct rule

52: SOLVE REAL-WORLD PROBLEMS WHICH DO NOT REQUIRE THE USE OF VARIABLES AND WHICH DO NOT INVOLVE PERCENT

Basics You'll Need to Know to Master This Competency

Having basic math competency and knowledge of conversions (within the metric or the English system, or percent to decimal, etc.)
Identifying irrelevant information

Sample Problems

1. An art gallery ordered 15 prints after receiving 13 requests for the print. Each print, which cost the gallery $35, was to be sold for $60. The gallery must pay a $5 service charge for each unsold print returned. If the gallery returned 4 prints, how much profit did the gallery make?
   (A) $235   (B) $255   (C) $275   (D) $305

2. A candy store ordered 12 special boxes of candy as gifts for its employees. The candy cost $5 a box and could be sold for $10 a box. After giving 10 boxes to its employees and selling 2 boxes to customers, how much did the store owner have to pay to her supplier.
   (A) $50   (B) $30   (C) $60   (D) $40

Sample Problem Solutions

1. (B) There were 15 ordered and 4 returned, so only 11 were sold. The profit on each print was $25 ($60 − $35) for a total of $275 (11 × $25). But 4 prints were returned at a service charge of $5 each, or $20, so that must be subtracted from the profit, leaving a net profit of $255.

2. (C) It doesn't matter whether the store owner gave the candy away or sold it. The owner still has to pay for all 12 boxes. 12 × $5 = $60.

If You Were Wrong, Here's Why

Excluding a necessary step
Using irrelevant information in the problem
Using a wrong operation

53: SOLVE REAL-WORLD PROBLEMS WHICH DO NOT REQUIRE THE USE OF VARIABLES AND WHICH DO REQUIRE THE USE OF PERCENT

Basics You'll Need to Know to Master This Competency

Having basic math competency and knowledge of conversions (within the metric or the English system, or percent to decimal, etc.)
Identifying irrelevant information

Sample Problems

1. By buying a smaller car, Sue was told that she would use only 65% as much gas. The actual amount of gas used by her larger car was 120 gallons last month. How much gas did Sue save by buying a smaller car?

    (A) 40 gallons   (B) 42 gallons
    (C) 63 gallons   (D) 78 gallons

2. By going to a discount store, Tom was told that he would spend only 75% as much for a TV. The regular price for a TV was $420. How much did Tom save by going to a discount store?

    (A) $315   (B) $115   (C) $105   (D) $95

Sample Problem Solutions

1. (B) The problem asks for how much was *saved*. Sue saved 35%. $120 \times .35 = 42$.

2. (C) $420 $\times$ .25 (% saved) = $105.

If You Were Wrong, Here's Why

Excluding a necessary step
Using irrelevant information in the problem
Using a wrong operation

54: SOLVE PROBLEMS THAT INVOLVE THE STRUCTURE AND LOGIC OF ARITHMETIC

Basics You'll Need to Know to Master This Competency

Understanding concepts from number theory or combinatorics

Sample Problems

1. Find the smallest positive multiple of 4 which leaves a remainder of 4 when divided by 5 and a remainder of 3 when divided by 7.

    (A) 24   (B) 44   (C) 52   (D) 59

2. How many whole numbers leave a remainder of 1 when divided into 55, and a remainder of 2 when divided into 29?

    (A) 0   (B) 2   (C) 3   (D) 4

Sample Problem Solutions

1. (A) The number 24 fulfills all the requirements. $4 \times 6 = 24$.
   $24 \div 5 = 4$, remainder 4. $24 \div 7 = 3$, remainder 3.

2. (C) The numbers 3, 9, and 27 fulfill the requirements. $55 \div 3 =$
   18, remainder 1. $55 \div 9 = 6$, remainder 1. $55 \div 27 = 2$, remainder
   1. $29 \div 3 = 9$, remainder 2. $29 \div 9 = 3$, remainder 2. $29 \div 27 = 1$,
   remainder 2.

If You Were Wrong, Here's Why

Not fulfilling all the conditions or relations
Not considering all cases
Misinterpreting the problem

55: SOLVE REAL-WORLD PROBLEMS INVOLVING PERIMETERS, AREAS, VOLUMES OF GEOMETRIC FIGURES

Basics You'll Need to Know to Master This Competency

Converting (for example, inches to feet) within the system (English
   or metric)
Identifying irrelevant information

Sample Problems

1. What will be the cost of covering a floor with linoleum if it
   measures 12 feet by 18 feet and linoleum costs $11.50 per square
   yard?
   (A) $276   (B) $828   (C) $1125   (D) $2484

2. A rectangular fish pond measures 3 feet by 42 inches. The outside
   dimensions of a path around the pond are 5¾ feet by 75 inches.
   What is the area of the path?
   (A) 305 sq ft
   (B) 305.25 sq ft
   (C) 3663 sq in
   (D) 3672 sq in

Sample Problem Solutions

1. (A) $12' \times 18' = 4$ yds $\times 6$ yds $= 24$ sq yds. $24 \times \$11.50 =$
   $276.

2. (C)

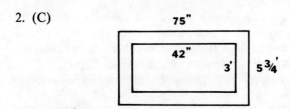

Change feet into inches. Then subtract the area of the fish pond from the area of the outside dimensions of the path. To find the area of the path:

$75'' \times 5\frac{3}{4}' = 75'' \times 69'' = 5175$ sq in
$42'' \times 3' = 42'' \times 36'' \quad = \underline{1512}$ sq in
$ 3663$ sq in

If You Were Wrong, Here's Why

Not Converting units
Using an incorrect conversion factor or formula
Estimating incorrectly

56: SOLVE REAL-WORLD PROBLEMS INVOLVING THE PYTHAGOREAN PROPERTY

Basics You'll Need to Know to Master This Competency

Knowing and understanding how to use the Pythagorean theorem

Sample Problems

1. A developer wants to construct a new jogging path connecting Path # 1 and Parkway as shown in the diagram. Construction costs have been estimated at $60 per linear foot. What is the estimated cost for constructing the new path?
   (A) $2,160,000
   (B) $3,132,000
   (C) $3,168,000
   (D) $31,680,000

2. A sculptor is going to construct a 12-foot tower in a park. The tower will by supported by three cables, each attached to the top of the tower and to points on the ground which are 5 feet from the tower's base. What is total length of these three cables?
(A) 13 ft   (B) 36 ft   (C) 39 ft   (D) 52 ft

Sample Problem Solutions

1. (C) let c = length in miles of the new jogging path.

$$a^2 + b^2 = c^2$$
$$6^2 + 8^2 = c^2$$
$$36 + 64 = 100$$
$$c = 10 \text{ miles}$$
$$10 \times 5280 \text{ ft} \times \$60 = \$3,168,000$$

2. (C) Use the Pythagorean theorem to solve. Let c = length in feet of one cable.

$$a^2 + b^2 = c^2$$
$$12^2 + 5^2 = c^2$$
$$144 + 25 = c^2$$
$$169 = c^2$$
$$13 = c$$

The problem asks for total length of three cables. $3 \times 13 = 39$ ft.

If You Were Wrong, Here's Why

Making an error in use of the Pythagorean theorem
Making an error in conversion of units of measure
Failing to find the final answer
Estimating incorrectly

57: SOLVE REAL-WORLD PROBLEMS INVOLVING THE USE OF VARIABLES

Basics You'll Need to Know to Master This Competency

Understanding linear or quadratic relationships, proportions, or any type of variation

Sample Problems

1. A game preserve wanted to estimate the number of lions living on its property. They caught and tagged 64 lions from the preserve and released them back into the preserve. Later they selected a sample of 256 lions. Of the 256 lions, 32 were tagged. Assuming that the proportion of tagged lions in the sample holds for all lions in the preserve, what is the best estimate of the number of lions in the preserve?
   (A) 128   (B) 116   (C) 576   (D) 512

2. Exercise equipment was purchased for $1460 and is assumed to have a resale value of $286 after 10 years. Assuming that the value depreciated linearly (steadily), what would be the value of the equipment after 5 years.
   (A) $587   (B) $730   (C) $873   (D) $1174

Sample Problem Solutions

1. (D)

   $$\frac{\text{tagged lions}}{\text{total number}} \quad \frac{64}{x} = \frac{32}{256}$$

   Cross multiplying

   $32x = 64(256)$
   $32x = 16,384$
   $x = 512$

2. (C) The value of the equipment after 5 years is found by finding the average depreciation per year and subtracting 5 times that amount from the original cost.

   $1460 - $286 = $1174 \div 10 = 117.40 (depreciation per year)
   $5 \times $117.40 = 587 (loss of value in 5 years)
   $1460 - $587 = 873 (value after 5 years)

If You Were Wrong, Here's Why

Incorrectly constructing a proportion, variation, or equation
Giving an intermediate value obtained during the process of solution
Incorrectly converting or misplacing a decimal point

Considering irrelevant information as relevant
Conforming to some, but not all, conditions

58: SOLVE PROBLEMS THAT INVOLVE THE STRUCTURE AND LOGIC OF ALGEBRA

Basics You'll Need to Know to Master This Competency

Being able to solve word problems involving
  A relationship between the two digits of an integer
  A relationship between two integers
  The sum of the two digits of an integer
  The sum of two integers
  Possible numerical values or algebraic properties of rational
   numbers

Sample Problems

1. The difference between a number and five more than three times the number is eight. What equation could be used to find x, the number?
 (A) $x - (5x + 3) = 8$
 (B) $x + (3x - 5) = 8$
 (C) $x - (3x + 5) = 8$
 (D) $x - 3x + 5 = 8$

2. Which of the following statements is false for every non-zero integer x?

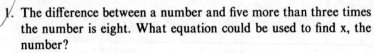

 (A) $\dfrac{4}{x} > 0$ (B) $\dfrac{4}{x} < 0$ (C) $\dfrac{4}{x} = \dfrac{60}{45}$ (D) $\dfrac{4}{x} = 0$

Sample Problems Solutions

1. (C) x = the number. 3x = three times the number. (3x + 5) = 5 more than 3 times the number. *Difference* means subtract and *is* becomes =. $x - (3x + 5) = 8$.

2. (D) No non-zero integer divided into 4 will ever give 0. A is true if x is replaced by 1. B is true if x is replaced by a negative integer. C is proved true by solving for x.

If You Were Wrong, Here's Why

Using a wrong operation
Omitting or misplacing parentheses in an otherwise correct equation
Letting the variable represent the wrong number
Failing to understand the problem or solve the relationships

59: SOLVE REAL-WORLD PROBLEMS INVOLVING THE NORMAL CURVE

Basics You'll Need to Know to Master This Competency

Understanding how to use a table listing proportions of a distribution which fall between 0 and $+3$ standard deviations to solve a word-problem involving a normal distribution

Sample Problems

Using the following table, solve the problems which are given.

Standard deviation above mean	Proportion of area between mean and indicated standard deviation above mean
.00	.000
.25	.099
.50	.192
.75	.273
1.00	.341
1.25	.394
1.50	.433
1.75	.460
2.00	.477
2.25	.488
2.50	.494
2.75	.497
3.00	.499

1. A normal distribution of weekly income has a mean of $250 and a standard deviation of $20. Approximately what proportion of the respondents earn between $240 and $260 a week?
(A) .19   (B) .34   (C) .38   (D) .48

2. A major corporation finds that the data on a qualification exam for training managers is normally distributed and has a mean score of 85 with a standard deviation of 5. If only applicants with scores 90 or above qualify, approximately what proportion of the applicants will be refused?
(A) 34%   (B) 84%   (C) 16%   (D) 68%

Sample Problem Solutions

1. (C) Note: Graph of the normal curve.

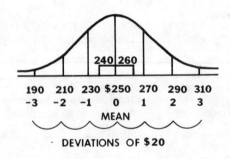

$240 is halfway ($-.50$) between $230 and $250 ($-1$ and 0). $260 is halfway (.50) between $250 and $270 (0 and 1). The respondents earn between $-.50$ and $+.50$. On the left side of the chart above, find .50. On the right side, across from .50, is the figure .192, the *proportion* of area between the mean and the standard deviation (.50) *above* the mean. (The chart can be used for scores above and below the mean)

The proportion for $250–260 (0 to .50) is   .192
The proportion for $240–250 ($-.50$ to 0) is .192
                                              .384, or .38

2. (B) Note: Graph of the normal curve.

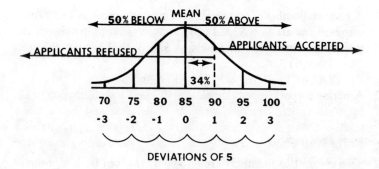

The score of 90 falls at 1 standard deviation above the mean. On the left side of the chart above find 1 or 1.00. On the right side, across from 1.00, is the figure .341 or 34%, the *proportion* of area between the mean and the standard deviation of 1. Since 50% of the scores lie to the right of the mean and 50% to the left, the number of applicants refused is 50% (left) + 34% (right) = 84%.

If You Were Wrong, Here's Why

Using the probability associated with one standard deviation from the
   mean when another deviation is appropriate
Using the probability associated with the area between the mean and
   a given deviation when the problem calls for using the area within
   ± this deviation from the mean
Using areas not within the specified limits

60: SOLVE REAL-WORLD PROBLEMS INVOLVING PROBABILITIES

Basics You'll Need to Know to Master This Competency

Understanding the probability of
   A single event, $A: P(A) = m/n$
   A complementary event, $\overline{A}: P(\overline{A}) = 1 - P(A)$
   The conjunction of two independent events, A and B:
      $P(A \text{ and } B) = P(A) \times P(B)$
   The disjunction of two mutually exclusive events, A and B:
      $P(A \text{ or } B) = P(A) + P(B)$

The conjunction of two dependent events, A and B:

$P(A \text{ and } B) = P(A) \times P(B)$

The disjunction of two events, A and B, that are not mutually exclusive:

$P(A \text{ or } B) = P(A) + P(B) - P(A \text{ and } B)$

Translation from odds to probability, or the converse

Sample Problems

1. Two committee members are chosen at random from a group of 100 people, consisting of 50 men and 50 women. What is the probability that the two representatives selected are either both men or both women?

   (A) $\dfrac{50}{100} \times \dfrac{49}{99}$

   (B) $2 \times \dfrac{50}{100} \times \dfrac{49}{99}$

   (C) $\dfrac{2}{50} \times \dfrac{2}{50}$

   (D) $\dfrac{2}{50} + \dfrac{2}{50}$

2. The odds *against* Champion winning a race are 3:12. With these odds, what is the probability that Champion will win a race?

   (A) $\dfrac{1}{4}$ (B) $\dfrac{4}{1}$ (C) $\dfrac{1}{5}$ (D) $\dfrac{4}{5}$

Sample Problem Solutions

1. (B) The probability of drawing two women is $(50/100) \times (49/99)$. Since the probability of drawing two men is the same, to arrive at the probability of *either* event occurring, multiply by 2.

2. (D) The odds of 3:12 against means in 3 races Champion loses and in 12 races Champion wins. That gives a total of 15 possibilities in all. As a result, the probability of Champion winning a race is 12/15 or 4/5.

If You Were Wrong, Here's Why

Using an incorrect operation
Giving the probability of a complementary event
Confusing the disjunction of an event with the conjunction
Using an incorrect sample space
Using an incorrect probability formula

61: DRAW LOGICAL CONCLUSIONS WHEN THE FACTS WARRANT THEM

Basics You'll Need to Know to Master This Competency

Understanding simple statements, statements with the connectives "and," "or," "if . . . then," and statements containing negations or quantifications.

Sample Problems

1. Study the information given below. If a logical conclusion is given, select that conclusion. If none of the conclusions given is warranted, select the option expressing this condition.

   If you work out with weights, you will improve your muscle tone. If you take aerobics, you will improve your muscle tone. You take aerobics and don't work out with weights.

   (A) You will not improve your muscle tone.
   (B) You will improve your muscle tone.
   (C) You run also.
   (D) None of the above is warranted.

2. Study the information given below. If a logical conclusion is given, select that conclusion. If none of the conclusions given is warranted, select the option expressing this condition.

   All people who go to school are intelligent. All intelligent people make lots of money. Jim makes lots of money.

   (A) Jim is intelligent.
   (B) Jim is not intelligent.
   (C) Jim went to school.
   (D) None of the above is warranted.

Sample Problem Solutions

1. (B) The "and" sentence indicates that you take aerobics. The second sentence states that if you take aerobics, you will improve your muscle tone.

2. (D) D is correct because A, B, and C cannot be logically concluded from the premises. A is invalid because many people who do not go to school may be intelligent. B is invalid. Jim may be intelligent. C is invalid because Jim may not have gone to school. Note that if the "all" in sentence one and the "all" in sentence two were changed to "only," then both A and C would be true.

If You Were Wrong, Here's Why

Using options which differ from the correct conclusion by a negation or connective

Using an incorrect assumption of the converse, or negation, of one of the given statements or premises

Using an incorrect quantification

MATHEMATICS POST-TEST

1. $-(2/3) - (-2) =$
   (A) $-2\frac{2}{3}$ (B) $1\frac{1}{3}$ (C) $-1\frac{1}{3}$ (D) $\frac{1}{3}$

   $\frac{-\cdot 2}{3} + \frac{2 \cdot 3}{1 \cdot 3} =$

2. $(-8) \times 2\frac{1}{4} =$
   (A) $-16\frac{1}{4}$ (B) -18 (C) 18 (D) 9

   $\frac{-2+6}{3} = \frac{4}{3} = 1\frac{1}{2}$

   $\frac{-8}{1} \cdot \frac{9}{4} =$ $\frac{-72}{4}$

3. $16.53 - .871 =$
   (A) 15.659 (B) -15.659 (C) 25.401 (D) 7.82

   16.530
   $.871$
   15.659

4. $-10.28 \div .04 =$
   (A) -257 (B) 25.7 (C) -2.57 (D) $.0257$

   -1028
   4

5. If 50 is decreased to 30, what is the percentage difference?
   (A) 20%   (B) 40%   (C) 30%   (D) 15%

   $\frac{20}{50} =$

6. Round 5464 miles to the nearest hundred miles.
   (A) 5000 miles   (B) 5400 miles
   (C) 5460 miles   (D) 5500 miles

   $5)\overline{20}$

7. What is the distance around this rectangle?

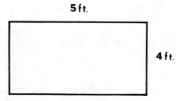

5 ft.

4 ft.

   (A) 16 ft   (B) 18 ft   (C) 18 sq ft   (D) 20 ft

8. What is the area of the pictured triangle?

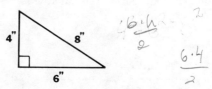

4"   8"

6"

$\frac{6 \cdot h}{2}$

$\frac{6 \cdot 4}{2}$

   (A) 18 sq in   (B) 24 sq in   (C) 12 sq in   (D) 12 in

9. $\sqrt{3} + \sqrt{12} =$
   (A) $\sqrt{15}$ (B) $3\sqrt{3}$ (C) 6   (D) 153

10. $3\sqrt{2} \times \sqrt{10} =$
    (A) 400   (B) $5\sqrt{5}$ (C) $6\sqrt{5}$ (D) 12

11. $4t - 2t \times 3 + 12t^2 \div 2 \times 3 =$
    (A) $18t^2 + 6t$ (B) $18t^2 - 2t$ (C) $2t^2 + 6t$ (D) $2t^2 - 2t$

12. $.00864 \div 4,320,000 =$
    (A) 2.00×10^{-9} (B) 2.00×10^{-2}
    (C) 2.00×10^{3} (D) 2.00×10^{9}

13. What is the volume of a 9 inch cube?
    (A) 639 cu in   (B) 729 cu in   (C) 729 sq in   (D) 81 sq in

14. If $2b - 6 \le 6b + 2$, then:
    (A) $b \le -2$ (B) $b \le 2$ (C) $b \ge -2$ (D) $b = 2$

15. The formula for finding the simple interest (I) on a loan is I = PRT. How much interest will Bill pay on his car loan if he finances \$5,000 (P) at a 13% simple interest rate (R) for 3 years (T)?
    (A) \$650   (B) \$1800   (C) \$1950   (D) \$2213

16. Given the following function, find $f(-2)$: $f(x) = 2x^3 - 3x^2 - x$
    (A) -28 (B) -26 (C) -20 (D) 6

17. Which is a linear factor of the following expression?
    $6x^2 + 5x - 4$
    (A) $2x + 2$ (B) $3x + 4$ (C) $3x - 4$ (D) $3x - 2$

18. Find the real roots of this equation: $x^2 - 3x - 3 = 0$

    (A) $\dfrac{-3 - \sqrt{15}}{2}$ and $\dfrac{-3 + \sqrt{15}}{2}$ (B) $\dfrac{3 - \sqrt{15}}{2}$ and $\dfrac{3 + \sqrt{15}}{2}$

    (C) $\dfrac{-3 - \sqrt{21}}{2}$ and $\dfrac{-3 + \sqrt{21}}{2}$ (D) $\dfrac{3 - \sqrt{21}}{2}$ and $\dfrac{3 + \sqrt{21}}{2}$

19. The graph below represents the yearly average snowfall for Colorado in inches for 1977–1982. Find the average snowfall for 1979.

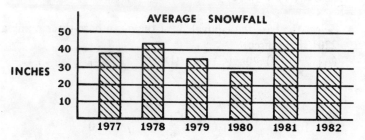

AVERAGE SNOWFALL

INCHES

(A) 40 inches   (B) 35 inches
(C) 31 inches   (D) 30 inches

20. What is the *median* of the data in the following sample? 6, 4, 2, 9, 4, 6, 5, 4

   (A) 3   (B) 4   (C) 4.5   (D) 5

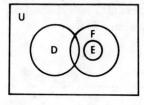

21. A florist has selected 6 different types of flowers to be used in small bud vases. Each vase will contain 2 different flowers. How many different combinations will the florist be able to make

   (A) 25   (B) 20   (C) 15   (D) 10

22. Sets D, E, F, and U are related as shown in the diagram.

```
U
   ┌─────────┐
   │    F    │
 D │   (E)   │
   └─────────┘
```

Which of the following statements is true, assuming none of the four regions is empty?

(A) Any element of set F is a member of set E.

(B) Any element of set D is a member of set F.

(C) Any element of set E is an element of set U.

(D) Membership in set U is a sufficient condition for membership in set D.

23. $5^2 + 6^2 =$
    (A) $(5 + 6)^2$ (B) $(5 + 6)^4$
    (C) $(5)(2) + (6)(2)$ (D) $(5)(5) + (6)(6)$

24. Select the base-ten equivalent of the given base-three numeral.
    2201 (base three)
    (A) 73   (B) 40   (C) 24   (D) 1485

25. $0.17 =$
    (A) $\dfrac{17}{100}\%$ (B) $1\dfrac{7}{10}\%$ (C) $\dfrac{17}{10}$ (D) $\dfrac{17}{100}$

26. Identify the symbol that should be placed in the box to form a
    true statement.

    $$4.51 \ \square \ 4.506$$

    (A) $=$ (B) $<$ (C) $>$

27. Forty people pick strawberries at a truck farm. The least
    productive person picks 125 quarts per week, and the most
    productive person picks 1200 quarts per week. Which of the
    following values could be a reasonable estimate of the total
    weekly harvest for the company?
    (A) 53,000   (B) 35,000   (C) 4600   (D) 1100

28. Which of the statements below is true for the figure shown, given
    that L1 and L2 are parallel lines?

    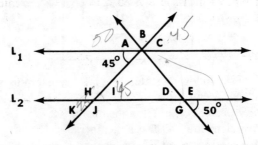

    (A) Since $m\angle I = 45°$, $m\angle E = 135°$
    (B) $m\angle J = m\angle C$
    (C) Since $m\angle K = 45°$, $m\angle B = 85°$
    (D) None of the above statements is true.

29. Which of the following is an acute angle?

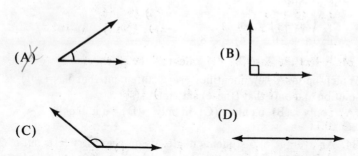

(A)

(B)

(C)

(D)

30. Which of the statements is true for the pictured triangles?

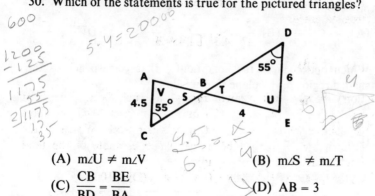

(A) m∠U ≠ m∠V   (B) m∠S ≠ m∠T

(C) $\dfrac{CB}{BD} = \dfrac{BE}{BA}$ (D) AB = 3

31. What type of measure is needed to express the interior of the figure shown below?

(A) equilateral
(B) square
(C) cubic
(D) linear

32. Which statement illustrates the distributive property of multiplication over addition?

(A) 4(x · y · z) = 4x · 4y · 4z   (B) y(2 + 3) = y(5)
(C) (x + y) · 4 = x(4) + y(4)   (D) xy = yx

33. For each of the three statements below, determine whether (-3) is a solution.

   i. $|2a + 3| = -a$

   ii. $(a + 2)(a - 4) \le -8$

   iii. $a^2 + 2a + 5 = -8$

Which option below identifies *every* statement that has (-3) as a solution and *only* that (those) statements(s)?

(A) i only (B) ii only (C) iii only (D) i and ii only

34. An average of 5 students made A's on chemistry tests out of 22 students. If n represents the number of students that make A's out of 360 students, select the equation that shows a correct proportion.

(A) $\dfrac{22}{5} = \dfrac{n}{360}$ (B) $\dfrac{5}{27} = \dfrac{n}{360}$ (C) $\dfrac{5}{22} = \dfrac{n}{360}$ (D) $\dfrac{n}{5} = \dfrac{22}{360}$

35. Which option gives the condition(s) that corresponds to the shaded region of the plane shown below.

(A) $2x + y < 4$

(B) $2x + y > 4$

(C) $2x - y > 4$

(D) $2x - y < 4$

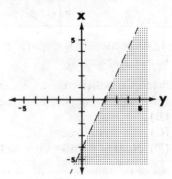

36. In an employment agency, half the applicants scored 90 on a placement test. Most of the remaining applicants scored 70 except for a few applicants who scored 20. Which of the following statements is true about the distributions of scores?

(A) The mode is less than the mean.

(B) The median and the mode are the same.

(C) The mean is greater than the mode.

(D) The median is greater than the mean.

37. A coin is tossed two times. What is the probability of getting either two heads or two tails, or one head and one tail?
    (A) 0   (B) .50   (C) .75   (D) 1

38. Select the statement which is the negation of the statement "Jones is a tailor, and Thomas is not a baker."
    (A) Jones is not a tailor, or Thomas is a baker.
    (B) Jones is not a tailor, and Thomas is a baker.
    (C) Jones is not a tailor, and Thomas is not a baker.
    (D) Jones is a tailor, and Thomas is a baker.

39. Select the statement below which is *not* logically equivalent to "If Tom takes physics, then Tom is intelligent."
    (A) If Tom is not intelligent, then Tom does not take physics.
    (B) If Tom is intelligent, then Tom takes physics.
    (C) Tom does not take physics, or Tom is intelligent.
    (D) Tom is intelligent, or Tom does not take physics.

40. Given that:

    i. All racists are ignorant.
    ii. Jim is ignorant.

    determine which conclusion can be logically deduced.
    (A) All ignorant people are racists.
    (B) Jim is a racist.
    (C) Jim is not a racist.
    (D) None of the above can be logically deduced.

41. All of the following arguments A–D have true conclusions, but one of the arguments is not valid. Select the argument that is *not* valid.

    (A) All humans have two legs, and all men are humans. Therefore, all men have two legs.
    (B) All cats have whiskers, and all Siamese are cats. Therefore, all Siamese have whiskers.
    (C) All men have a heart, and all humans have a heart. Therefore, all men are humans.
    (D) All arachnids have eight legs, and all spiders are arachnids. Therefore, all spiders have eight legs.

42. Identify the missing term in the following arithmetic progression.

$$-\frac{1}{3}, -\frac{2}{3}, -1, -\frac{4}{3}, -\frac{5}{3}, \underline{\hspace{1cm}}$$

(A) $-\frac{7}{3}$ (B) -2 (C) 2 (D) $\frac{7}{3}$

43. Select the property or properties of operation(s) illustrated in this equation: $6(7 \times 4) = (6 \times 7)4$ *Assoc.*
    (A) $a(bc) = (ab)c$
    (B) $a(bc) = (bc)a$
    (C) $a(bc) = ab \times ac$
    (D) $a(b + c) = (a + b)c$

44. Select the property used to justify the following statement:

$$\text{If } -4x < 9, \text{ then } x > \frac{9}{-4}$$

    (A) If $a > b$, then $a + c > b + c$.
    (B) If $ac > bc$ and $c > 0$, then $a > b$.
    (C) If $ac < bc$ and $c < 0$, then $a > b$.
    (D) If $a > b$ and $b > c$, then $a > c$.

45. Study the examples illustrating ways of combining objects two at a time.

3 objects	4 objects	5 objects
p, q, r	t, u, v, w	a, b, c, d, e
(p, q)	(t, u)	(a, b) (b, d)
(p, r)	(t, v)	(a, c) (b, e)
(q, r)	(t, w)	(a, d) (c, d)
	(u, v)	(a, e) (c, e)
	(u, w)	(b, c) (d, e)
	(v, w)	

How many two member combinations can be formed from a set containing 7 objects?
(A) 15   (B) 21   (C) 28   (D) 42

46. Read each of the following valid arguments, then select the symbolic form of the reasoning pattern illustrated by both arguments.

Jill will get an A if she reads 10 books. Jill read 10 books. Therefore, Jill will get an A.

If Max doesn't make the football team, Ruth won't date him. Max doesn't make the football team. Therefore, Ruth won't date Max

(A) $\sim p \rightarrow \sim q$ (B) $p \rightarrow q$ (C) $p \rightarrow q$ (D) $p \rightarrow q$
    $\sim p$ p q p
    $\overline{}$ $\overline{}$ $\overline{}$ $\overline{}$
    $\therefore \sim q$ $\therefore q$ $\therefore p$ $\therefore \sim q$

47. Select the rule of logical equivalence which *directly* (in one step) *transforms* statement i into statement ii.

   i. If x^4 is even, then x is even.
   ii. If x is not even, then x^4 is not even.

   (A) "If p, then q" is equivalent to "(not p) or q."
   (B) "Not (p and q)" is equivalent to "not p, or not q."
   (C) "If p, then q" is equivalent to "If not q, then not p."
   (D) The correct equivalence rule is not given.

48. A clothing store purchased 30 shirts and sold 20 shirts during a sale. Each shirt was purchased for $10 and sold for $20. Unsold shirts were returned to the manufacturer and a refund of $9 per shirt was made to the store. How much profit did the store make.
   (A) $600   (B) $400   (C) $200   (D) $190

49. Out of a herd of 360 horses, 85% were able to be ridden. How many horses could not be ridden?
   (A) 306   (B) 298   (C) 54   (D) 44

50. Find the smallest positive multiple of 3 which leaves a remainder of 3 when divided by 4 and a remainder of 2 when divided by 5.
   (A) 18   (B) 27   (C) 39   (D) 42

51. What will be the cost of replacing a rectangular roof measuring 15 ft by 18 ft if the roof material costs $65 for bundles covering 5 sq yds and the labor costs $275?
    (A) $765   (B) $665   (C) $565   (D) $390

52. A man wants to construct a slide from the top of his balcony to the edge of a pool below. Construction costs have been estimated at $6 per linear half-foot. What is the estimated cost for constructing the slide?

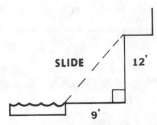

SLIDE   12'

9'

    (A) $90   (B) $180   (C) $192   (D) $360

53. Suppose that two pounds of flour makes four loaves of bread. If 80 pounds of flour are available, how many loaves of bread can be made?
    (A) 320   (B) 160   (C) 40   (D) 20

54. The sum of two whole numbers is known to be odd. Which of the following statements is true about these two numbers?
    (A) Both of the numbers may be even.
    (B) Both of the numbers may be odd.
    (C) Only one of the numbers is even.
    (D) The difference between the two numbers may be even.

55. Two mice are chosen at random from a group of 60 mice, consisting of 30 females and 30 males. What is the probability that the two mice selected are either both female or both male?

    (A) $2 \times \dfrac{30}{60} \times \dfrac{30}{60}$ (B) $2 \times \dfrac{30}{60} \times \dfrac{29}{59}$

    (C) $\dfrac{2}{60} \times \dfrac{2}{60}$ (D) $\dfrac{30}{60} \times \dfrac{29}{50}$

56. Study the information given below. If a logical conclusion is given, select that conclusion. If none of the conclusions given is warranted, select the option expressing this condition.

If you are allergic to cats, your eyes will itch. If you are allergic to dogs, your eyes will itch. You are not allergic to dogs and are allergic to cats.

(A) You do not have a cat.
(B) You have a dog.
(C) You don't have any pets.
(D) None of the above is warranted.

$p \to q$

$r \to q$

$\sim r \wedge p$

MATHEMATICS POST-TEST ANSWER KEY AND ANALYSIS

ANSWER KEY

1. (B)	13. (B)	24. (A)	35. (C)	46. (B)
2. (B)	14. (C)	25. (D)	36. (D)	47. (C)
3. (A)	15. (C)	26. (C)	37. (D)	48. (D)
4. (A)	16. (B)	27. (B)	38. (A)	49. (C)
5. (B)	17. (B)	28. (C)	39. (B)	50. (B)
6. (D)	18. (D)	29. (A)	40. (D)	51. (B)
7. (B)	19. (B)	30. (D)	41. (C)	52. (B)
8. (C)	20. (C)	31. (C)	42. (B)	53. (B)
9. (B)	21. (C)	32. (C)	43. (A)	54. (C)
10. (C)	22. (C)	33. (A)	44. (C)	55. (B)
11. (B)	23. (D)	34. (C)	45. (B)	56. (D)
12. (A)				

SCORE: _____48_____ (number of correct answers)

TIME: _____

ANALYSIS

1. (B) Competency 1. To subtract negative and/or positive numbers, change the sign of the number being subtracted and then add.

$$-\frac{2}{3} - (-2) = -\frac{2}{3} + (+2) = -\frac{2}{3} + \left(+\frac{6}{3} \right) = \frac{4}{3} = 1\frac{1}{3}$$

2. (B) Competency 2. See the examples and rules on multiplication and division in Competency 2 of the Mathematics Competencies Tested section. Remember to convert the mixed number to an improper fraction.

$$-\frac{\overset{2}{\cancel{8}}}{1} \times \frac{9}{\underset{1}{\cancel{4}}} = -18$$

3. (A) Competency 3. Remember to align the decimals and add a zero.

$$\begin{array}{r} 16.530 \\ -\ .871 \\ \hline 15.659 \end{array}$$

4. (A) Competency 4. Remember that $-\div + = -$.

$$.04\sqrt{-10.28} = 4.\sqrt{-1028}.$$

with -257 noted above.

5. (B) Competency 5.

$$\frac{\text{change}}{\text{starting point}} = \text{percent change}$$

change $= 50 - 30 = 20$

starting point $= 50$

$$\frac{20}{50} = \frac{2}{5} = \frac{4}{10} = 40\%$$

6. (D) Competency 6. The problem asks for the nearest *hundred* miles, so the answer will be either 5400 miles or 5500 miles. To determine which, look at the two numbers to the right of 54. They are 64, and since 64 is closer to 100 than it is to 0, you round up to 5500.

7. (B) Competency 7. Distance around is the same as perimeter.

$p = 2(l + w)$ or $2l + 2w$
$p = 2(9) = 18$ ft

8. (C) Competency 8. $A = \frac{1}{2}bh = \frac{1}{2}(6)(4) = 12$ sq in.

9. (B) Competency 9. $\sqrt{3} + \sqrt{12} = \sqrt{3} + \sqrt{4 \times 3} = \sqrt{3} + \sqrt{4}\sqrt{3} = \sqrt{3} + 2\sqrt{3} = 3\sqrt{3}$. Note that $\sqrt{3}$ and $\sqrt{12}$ are not like terms, so they cannot be added as is. But $\sqrt{12}$ can be simplified into $2\sqrt{3}$ as shown above, and then they are like terms which can be added.

10. (C) Competency 10. To multiply square roots, multiply the numbers under the signs and simplify.

$3\sqrt{2} \times \sqrt{10} = 3\sqrt{2 \times 10} = 3\sqrt{20} = 3\sqrt{4 \times 5} = 3\sqrt{4} \times \sqrt{5}$
$(\sqrt{4} = 2, 2 \times 3 = 6) = 6\sqrt{5}$

11. **(B) Competency 11.** Rules on order of operations: Working from *left* to *right* (1) do all operations in the *grouping symbols*, (2) do all *exponents (powers)*, (3) do all multiplication and division, (4) do all addition and subtraction.

$$4t - (2t \times 3) + (12t^2 \div 2) \times 3 = 4t - 6t + 6t^2 \times 3 =$$
$$4t - 6t + 18t^2 = 18t^2 - 2t$$

12. **(A) Competency 12.** Remember, whole numbers (4,320,000) have positive powers, and fractions (.00864) have negative powers.

$$.00864 = 8.64 \text{ (moved 3 digits to right)}$$

$$4,320,000 = 4.32 \text{ (moved 6 digits to left)}$$

To solve $8.64 \div 4.32 = \underline{2.00}$ (first figure)

Subtract the powers $-3 - 6 = \underline{-9}$ (final power of 10)

$$.00864 \div 4,320,000 = \underline{2.00} \times 10^{\underline{-9}}$$

13. **(B) Competency 13.** $V = s^3$, $V = 9^3$, $V = 729$ cu in.

14. **(C) Competency 14.** To work with an inequality, treat it exactly like an equation, *except* if you multiply or divide *both* sides by a negative number, you must *reverse* the direction of the inequality sign.

$$2b - 6 \leq 6b + 2 = 2b - 6b \leq 2 + 6 = \frac{-4b}{-4} \leq \frac{8}{-4} = b \geq -2$$

15. **(C) Competency 15.** $I = PRT$, $I = (\$5000)(.13)(3)$, $I = \$1950$.

16. **(B) Competency 16.** To solve, substitute -2 for x in the given equation.

$$f(-2) = 2(-2)^3 - 3(-2)^2 - (-2) = 2(-8) - 3(4) + 2 =$$
$$-16 - 12 + 2 = -16 - 10 = -26$$

17. **(B) Competency 17.** The factors for $6x^2 + 5x - 4$ are:

$$(3x + 4)(2x - 1)$$

Check by multiplying out:

$$(3x + 4)(2x - 1)$$

first term = $(3x)(2x) = \underline{6x^2}$
middle term = the sum of $(3x)(-1) = 3x$ and $(4)(2x) = 8x$ or
$-3x + 8x = \underline{5x}$
last term = $(4)(-1) = \underline{-4}$

18. (D) Competency 18. Given $x^2 - 3x - 3$; $a = 1$, $b = -3$, $c = -3$.

Substitute the numbers for a, b, and c into

$$x = \frac{-b \pm \sqrt{b^2 - 4ac}}{2a} \quad \text{(quadratic formula)}$$

$$x = \frac{-(-3) \pm \sqrt{(-3)^2 - 4(1)(-3)}}{2(1)}$$

$$x = \frac{3 \pm \sqrt{9 + 12}}{2} = \frac{3 \pm \sqrt{21}}{2} = \frac{3 - \sqrt{21}}{2} \text{ and } \frac{3 + \sqrt{21}}{2}$$

19. (B) Competency 19. Find the bar labeled 1979 at the bottom. Then follow the top of the bar across to the left and see where the top measures on the inches scale. 1979 falls midway between 30 inches and 40 inches, so the answer is 35 inches.

20. (C) Competency 20. The median is the score in the middle. When there are two scores in the middle, add them together and divide by 2 to find the median. Note: Don't forget to arrange them in order of size.

$$2, 4, 4, \underline{4, 5}, 6, 6, 9$$

$$(4 + 5) \div 2 = 4.5$$

21. (C) Competency 21. The question asks for different combinations of two different flowers per vase. C(n, r) denotes this situation and is read "the number of combinations of n things taken r at a time." The formula used is

$$C(n, r) = \frac{n!}{r!(n - r)!}$$

where n = 6 and r = 2 (6 different flowers taken 2 at a time).
Therefore, the equation is

$$\frac{6!}{2!(6 - 2)!} = \frac{6!}{2!4!} = \frac{6 \cdot 5 \cdot \cancel{4} \cdot \cancel{3} \cdot \cancel{2} \cdot \cancel{1}}{2 \cdot 1 \cdot \cancel{4} \cdot \cancel{3} \cdot \cancel{2} \cdot \cancel{1}} = \frac{30}{2} = 15$$

22. (C) Competency 22. C is correct because set E is contained in the
rectangular region of set U.

A is false.

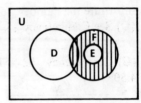

The shaded area shows elements of set
F that are not in set E.

B is false.

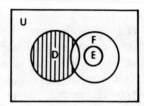

The shaded area shows elements of set
D that are not in set F.

D is false.

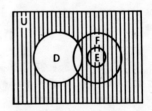

The shaded area shows elements of set
U that are not in set D.

23. (D) See Competency 23.

24. (A) Competency 24.

$$2 \quad 2 \quad 0 \quad 1 \text{ (base-three number)}$$
$$3^3 \quad 3^2 \quad 3^1 \quad 3^0 \text{ (place values in base three)}$$

To find the equivalent in base ten:

$2 \cdot 3^3 + 2 \cdot 3^2 + 0 \cdot 3^1 + 1 \cdot 3^0 = 2 \cdot 27 + 2 \cdot 9 + 0 \cdot 3 +$
$1 \cdot 1 = 54 + 18 + 0 + 1 = 73 \text{ (base ten)}$

25. (D) See Competency 25.

26. (C) Competency 26. $4.51 = 4.510$; therefore, it is greater than 4.506.

27. (B) Competency 27.

$\left. \begin{array}{l} 40 \times 1200 = 48,000 \\ 40 \times 125 = 5,000 \end{array} \right\}$ 35,000 falls between the two scores.

28. (C) Competency 28.
    $\angle C = 45°$ (vertical angles are equal)
    $\angle K = \angle C = 45°$ (alternate exterior angles are equal)
    $\angle A = 50°$ (vertical angles)
    $180° - (\angle A + \angle C) = \angle B = 85°$

29. (A) Competency 29. An acute angle is less than $90°$.

30. (D) Competency 30.

$$\frac{AC}{DE} = \frac{AB}{BE}$$

$$\frac{4.5}{6} = \frac{AB}{4}$$

$$6 \, AB = 4(4.5)$$
$$6AB = 18$$
$$AB = 3$$

31. (C) Competency 31. Volume is measured in cubic units.

32. (C) Competency 32. Distributive:

$$a(b + c) = ab + ac$$
$$4(x + y) = 4x + 4y$$

33. (A) Competency 33.

i. $|2(-3) + 3| = -(-3)$ ii. $(-3 + 2)(-3 - 4) \leq -8$
  $|-6 + 3| = 3$ $(-1)(-7) \leq -8$
    $|-3| = 3$, true $7 \leq -8$, false

iii. $-3^2 + 2(-3) + 5 = -8$
    $9 - 6 + 5 = -8$
        $8 = -8$, false

34. (C) Competency 34. Be sure to keep the comparisons in the proportion the same.

$$\frac{n \text{ students}}{\text{total students}} \qquad \frac{5}{22} = \frac{n}{360}$$

35. (C) Competency 35. Choice A would look like

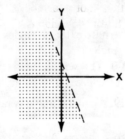

B would be the opposite side of A. D would be the opposite side of C.

36. (D) Competency 36. The *median* is the score in the middle, but you have

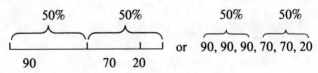

The *median* is found by $(90 + 70) \div 2 = \underline{80}$. You cannot find the exact *mean* (the average), so you have to estimate, noting that 50% of the scores are 90, *most* of the rest are 70, and *a few* are 20. For example:

$$50 \times 90 = 4500$$
$$40 \times 70 = 2800$$
$$10 \times 20 = \underline{200}$$
$$7500$$

$7500 \div 100 = 75$ (the *estimated mean*)
The median is greater than the mean.

The *mode* is the most frequent (greatest number of) score, and since 50% of the scores are 90, 90 is the mode.

37. **(D)** Competency 38. All the possible probabilities are covered. Choice A means the event cannot possibly occur. B and C mean that there are possibilities other than those given in the question.

38. **(A)** Competency 39. The sentence is in the form "p and q," which has a negation "not p, or not q." Remember, "Thomas is not a baker" = q. So the negation is "Thomas is a baker."

39. **(B)** Competency 40. The sentence is in the form "if p, then q," which is equivalent to "if not q, then not p," "not p or q," and "q or not p." Choice B does not fit any of these forms.

40. **(D)** Competency 41. Choices A, B, and C cannot be deduced.

41. **(C)** Competency 42. When you are given several arguments and asked to give the one that is valid or invalid, check the arguments for a pattern.

       A   B   C   B
(C) All men have a heart and all humans have a heart.

          A   C
Therefore, all men are humans. (AB, CB, AC)

                    A   B   C   A
(A) All humans have two legs and all men are humans.

                    C   B
Therefore, all men have two legs.

(AB, CA, CB—arguments B and D also have this pattern)

42. (B) Competency 43. In an arithmetic progression, look for the common difference (d) between the terms.

$$-\tfrac{1}{3} + d = -\tfrac{2}{3}$$
$$d = -\tfrac{2}{3} + \tfrac{1}{3}$$
$$d = -\tfrac{1}{3}$$

$-(1/3)$ is then added to each term to find the next term.

$$-\tfrac{5}{3} + (-\tfrac{1}{3}) + (-\tfrac{6}{3}) = -2$$

43. (A) Competency 44. Let a = 6, b = 7, and c = 4. Then substitute the numbers into the answers to see which one matches the problem.

$$a(bc) = (ab)c$$
$$6(7 \times 4) = (6 \times 7)4$$

44. (C) Competency 48. C gives the multiplicative property of inequalities when c < 0 (negative). This allows both sides of the first statement to be multiplied by $-(1/4)$ to obtain the second statement.

$$-\frac{1}{4}(-4x) < -\frac{1}{4}(9) = x > \frac{9}{-4}$$

45. (B) Competency 49.

$$C = \frac{n!}{r!(n-r)!} = \frac{7!}{2!(7-2)!} = \frac{7!}{2!5!} = \frac{7 \cdot 6 \cdot \cancel{5} \cdot \cancel{4} \cdot \cancel{3} \cdot \cancel{2} \cdot \cancel{1}}{2 \cdot 1 \cdot \cancel{5} \cdot \cancel{4} \cdot \cancel{3} \cdot \cancel{2} \cdot \cancel{1}}$$

$$= \frac{7 \cdot 6}{2 \cdot 1} = \frac{42}{2} = 21$$

46. (B) Competency 50. Note: "Jill will get an A if she reads 10 books" is the same as "If Jill reads 10 books, then she will get an A," which is in the form "if p, then q," or $p \rightarrow q$. "Jill read 10 books" = p. "Therefore, Jill will get an A" = $\therefore q$. So the argument looks like

$$p \rightarrow q$$
$$\underline{p}$$
$$\therefore q$$

47. (C) Competency 51. Statement i is in the form "if p, then q," or $p \rightarrow q$. Statement ii is in the form "if not q, then not p," or $\sim q \rightarrow \sim p$. $p \rightarrow q \equiv \sim q \rightarrow \sim p$.

48. (D) Competency 52.

$20 \times \$20 = \$400$
$30 \times \$10 = \$300$
$\$400 - \$300 = \$100$
$\$100 + \$90$ (refund) $= \$190$

49. (C) Competency 53. 15% could not be ridden.

$.15 \times 360 = 54$ horses that could not be ridden

50. (B) Competency 54. The number 27 fulfills all the requirements.

$3 \times 9 = 27$
$27 \div 4 = 6$, remainder 3
$27 \div 4 = 5$, remainder 2

51. (B) Competency 55.

$15 \text{ ft} \times 18 \text{ ft} = 5 \text{ yds} \times 6 \text{ yds} = 30 \text{ sq yds}$
$30 \div 5 = 6$ bundles of roofing at $65 each
$6 \times \$65 = \$390$
$\$390 + \$275$ (labor) $= \$665$

52. (B) Competency 56. Let c = length in feet of slide.

$$a^2 + b^2 = c^2$$
$$12^2 + 9^2 = c^2$$
$$144 + 81 = c^2$$
$$225 = c^2$$
$$15 = c$$

$6 per ½ ft × 2 = $12 per ft
$12 × 15 = $180

53. (B) Competency 57.

$$\frac{\text{pounds of flour}}{\text{loaves of bread}} \qquad \frac{2}{4} = \frac{80}{x}$$

$$2x = 320$$
$$x = 160$$

54. (C) Competency 58.
    (C) is true—odd plus even = odd
    (A) is false—even + even = even
    (B) is false—odd + odd = even
    (D) is false—odd − even = odd

55. (B) Competency 60. Probability that both are females:

$$\frac{30}{60} \times \frac{29}{59}$$

The probability that both are males is the same as the probability that both are females. Thus, the probability of *either* occurrence:

$$2 \times \frac{30}{60} \times \frac{29}{59}$$

56. (D) Competency 61. A, B, and C are not valid because they don't follow logically from the premises.

Part VI: Complete Practice CLAST

Instructions for Taking the Complete Practice CLAST

Simulate actual test conditions by taking the following practice CLAST in a single four hour and ten minute period. Follow the schedule and sequence you will encounter on CLAST day.

FORMAT OF THE CLAST		
Test Sequence	*Time Allowed*	*Approximate Number of Questions*
1. Essay	60 minutes	1 essay
2. break	5 minutes	
3. Grammar and Reading	80 minutes	37 44
4. break	15 minutes	
5. Mathematics	90 minutes	56

ANSWER SHEET FOR COMPLETE PRACTICE CLAST
(Remove This Sheet and Use It to Mark Your Answers)

GRAMMAR TEST

1 A B C D E	11 A B C D E	21 A B C D E	31 A B C D E
2 A B C D E	12 A B C D E	22 A B C D E	32 A B C D E
3 A B C D E	13 A B C D E	23 A B C D E	33 A B C D E
4 A B C D E	14 A B C D E	24 A B C D E	34 A B C D E
5 A B C D E	15 A B C D E	25 A B C D E	35 A B C D E
6 A B C D E	16 A B C D E	26 A B C D E	36 A B C D E
7 A B C D E	17 A B C D E	27 A B C D E	37 A B C D E
8 A B C D E	18 A B C D E	28 A B C D E	
9 A B C D E	19 A B C D E	29 A B C D E	
10 A B C D E	20 A B C D E	30 A B C D E	

READING TEST

1 A B C D E	12 A B C D E	23 A B C D E	34 A B C D E
2 A B C D E	13 A B C D E	24 A B C D E	35 A B C D E
3 A B C D E	14 A B C D E	25 A B C D E	36 A B C D E
4 A B C D E	15 A B C D E	26 A B C D E	37 A B C D E
5 A B C D E	16 A B C D E	27 A B C D E	38 A B C D E
6 A B C D E	17 A B C D E	28 A B C D E	39 A B C D E
7 A B C D E	18 A B C D E	29 A B C D E	40 A B C D E
8 A B C D E	19 A B C D E	30 A B C D E	41 A B C D E
9 A B C D E	20 A B C D E	31 A B C D E	42 A B C D E
10 A B C D E	21 A B C D E	32 A B C D E	43 A B C D E
11 A B C D E	22 A B C D E	33 A B C D E	44 A B C D E

ANSWER SHEET FOR COMPLETE PRACTICE CLAST
(Remove This Sheet and Use It to Mark Your Answers)

MATHEMATICS TEST

1 A B C D E	15 A B C D E	29 A B C D E	43 A B C D E
2 A B C D E	16 A B C D E	30 A B C D E	44 A B C D E
3 A B C D E	17 A B C D E	31 A B C D E	45 A B C D E
4 A B C D E	18 A B C D E	32 A B C D E	46 A B C D E
5 A B C D E	19 A B C D E	33 A B C D E	47 A B C D E
6 A B C D E	20 A B C D E	34 A B C D E	48 A B C D E
7 A B C D E	21 A B C D E	35 A B C D E	49 A B C D E
8 A B C D E	22 A B C D E	36 A B C D E	50 A B C D E
9 A B C D E	23 A B C D E	37 A B C D E	51 A B C D E
10 A B C D E	24 A B C D E	38 A B C D E	52 A B C D E
11 A B C D E	25 A B C D E	39 A B C D E	53 A B C D E
12 A B C D E	26 A B C D E	40 A B C D E	54 A B C D E
13 A B C D E	27 A B C D E	41 A B C D E	54 A B C D E
14 A B C D E	28 A B C D E	42 A B C D E	56 A B C D E

ESSAY TEST

DIRECTIONS FOR ESSAY

You will have 60 minutes to plan, write, and proofread an essay on one of the topics below.

> TOPIC 1. An idea presented in modern times which has had harmful effects.

OR

> TOPIC 2. The most ridiculous practice in education today.

Read the two topics again and select the one on which you wish to write your essay. In order for your essay to be scored, it *must* be on *only one* of these topics.

In your essay, you should introduce the subject and then either

—explain the subject you have chosen, or
—take a position about your subject and support it.

At least two evaluators will read your essay and assign it a score. They will pay special attention to whether you

—have a clear thesis or main idea,
—develop your thesis logically and in sufficient detail,
—use well-formed sentences and paragraphs,
—use language appropriately and effectively, and
—follow standard practices in spelling, punctuation, and grammar.

Take a few minutes to think about what you want to say before you start writing. Leave yourself a few minutes at the end of the period to proofread and make corrections.

You may cross out or add information as necessary. Although your handwriting will not affect the score, you should write as legibly as possible so the evaluators can easily read your essay.

You may use the following page to plan your essay before you begin to write in the answer folder.

Do not begin until you are told to do so.

ENGLISH LANGUAGE SKILLS TEST

Time: 70 Minutes
81 Questions

GRAMMAR TEST

Suggested Time: 20 Minutes
37 Questions

I. **DIRECTIONS:** Complete each sentence by choosing the most effective word or phrase which conforms to standard written English.

1. In an effort to end rioting, the government declared
   _____ law.
   A. marshal
   B. martial
   C. marital

2. In _____ she made her first trip to Europe.
   A. the year 1985
   B. nineteen hundred and eighty five
   C. the calendar year of 1985
   D. 1985

3. Sara and Tara were embarrassed to discover that they both wore the _____ dress to the party.
   A. same exact
   B. same
   C. very same
   D. same identical

4. Developing the _____ of exercising daily has made her healthier.
   A. addiction
   B. habit
   C. ritual

5. Unable to agree on anything, the couple argued _____.
   A. on a daily basis
   B. day in and day out
   C. daily
   D. every single day

6. Some writers express their meaning openly while others prefer to
   _____ their message.
   A. imply
   B. insinuate
   C. infer

II. **DIRECTIONS:** Choose the sentence that expresses the thought
most clearly and effectively and that has no errors in structure.

7. A. He decided that the way to overcome hardship is to set goals,
       work toward those goals, and keeping a good attitude.

   B. He decided that the way to overcome hardship is by setting
      goals, to work toward those goals, and that a good attitude is
      important.

   C. He decided that the way to overcome hardship is to set goals,
      work toward those goals, and keep a good attitude.

8. A. Having experienced only Canadian winters, Florida's mild
      climate astonished the tourist.

   B. Having experienced only Canadian winters, the tourist was
      astonished by Florida's mild climate.

   C. Having experienced Canadian winters, the tourist was only
      astonished by Florida's mild climate.

9. A. Jogging remains a popular exercise even though doctors warn
      that it can lead to serious injury.

   B. Jogging remains a popular exercise, and doctors warn that it
      can lead to serious injury.

   C. Jogging remains a popular exercise; doctors warn that it can
      lead to serious injury.

10. A. The state legislature passed a law requiring all automobile passengers to wear seat belts in 1986.

  B. The state legislature passed a 1986 law requiring all automobile passengers to wear seat belts.

  C. In 1986, the state legislature passed a law requiring all automobile passengers to wear seat belts.

11. A. The boat made its way under the bridge, and the owner was at the wheel, but he was still half asleep.

  B. As the boat made its way under the bridge, the owner, who was still half asleep, was at the wheel.

  C. The boat made its way under the bridge while the owner was at the wheel, and he was still half asleep.

12. A. School regulations prohibit eating, cigarettes, and drinking in classrooms.

  B. School regulations prohibit eating, smoking, and drinking in classrooms.

  C. School regulations prohibit food, cigarettes, and drinking in classrooms.

13. A. He neither could eat nor sleep for two days after visiting the dentist.

  B. After visiting the dentist, his eating and sleeping were disrupted for two days.

  C. He could neither eat nor sleep for two days after visiting the dentist.

14. A. Sam keeps gaining weight because he loves to eat but hates exercising.

  B. Sam keeps gaining weight because he loves eating but hates to exercise.

  C. Sam keeps gaining weight because he loves to eat but hates to exercise.

15. A. As soon as the last passenger sat down, the driver started the bus and turned it onto the highway.

   B. The last passenger sat down, and the driver started the bus, and he turned it onto the highway.

   C. The last passenger sat down, and after that the driver started the bus, and then he turned it onto the highway.

III. DIRECTIONS: Each item below <u>may</u> contain an error in sentence construction; a fragment, a comma splice, or a fused (run-on) sentence. <u>NO ITEM HAS MORE THAN ONE ERROR.</u> Mark the letter which precedes the group of words containing the error. Mark <u>E</u> if there is no error.

16. <u>(A)</u> As her first weeks in college passed, Nancy gained confidence in herself. <u>(B)</u> Especially after taking a test and earning a perfect score on it. <u>(C)</u> Soon she lost her fear of tests; in fact, she began to enjoy them. <u>(D)</u> When she received her grades, which arrived in the mail on her birthday, she was overjoyed to see only A's on her transcript. <u>(E) No error</u>

17. <u>(A)</u> Having the feeling that we were being watched, we walked further into the woods. <u>(B)</u> Suddenly, we saw a large claw print in the muddy path. <u>(C)</u> With our eyes opened wide, we stared at each other, and then both of us started moving cautiously. <u>(D)</u> Something, we knew, was watching our every step. <u>(E) No error</u>

18. <u>(A)</u> Creative ideas can't be forced to occur at will; they just come at the most unexpected times. <u>(B)</u> Most people have had brilliant ideas in the shower or while driving, but by the time they sit down to write, the thoughts have vanished. <u>(C)</u> Those ideas must be written down the best place for them is a notebook. <u>(D)</u> Anything from an appointment calendar to an old envelope can be used to keep a record of fleeting ideas. <u>(E) No error</u>

IV. DIRECTIONS: Mark "A" if the first alternative within the parentheses is correct; mark "B" if the second alternative is correct.

19. When she was a child, her family (use, used) to
             A   B
    vacation each summer.

20. The nervous patient tried to sit (calm, calmly) while the nurse
                    A   B
    medicated him.

21. Some of the color used in the old painting (is, are)
                    A   B
    beginning to fade.

22. Every girl was eager to tell (their, her) own
             A   B
    version of the story.

23. Philosophers have always speculated about the nature of
    (existence, existance).
    A   B

24. The lights went out, leaving his wife and (he, him) in the dark.
                    A   B

25. Barry began to behave (peculiarly, peculiar) after he inherited
             A   B
    a fortune.

26. The school (accepted, excepted) almost everyone
        A   B
    who applied for admission.

27. Neither heat nor insects (are, is) able to discourage
                    A   B
    the Florida home gardener.

28. Although they argued often, this (argument, arguement)
                    A   B
    was the worst yet.

29. The committee makes (their, its) recommendations
                    A   B
    at the end of each meeting.

30. The confrontation between the other driver and (I, me)
                                                A B
    was loud but harmless.

31. Susan refused the nomination even though she (would have,
                                                  A

    would of) been proud to win the election.
    B

32. Statistics (are, is) a required course for computer
               A   B
    science majors.

33. Most people can pass the driving test (easy, easily).
                                            A   B

34. Each new car has (its, it's) own special features.
                      A   B

V. **DIRECTIONS:** The items below <u>may</u> contain errors in punctua-
   tion. <u>NO ITEM HAS MORE THAN ONE ERROR UNDER-
   LINED</u>. Mark the letter which locates an error in punctuation.
   Mark <u>E</u> if there is no error.

35. By day the director held auditions for the new play ; by night
                                                       A
    he conferred with designers. He sat , like a king at court ,
                                        B   C
    on a high-backed canvas chair , giving orders and calling
                                   D
    for silence. No error
                 E

36. Severe depression can result from feelings of : loneliness ,
                                                 A   B
    grief, or fear. Many people experience these feelings ;
                                                          C
    however , not everyone who does becomes seriously depressed.
            D
    No error
    E

IV. DIRECTIONS: The item below <u>may</u> contain an error in capitalization. <u>THERE IS NOT MORE THAN ONE ERROR UNDERLINED.</u> Mark the letter which locates the error in capitalization. Mark <u>E</u> if there is no error.

37. As the plane traveled <u>west</u>, the <u>senator</u> reviewed the
                 A   B

legislation he was planning to support in the U.S. <u>Senate.</u>
  C

<u>Glancing</u> out the window, he saw sun glinting on the Colorado river far below. <u>No error</u>
D   E

READING TEST

Suggested Time: 60 Minutes
44 Questions

Passage 1

It's difficult to believe that in 1841 people actually lined up on the New York piers to learn what happened in the latest installment of a Dickens novel; "How's little Nell?" they shouted. It's easier to believe that in 1987 students
5 shelve Dickens as long as possible. They cajole and tease and try to worm their way out of reading him. "But I had to read *A Christmas Carol* in the eighth grade and hated it. Will this be any better?" And these students are the brightest in the school. They are, in our lexicon of labels, the sophomore
10 honors gifted, which means a tenth grader with a 130+ IQ and an academic orientation. They are intelligent, conscientious and responsible. They honestly "gave Dickens another shot" and were honestly miserable.

Nevertheless we read it because I—the one who is certi-
15 fied to know what is good for everybody, who had indeed been using it as part of the curriculum for ten years, who had files of Dickens paraphernalia, who could traipse up and down Bloom's entire ladder with Dickens—I said we would. There were, after all, three sound reasons for studying him,
20 especially through *A Tale of Two Cities:* the quality of the genre, the masterful techniques, and the thematic perspective. I promised students that by Book III (at the latest) they, too, would be engrossed, and, to sweeten the engrossment, added two topics to their choices for final compositions—
25 Why Dickens Is Okay After All, and Why I Still Hate Dickens. On those final papers, four chose various topics, one chose the former, and twenty-two embraced the latter. Reading those papers and coincidentally seeing the film *Brazil* converged to underscore that Dickens is not the mode
30 of critical thinking I once thought he was and that gifted students are indeed willing, growing people—people who took all the techniques learned in the argumentation unit and applied to each of those three sound reasons.

First, they analyzed that "quality of the genre," looking at
35 and being amused by the fourteen characteristics of the
Victorian novel. Okay, they assessed, so you have doubles, a
victimized woman, a brutal aristocrat . . . but so do *The
Colbys, Dallas,* and *Hotel.* TV has copied, modernized, and
visualized him. Say, why don't we study a TV series?
40 Because "there's more" to Dickens, I whispered.

1. Identify the statement below which gives the most accurate
   statement of the central idea of this passage.
   A. Students can apply techniques of argumentation to discus-
      sion of literature.
   B. Studying Dickens can be a necessary experience for high
      school students.
   C. Many gifted students are reluctant to study Dickens.
   D. Studying a television series would have been more enjoyable
      than studying Dickens.

2. The examples of *Dallas* and *The Colbys* were used to illustrate
   that
   A. modern TV series are more interesting than old novels.
   B. studying a TV series would be enjoyable.
   C. studying a TV series would be less challenging than a
      Dickens novel.
   D. modern TV series often have the same characteristics as a
      Dickens novel.

3. In this context, the word cajole (line 5) means
   A. lie.
   B. coax.
   C. deceive.
   D. laugh at.

4. In this context, the word traipse (line 17) means
   A. quote.
   B. teach.
   C. travel.
   D. visualize.

5. In the sentence "They honestly 'gave Dickens another shot' and were honestly miserable." the author indicates that his or her purpose is to
   A. present an account of why intelligent students have difficulty studying and appreciating Dickens's novels.
   B. present a strong case for not studying Dickens's novels in high school.
   C. present a proposal for curriculum reform.
   D. attack the works of Charles Dickens.

6. In developing the passage, the organizational pattern used by the author could be described as
   A. contrast and comparison.
   B. cause and effect.
   C. definition.
   D. generalization and example.

7. The author's statement "They are intelligent, conscientious, and responsible." (in lines 11–12) is a statement of
   A. fact.
   B. opinion.

Passage 2

NASA has formed a new Office of Exploration to provide a structure within the space agency that will first study manned lunar base and manned Mars mission concepts, and then provide the foundation from which such projects could be executed.

Astronaut Sally K. Ride, who has been coordinating space goal studies, was named as acting assistant administrator for the office. Ride has resigned from NASA effective this autumn, however, to take a position at Stanford University.

A significant problem for any new, substantial U.S. space goal is the lack of a structure or process within NASA to support it. The agency is rigidly structured for the shuttle, the space station, space science and applications, and aeronautics, but there has been no effective structure to nurture projects such as a manned lunar or Mars initiative. The new office will focus on Mars and lunar base questions and issues raised by recent space-goal study efforts.

While this is under way, the Office of Space Science and Applications will continue to study the major earth observation and advanced planetary initiatives also considered as inherent parts of the space-goals study.

A separate study in NASA is examining how the new initiative should be presented as a U.S. policy issue and how the White House should be involved. There is significant frustration within NASA that Administrator James C. Fletcher has been ineffective in promoting the agency's interests, and that the White House has been uninterested in working aggressively with NASA on these issues.

NASA and the National Security Council are trying to schedule a briefing for President Reagan on the Soviet space program to demonstrate the significance of the Soviet efforts.

"There are considerable—even urgent—demands for a major initiative that would re-energize America's space program and stimulate development of new technology to help the nation remain pre-eminent both in space and in the world's high-tech market place," Fletcher said last week. "This office is a step in responding to that demand," he said.

8. In this passage, the author reflects bias by people within NASA against
   A. NASA.
   B. Astronaut Sally K. Ride.
   C. Administrator James C. Fletcher.
   D. the Office of Space Science and Applications.

9. If the author were delivering this passage orally, his or her tone of voice would probably be
   A. reverent.
   B. outraged.
   C. caustic.
   D. formal.

10. Is Fletcher's argument logically valid or invalid when he states that if we "... re-energize America's space program and stimu-late development of new technology ..." we will "... help the nation remain pre-eminent both in space and in the world's high-tech market place ..."?
   A. valid.
   B. invalid.

11. Sally Ride's resignation from NASA was probably a result of
   A. frustration with her job.
   B. lack of promotion and advancement.
   C. pressure from the president and others.
   D. being offered a position at Stanford.

DIRECTIONS: In the following sentence, a certain relationship between parts of the sentence can be identified. Read the sentence carefully; then choose the word or phrase which identifies the relationship between parts of the sentence.

Passage 3

Even if each network used satellite images every day, only a few thousand images would be used each year; hence, the system's development and operating costs could be paid back only if networks were willing to pay $35,000 to $75,000 per year.

12. What is the word or phrase which identifies the relationship between parts of the sentence?
   A. summary
   B. cause and effect
   C. comparison and/or contrast
   D. statement and clarification

DIRECTIONS: The following passage has several words deleted: Choose the word which best completes the passage. Choices for each item are given below the passage.

Passage 4

It is argued that since young pupils will read popular literature anyway, we ought to teach the classics in school because _____13_____ they will never know anything about them. I do not say that the argument lacks merit; _____14_____ it has an ugly aspect, when stripped of its sophistry. It amounts to admitting that because the classics are disagreeable anyway, we had better teach them in school along with the other disagreeable subjects. _____15_____, it invalidates the very assumptions on which the teaching of the classics is based; the assumptions, _____16_____, that their teaching will carry over into life. . . . It reduces literature to a more or less disagreeable task to be conscientiously got through for some mysterious reason that neither teacher nor pupil can understand. It makes the teacher admit defeat before the battle is begun.

13. The missing word in space 13 is
    A. finally.
    B. otherwise.
    C. likewise.
    D. evidently.

14. The missing word in space 14 is
    A. but.
    B. since.
    C. until.
    D. by.

15. The missing word in space 15 is
    A. Still.
    B. Moreover.
    C. Conversely.
    D. About.

16. The missing word in space 16 is
    A. likewise.
    B. beyond.
    C. until.
    D. namely.

Passage 5

I have observed Dr. Smith drink wine daily and in large quantities. Shall we, in keeping him as our family doctor, commit our health to a wino?

17. Is the author's argument logically valid or invalid?
    A. valid
    B. invalid

DIRECTIONS: The following passage has words or phrases deleted. For each blank, choose the word or phrase which best completes the passage. Choices for each item are given below the passage.

Passage 6

Add one more environmental disaster to the list of potential dire consequences of the greenhouse effect. A general
warming of the earth because of increasing amounts of
carbon dioxide and other gases in the atmosphere might not
5   only melt the polar ice caps and drastically alter weather
patterns but also cause more ferocious storms. Writing in
Nature, M.I.T. Meteorologist Kerry Emanuel warned that a
warmer climate could result in hurricanes packing up to 50%
more destructive power. This could happen, he suggests,
10   within 40 to 80 years, when some scientists think CO_2 levels
will have doubled and ocean temperatures will have
increased by 2°C to 3°C.   18   the energy of warm,
rising air is the driving force behind hurricanes, a warmer
ocean would translate into stronger storms.
15   "What is very speculative at this point," Emanuel says, "is
how the earth's climate will respond." One variable that
could offset the rise in CO_2 levels, for example, would be a
change in cloud cover, which would cut down on the sunlight
reaching the surface of the earth.   19   it is too early to
20   sound alarms, says Emanuel, his purpose is to make it clear
"the consequences of the changes that are occurring are
quite severe."

18. The missing word or phrase in space 18 is
   A. As a matter of fact.   B. For example.
   C. Accordingly.   D. Because.

19. The missing word or phrase in space 19 is
   A. Afterward.   B. Although.
   C. Evidently.   D. For instance.

20. What is the relationship between the sentence beginning in line 1
   ("Add one more environmental . . .") and the sentence beginning
   in line 2 ("A general warming of the . . .")?
   A. cause and effect
   B. comparison and contrast
   C. statement and clarification
   D. reverses meaning

Passage 7

Since their formation in 1775, the Marines have evolved into an arm of American foreign policy based on rapier-sharp discipline, a powerful code of integrity, and a lustrous reputation as the nation's truest warriors. With just 196,000 members, the Marine Corps regards itself as the elite military service, though it is technically an arm of the Navy. But what most distinguishes the Marine Corps, forging the powerful esprit and the ideal of *Semper Fidelis,* is the basic training.

Gone from the modern training lexicon are the physical brutality and psychological abuse that once made camps like Parris Island, S.C., seem the American counterpart of Devil's Island. Boot camp is still rigorous, and some drills involve live ammunition; 37 enlistees have died during training at the Marine Corps Recruit Depot in San Diego since 1970. But Marine regulations adopted in 1976 forbid drill instructors from touching recruits except to correct their position during instruction or to prevent injury. Punitive push-ups are now limited to just five minutes, with a 30 second break midway. Mental harassment is frowned upon. "We don't use negative reinforcement anymore," says Lieut. John Coonradt at the M.C.R.D.

Marine recruits are supposed to run no farther than five miles, and jogging routes are lined with emergency telephones and water hoses. Regulations require that ambulances be present during all activities involving "heights or fights." As three platoons of recruits in San Diego waited to begin close-combat training last week, a drill instructor complained, "We can't start without an ambulance present."

21. The main idea expressed in this passage is that
    A. Marines regard themselves as the elite military force.
    B. Marine basic training has recently changed.
    C. Marines may not be struck by instructors.
    D. punitive push-ups are now limited to 5 minutes.

22. The example of needing an ambulance present is used to
    A. show the potential violence of basic training.
    B. show the necessity for "playing it safe" these days.
    C. illustrate that some drills are harsher than others.
    D. illustrate the changes in basic training.

23. The last sentence of the first paragraph ("But what most distinguishes the Marine Corps, ... is the basic training.") indicates that the author's purpose is to
    A. state a problem in the Marine Corps.
    B. classify types of basic training.
    C. describe the uniqueness of this basic training.
    D. analyze the Marine Corps.

24. In developing the passage, the organizational pattern used by the author could be described as
    A. time order.
    B. simple listing.
    C. definition.
    D. statement and clarification.

25. The statement in sentence one of the first paragraph ("Since their formation . . .") is a statement of
    A. fact.
    B. opinion.

26. In this passage, the author shows bias in favor of the
    A. old Marine Corps.
    B. present day Marine Corps.
    C. use of live ammunition.
    D. use of push-ups for punishment.

27. The author of this passage has created a tone that could be described as
    A. cheerful.
    B. outraged.
    C. objective.
    D. excited.

28. The writer of the passage probably feels that the new basic training is
    A. bad.
    B. good.
    C. producing less competent Marines.
    D. abusive.

Passage 8

I am rather troubled about the moral fibre of this censor who reads the subversive books. . . . if the book has no effect on that censor, why should it have any effect on me; I insist that my moral fibre is just as strong as his, and I insist that freedom, if it means anything, means that I have a right to be contaminated. Who are these people who arrogate to themselves the right to be contaminated, but deny it to me? . . . For whom is this restricting done? . . . I assume it would probably be applied to youth. Our censors are always saving youth. It does not strike me that middle-age and old-age have made tremendous success of the world as it is; and my own experience is that youth has a certain self-restraint and idealism, and that as you get older you become a little more cynical. If there is any crowd that needs saving, it is middle-age and old-age, and not youth.

29. Which of the following statements shows a biased attitude expressed by the author in this passage?
    A. "If there is a crowd that needs saving, it is middle-age and old-age, and not youth."
    B. "I am rather troubled by the moral fiber of this censor . . ."
    C. "I insist that my moral fiber is just as strong as his . . ."
    D. "Our censors are always saving youth."

30. If the author were delivering this passage orally, his or her tone would be
    A. objective.
    B. outspoken.
    C. amused.
    D. reverent.

31. When the author says that ". . . if the book has no effect on that censor, why should it have any effect on me?" the argument is logically
    A. valid.
    B. invalid.

32. The author implies that censorship is
    A. reasonable.
    B. unreasonable.
    C. best for youth.
    D. often necessary.

33. The author's statement that "If there is a crowd that needs saving, it is middle-age and old-age, and not youth." is a statement of
   A. fact.
   B. opinion.

34. In developing the passage, the overall pattern used by the author could be described as
   A. clarification.
   B. summary.
   C. simple listing.
   D. time order.

35. The first sentence ("I am rather troubled . . .") indicates that the author's purpose is to
   A. encourage people to not read subversive books.
   B. encourage people to read subversive books.
   C. suggest inconsistencies in supposed impact of subversive books.
   D. analyze what a subversive book is.

Passage 9

All the neighborhood children have jobs after school and they have never been in trouble with the police. If our son had an after-school job, he would not get in trouble either.

36. Is the author's argument logically valid or invalid?
   A. valid
   B. invalid

Passage 10

It's easy to switch on the television set when there's nothing else to do. But many people watch TV not just because it's convenient, but because it provides escape from the anxiety they feel during idle moments.
5   Psychologist Robert W. Kubey has looked at television's role during idle time by having 107 married, divorced, and single men and women complete questionnaires describing what they were doing and how they felt whenever an electronic pager signaled them. Each participant was paged

10 from seven to nine times a day over one week. All were employed, and ranged in age from 18 to 63 years old.

Kubey found that the heaviest viewers of television reported more negative feelings when alone and when they had nothing to do than did those who watched TV least.
15 Heavy TV viewers reported more positive feelings in structured situations, such as working, engaging in hobbies, or doing housework. Overall, they reported unpleasant fantasies, thoughts, and feelings more frequently than did light viewers. For them, Kubey says, "Television seems to offer a
20 ready means of structuring attention that permits both escape from and avoidance of the discomfort that normally occurs during idle time."

The results also suggest that lack of structure is more troublesome than the solitude that so often accompanies idle
25 time. The heavy TV viewers consistently were in better spirits when involved in an activity, whether with others or alone, than when they had nothing to do.

But using television to overcome the discomfort idle time may bring only makes matters worse. People who increas-
30 ingly depend on TV may become less capable of filling their free time when it isn't around. "Heavy viewing of the rapid montage of much contemporary television may help reinforce an intolerance in the heavy viewer for daily activities that are not chock full of sight and sound," Kubey says.

37. The central idea expressed in this passage is that television
  A. makes time pass faster.
  B. makes work more enjoyable.
  C. overcomes discomfort idle time brings.
  D. makes us less capable of handling spare time without television.

38. All of the following were findings of Dr. Kubey except that heavy TV
  A. viewers report frequent, unpleasant fantasies.
  B. viewing often causes arguments.
  C. viewers are in better spirits when involved in an activity.
  D. viewers have positive feelings.

39. As used in line 32, the word <u>montage</u> means
   A. jumble.
   B. movement.
   C. color.
   D. landscape.

40. The first sentence of the third paragraph ("Kubey found that the . . .") indicates that the author's purpose is to
   A. state a problem in TV watching.
   B. describe the results of a survey.
   C. define "excessive" TV watching.
   D. argue for legal remedies.

41. In developing the passage, the organizational pattern used by the author could be described as
   A. definition.
   B. cause and effect.
   C. contrast and comparison.
   D. simple listing.

42. The author's statement (in lines 17–18) that heavy TV viewers experienced "unpleasant fantasies, thoughts and feelings . . ." is a statement of
   A. fact.
   B. opinion.

43. The author of this passage has created a tone that could be described as
   A. analytical.
   B. arrogant.
   C. ambivalent.
   D. evasive.

44. From this passage, you could infer that TV probably has
   A. an impact on only heavy viewers.
   B. an unpredictable impact on our lives.
   C. a greater impact on our lives than we have realized.
   D. no real impact on our lives.

MATHEMATICS TEST

Time: 90 Minutes
56 Questions

1. $-2\frac{1}{3} + (-1\frac{1}{4}) =$
   (A) $3\frac{7}{12}$ (B) $-1\frac{1}{12}$ (C) $-1\frac{1}{2}$ (D) $-3\frac{7}{12}$

2. $5 \div 3\frac{1}{3} =$
   (A) $1\frac{2}{3}$ (B) $\frac{2}{3}$ (C) $1\frac{1}{2}$ (D) $16\frac{2}{3}$

3. $-1.84 + (-.031) =$
   (A) 2.15 (B) -1.871 (C) -1.809 (D) 1.871

4. $1.89 \times (-.023) =$
   (A) .04347 (B) $-.0945$ (C) $-.04347$ (D) .0945

5. If you decrease 32 by 25% of itself, what is the result?
   (A) 24 (B) 8 (C) 28 (D) 9

6. Round the measurement of the length of the pictured triangle to the nearest ¼ inch.

   (A) 1 in
   (B) 1¼ in
   (C) 1½ in
   (D) 1¾ in

   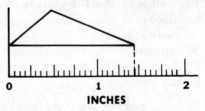

7. What is the distance around this polygon, in centimeters?

   (A) 2.3 cm
   (B) 23 cm
   (C) 230 cm
   (D) 2300 cm

   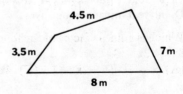

8. What is the area of the pictured triangle?

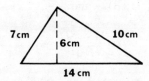

   (A) 31 sq cm   (B) 42 cm   (C) 42 sq cm   (D) 84 sq cm

9. $\sqrt{18} - \sqrt{2} =$
   (A) 4   (B) $9\sqrt{2}$ (C) $2\sqrt{2}$ (D) $-2\sqrt{2}$

10. $\dfrac{4}{\sqrt{3}} =$
    (A) $\dfrac{4}{3}$ (B) $\dfrac{4\sqrt{3}}{9}$ (C) $\dfrac{4\sqrt{3}}{3}$ (D) $4\sqrt{3}$

11. $5t - 3t \times 2 + 18t^2 \div 3 \times 2 =$
    (A) $12t^2 + 4t$ (B) $12t^2 - t$ (C) $3t^2 + 4t$ (D) $3t^2 - t$

12. $(1.4 \times 10^{-4}) \times (5.2 \times 10^7) =$
    (A) .00728   (B) .0728   (C) 7280.   (D) 7.28

13. If $3b - 5 \geq 5b + 3$, then
    (A) $b \geq -4$ (B) $b \leq -4$ (C) $b \leq 4$ (D) $b \geq 4$

14. The formula for converting a Celsius temperature to Fahrenheit is $F = \frac{9}{5}C + 32°$. What is the Fahrenheit temperature when the Celsius temperature is 45°?
    (A) 137°   (B) 113°   (C) 49°   (D) 95°

15. Given the following function, find $f(-2)$.
    $f(x) = x^3 - 3x^2 - 2x$
    (A) -24 (B) -16 (C) 0   (D) 8

16. Which is a linear factor of the following expression?
    $8x^2 - 2x - 3$
    (A) $x - 1$ (B) $2x - 1$ (C) $4x - 3$ (D) $x + 1$

17. What are the real roots of this equation: $8x^2 - 3 = 2x$?

(A) $-\dfrac{1}{2}$ and $\dfrac{3}{4}$ (B) $\dfrac{1}{2}$ and $-\dfrac{3}{4}$

(C) $-\dfrac{1}{2}$ and $\dfrac{1}{4}$ (D) $\dfrac{1 - \sqrt{7}}{4}$ and $\dfrac{1 + \sqrt{7}}{4}$

18. The graph below represents the annual average growth in inches of a teenager for 1982 through 1987. What is the average growth for 1985?

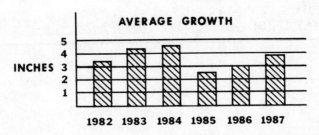

(A) 3 inches   (B) 2.5 inches   (C) 2 inches   (D) 1.5 inches

19. What is the *mean* of the data in the following sample? 11, 4, 5, 2, 4, 7, 10, 4, 7
(A) 4   (B) 5   (C) 6   (D) 7

20. If a company has 9 applicants and 4 job openings, how many ways can the openings be filled?
(A) 36   (B) 126   (C) 3024   (D) 3192

21. Sets J, K, L, and U are related as shown in the diagram.

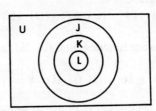

Which of the following statements is true, assuming none of the four regions is empty?
(A) An element which is a member of set K is also a member of set L.
(B) An element which is a member of set J is also a member of set K.
(C) An element which is a member of set K is also a member of set´J.
(D) No element is a member of all four sets J, K, L, and U.

22. $(6 \cdot 4)^2 =$
   (A) $(6 \times 2)(4 \times 2)$ (B) $(6 \times 4)(6 \times 4)$
   (C) $(6 \times 6)(4 \times 4)$ (D) $(6)(4)(4)$

23. Select the place value associated with the underlined digit. 42031 (base five)
   (A) 5^0 (B) 5^1 (C) 5^2 (D) 5^3

24. $^{19}/_{25} =$
   (A) .76   (B) 0.076   (C) 7.6%   (D) 0.76%

25. Identify the symbol that should be placed in the box to form a true statement.

$$\frac{1}{5} \ \square \ -\frac{2}{3}$$

(A) $=$ (B) $<$ (C) $>$

26. In a herd of 35 elephants, the smallest elephant weighs 500 pounds and the largest weighs 12,000 pounds. Which of the following values could be a reasonable estimate of the total weight of the herd?
   (A) 500,000 lbs   (B) 350,000 lbs
   (C) 10,000 lbs   (D) 6250 lbs

27. Which of the statements below is true for the figure shown, given that L_1 and L_2 are parallel lines?

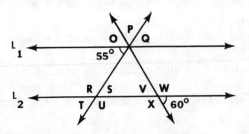

(A) Since m∠ T = 55°, m∠ P = 55°
(B) Since m∠ V = 60°, m∠ S = 60°
(C) m∠ P = m∠ W
(D) None of the above statements is true.

28. Which of the following is an isosceles, acute triangle?

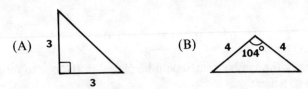

(A)   3

     3

(B)   4   104°   4

(C)   6   40°   6

     4

(D)   4   6

         7

29. Which of the statements is true for the pictured triangles?

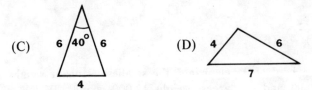

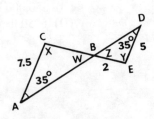

(A) $m\angle W \neq m\angle Z$ (B) $m\angle X \neq m\angle Y$

(C) $CB = 3$ (D) $\dfrac{EC}{EB} = \dfrac{DB}{DA}$

30. What type of measure is needed to express the area of the figure shown below?

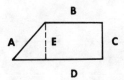

(A) cubic   (B) surface   (C) square   (D) linear

31. Which statement illustrates the associative property of addition?
    (A) $(x + y) + z = (y + x) + z$
    (B) $(x + y) + z = x + (y + z)$
    (C) $x(y + z) = x(z + y)$
    (D) $xy = yx$

32. For each of the statements below, determine whether $\frac{1}{5}$ is a solution.

    i. $3x - \dfrac{4}{5} < 0$

    ii. $(10x - 3)(5x + 4) = 5$

    iii. $5t - 3 = -10t$

    Which option below identifies *every* statement that has $\frac{1}{5}$ as a solution and *only* that (those) statement(s)?
    (A) i only   (B) ii only   (C) ii and iii only   (D) i and iii only

33. The distance a train travels is held constant while its time and rate of speed vary. If it travels for 8 hours at a rate of 90 miles per hour, select the statement of the condition when the train travels for t hours at a rate of 65 miles per hour.
    (A) $\dfrac{90}{8} = \dfrac{65}{t}$ (B) $\dfrac{90}{65} = \dfrac{8}{t}$ (C) $\dfrac{8}{90} = \dfrac{t}{65}$ (D) $\dfrac{90}{65} = \dfrac{t}{8}$

34. Which shaded region identifies the portion of the plane in which $x \leq 3$, $y \geq 0$, and $x \geq 0$?

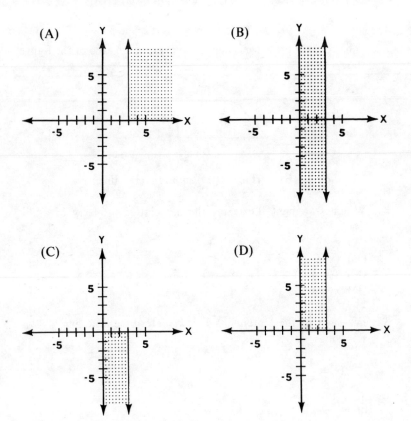

35. The graph on the following page represents the distribution of ratings from an audience at Zinc Television Studio on a program about whales. Select the statement that is true about the distribution of ratings.

(A) The mean is less than the mode.

(B) The mode is greater than the mean.

(C) The median is less than the mode.

(D) The median is greater than the mode.

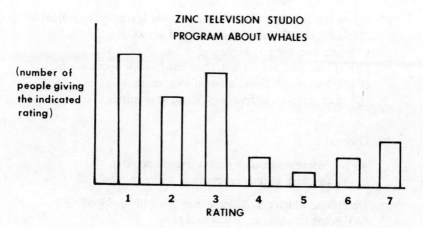

36. A beauty parlor wants to find out which shampoos are popular with its customers. The beauty parlor decides to conduct a survey of a sample of its customers. Which of the following procedures would be most appropriate for obtaining a statistically unbiased sample of the beauty parlor's customers?
   (A) surveying the first hundred customers from an alphabetical listing of customers
   (B) surveying a random sample of customers from a list of customers
   (C) having customers voluntarily mail in their preferences
   (D) surveying a random sample of customers from other beauty parlors

37. A bag contains 2 yellow, 4 blue, and 6 red stones. Two stones are drawn from the bag at random without replacement. What is the probability that neither is yellow?
   (A) $\dfrac{10}{12} \times \dfrac{2}{12}$ (B) $\dfrac{10}{12} \times \dfrac{9}{11}$ (C) $\dfrac{10}{12} \times \dfrac{9}{12}$ (D) $\dfrac{100}{132}$

38. Select the negation of the statement, "If I live in Florida, I live in America."
   (A) If I live in Florida, I do not live in America.
   (B) If I do not live in Florida, I do not live in America.
   (C) I live in Florida, and I do not live in America.
   (D) I live in Florida, and I live in America.

39. Select the statement below which is *not* logically equivalent to "If Sue goes swimming, then Sue will get wet."
    (A) Sue does not go swimming, or Sue will get wet.
    (B) If Sue does not get wet, then Sue has not been swimming.
    (C) If Sue is wet, then Sue went swimming.
    (D) Sue gets wet, or Sue does not go swimming.

40. Given that:

    i. No people who assign homework are popular.
    ii. All teachers assign homework.

    Determine which conclusion can be logically deduced.
    (A) Some teachers are not popular.
    (B) All teachers are popular.
    (C) No teachers are popular.
    (D) none of the above

41. All of the following arguments A–D have true conclusions, but one of the arguments is not valid. Select the argument that is *not* valid.
    (A) If you are bald, then you have no hair. You have hair. Therefore, you are not bald.
    (B) If you are standing in the rain, then you are wet. You are not wet. Therefore, you are not standing in the rain.
    (C) If you wear dentures, then you have no teeth. You do not wear dentures. Therefore, you have teeth.
    (D) If the sun is shining, then it is daytime. It is not daytime. Therefore, the sun is not shining.

42. Identify the missing term in the following geometric progression.

$$9, -6, 4, -\frac{8}{3}, \frac{16}{9}, \underline{\hspace{2em}}$$

(A) $\frac{24}{21}$ (B) $\frac{32}{27}$ (C) $-\frac{32}{27}$ (D) $-\frac{24}{21}$

43. Select the property or properties of operations(s) that could be used to simplify the given numerical expression in the least number of computational steps.

$$.63(47.1) + .63(2.5)$$

(A) commutative property of addition and distributive property
(B) distributive property only
(C) associative property of multiplication only
(D) distributive property and associative property of multiplication

44. Select the property used to justify the following statement.

$$\text{If } x + 3 = 8, \text{ then } x = 5$$

(A) If $a = b$, then $ac = bc$.
(B) If $a = b$, then $a + c = b + c$
(C) If $a = b$ and $b = c$, then $a = c$.
(D) If $a = b$, then $b = a$.

45. For the following sets of numbers, the value of x represents the same type of measure of central tendency.

15	9	14
20	13	18
25	16	18
30	22	18
35	35	21
x = 25	41	x = 18
	x = 19	

What is the value of x for the following set of numbers?

12	(A) 12
12	(B) 14
12	(C) 15
16	(D) 18
18	
20	
x =	

46. Read each of the following valid arguments, then select the symbolic form of the reasoning pattern illustrated by both arguments.

Jane is going to college, or she is going to get a job. Jane is not going to get a job. Therefore, she is going to college.

Bob is handsome or intelligent, and his D average indicates he isn't intelligent. Therefore, Bob is handsome.

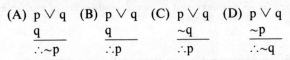

47. Select the rule of logical equivalence which *directly* (in one step) *transforms* statement i into statement ii.

  i. There are no dogs that are not animals.
 ii. All dogs are animals.

(A) "None are p" is equivalent to "all are not p."
(B) "None are not p" is equivalent to "all are p."
(C) "Not all are p" is equivalent to "some are not p."
(D) "Not (not p)" is equivalent to "p."

48. A furniture store ordered 5 chairs for 5 people. Each chair cost $100 and was sold for $150. One person paid for his chair in advance but didn't pick it up. How much profit did the store make?
(A) $750   (B) $500   (C) $250   (D) $200

49. By getting a major tune-up, Ken was told he would use only 64% as much gas. His untuned car used 150 gallons last month. How much gas would he save by getting a tune-up?
(A) 99 gallons   (B) 96 gallons
(C) 51 gallons   (D) 54 gallons

50. The outside dimensions of a picture frame are 2¾ feet by 42 inches and its inside dimensions are 2 feet by 33 inches. What is the area of the frame?
(A) 49.5 sq ft   (B) 582 sq in   (C) 4⅛ sq ft   (D) 2178 sq in

51. A 10-foot ladder is placed against a perpendicular tree. The bottom of the ladder is 6 feet from the tree. How far up the tree does the ladder reach?
(A) 5 ft (B) 6 ft (C) 7 ft (D) 8 ft

52. Stereo equipment was purchased for $2340 and is assumed to have a scrap value of $456 after 10 years. Assuming that the value depreciated linearly (steadily), what would be the value of the equipment after 6 years?
(A) $1143.60 (B) $1130.40 (C) $1884 (D) $1209.60

53. The product of two whole numbers is known to be odd. Which of the following statements is true about these two numbers?
(A) Both of the numbers may be even.
(B) Only one of the numbers is even.
(C) Both of the numbers are odd.
(D) The difference between the two numbers may be odd.

54. The probability an event will not occur is $3/8$. What are the odds in favor of the event?
(A) $8/3$ (B) $15/64$ (C) $5/3$ (D) $3/5$

55. Study the information given below. If a logical conclusion is given, select that conclusion. If none of the conclusions given is warranted, select the option expressing this condition.

All athletes are attractive. Some attractive people are models. Tom is a model.

(A) Tom is an athlete.
(B) Tom is not an athlete.
(C) Some athletes are models.
(D) None of the above is warranted.

56. How many whole numbers leave a remainder of 2 when divided into 65, and a remainder of 1 when divided into 22?
(A) 5 (B) 3 (C) 2 (D) 0

COMPLETE PRACTICE CLAST ANSWERS, ANALYSIS, AND REVIEW GUIDE

GRAMMAR TEST

ANSWERS AND ANALYSIS

QUESTION	ANSWER	ANALYSIS	REMINDER
1	B	word choice	*Martial law* is that invoked by a government in an emergency, such as rioting.
2	D	wordiness	In this case, as in many of these questions, the shortest answer is the best.
3	B	wordiness	Choices A, C, and D are redundant. *Same* gives the intended meaning concisely.
4	B	word choice	*Addiction* is not a good choice because it suggests something harmful, and *ritual* often has a religious connotation.
5	C	wordiness	*Daily* says in one word what the other choices say in three or four.
6	A	word choice	*Infer* means the opposite of the intended meaning. *Insinuate* suggests something underhanded, a mean-

QUESTION	ANSWER	ANALYSIS	REMINDER
			ing not supported by the sentence.
7	C	parallelism	Choice C uses parallel verbs: *set, work, keep.*
8	B	modification	Choice B makes it clear that the *tourist* experienced the winters. The placement of *only* in C creates an illogical meaning.
9	A	subordination	Choice A makes clear the relationship between the two ideas.
10	C	modification	Choice A suggests that the belts need to be worn only in 1986.
11	B	subordination	Choices A and C are typical examples of unhelpful coordination.
12	B	parallelism	Only choice B uses parallel verbs: *eating, smoking,* and *drinking.*
13	C	modification	The correct form is *could neither eat nor sleep.*
14	C	parallelism	Choice C is parallel: *to eat, to exercise.*
15	A	subordination	All choices show the progression of events, but only choice A does so concisely while making clear the relationship of the events.

QUESTION	ANSWER	ANALYSIS	REMINDER
16	B	fragment	Choice B contains no verb.
17	E	sentence errors	The item is correct as given.
18	C	fused sentence	The *down _ the* creates a fused sentence.
19	B	verb form	Don't let the "sound" of conversational English confuse you. The standard verb form is *used to.*
20	B	adverb	The adverb *calmly* modifies the verb *sit.*
21	A	subject-verb agreement	The singular subject *color* takes the singular verb *is.*
22	B	noun-pronoun agreement	The pronoun *her* agrees with the singular *Every.*
23	A	spelling	Review the spelling list in section 5.
24	B	case	*He* is incorrect because it is not the subject of a verb.
25	A	adjective	The adverb *peculiarly* modifies the verb *behave.*
26	A	verb form	*Excepted* means *excluded* and would make no sense in this sentence.
27	A	subject-verb agreement	The plural word *insects* is the closer term to the verb and thus takes the plural *are.*

QUESTION	ANSWER	ANALYSIS	REMINDER
28	A	spelling	Review the spelling list in section 5.
29	B	noun-pronoun agreement	*Committee* here takes the pronoun *its*. The singular verb *makes* should alert you to that fact.
30	B	case	*I* is incorrect because it is not the subject of a verb.
31	A	verb form	Don't confuse informal, conversational English with standard written English.
32	B	subject-verb agreement	*Statistics* is the name of the course and is singular.
33	B	adverb	*Easily* is an adverb modifying the verb *pass*.
34	A	case	*It's* means *it is*. The possessive pronoun *its* is required here.
35	E	punctuation	All punctuation in this item is used correctly.
36	A	punctuation	Colons do not belong after introductory words such as *of*.
37	D	capitalization	*River* must be capitalized as part of the name of a specific river.

SCORE: _____ (number of correct answers)
TIME: _____

REVIEW GUIDE

IF YOU MISSED QUESTIONS	REVIEW SECTIONS
1–6	6 (p. 76)
7–15	4 (p. 52)
16–18	1, 3 (pp. 27, 48)
19–34	5 (p. 63)
35–36	2 (p. 37)
37	5 (p. 63)

READING TEST

ANSWERS AND ANALYSIS

QUESTION	ANSWER	ANALYSIS	REMINDER
1	C	central idea	The other choices may be true, but they do not give the central idea. The passage basically concerns students' reluctance concerning the study of the works of Dickens.
2	D	details	You might assume, from the context, that B is true, but D is the best choice because the passage specifically compares the characteristics of the novels and those of TV series.
3	B	word meaning	Since the students are trying *to worm their way out* of something, *coax* is the most reasonable choice.

QUESTION	ANSWER	ANALYSIS	REMINDER
4	C	word meaning	The meaning of the word must have something to do with going *up and down* a *ladder* (even if only figuratively). The only choice having to do with movement is *travel*.
5	A	author's purpose	Nothing in the sentence or in the passage as a whole suggests the other choices.
6	D	pattern	The generalization concerns students' reluctance in studying Dickens. The passage then gives examples of that reluctance.
7	B	fact/opinion	The statement is an opinion of the writer and cannot be validated, only assumed. The terms *intelligent, conscientious,* and *responsible* can have widely varying meanings depending on the situation.
8	C	bias	Bias can be stated (as this was), not just assumed or implied.
9	D	tone	The vocabulary of the passage suggests objectivity, and a formal tone would be appropriate.

QUESTION	ANSWER	ANALYSIS	REMINDER
10	A	valid/invalid	The key word is *help*. That qualifying word avoids exaggeration which could invalidate the argument.
11	D	conclusion	This choice is explicitly stated in the passage. The other choices may or may not be true; the passage gives no indication.
12	B	relationship within sentence	The clue word is *hence*.
13	B	relationship within sentence	The word *otherwise* suggests contrast—between what will happen if the classes are taught and what will happen if they are not.
14	A	relationship within sentence	Again, a contrast is indicated—between possible *merit* and the *ugly aspect. But* indicates a contrast.
15	B	relationship between sentences	No contrast is indicated here. Two negatives (*admitting that . . . the classics are disagreeable* and invalidating the *assumptions*) call for a word indicating that parallel—*Moreover*.
16	D	relationship within sentence	The word before the blank is *assumptions*. The words following

QUESTION	ANSWER	ANALYSIS	REMINDER
			the blank *name* the assumptions. *Namely* is the logical choice.
17	B	valid/invalid	The word *wino* is emotional and imprecise. Drinking wine, even a lot of it, doesn't necessarily mean that a person would fit into this category.
18	D	relationship between sentences	The first part of the sentence gives a reason for the occurrence mentioned in the second part. *Because* appropriately introduces this reason.
19	B	relationship between sentences	*Although* is a qualifying word appropriate to the idea presented. *Although* Emanuel does not wish to sound alarms, the scientist *does* want to make consequences clear.
20	C	relationship between sentences	The first sentence says *Add one more;* the second statement clarifies the *one more* by naming it.
21	B	central idea	Choice A is an introductory detail. Choices C and D are examples of the changes mentioned in B.
22	D	details	The passage is about the changes in basic

QUESTION	ANSWER	ANALYSIS	REMINDER
			training. Having an ambulance present is one of those changes.
23	C	author's purpose	The purpose of the passage is to describe the central idea, the changes in basic training. These changes are what partially distinguish—make unique—that training.
24	D	pattern	See the explanation for question 23.
25	B	fact/opinion	The vocabulary choice makes this statement obviously opinion.
26	B	bias	The vocabulary of the entire passage is laudatory, especially concerning the present-day Corps.
27	C	tone	This is a somewhat difficult judgment to make. Because of the very positive statements of the author, choices A and B might seem tempting. In general, however, the facts are presented in an objective way, making C the *best* choice.
28	B	conclusion	Because of the positive approach of the passage, choices A, C, and D may be immediately eliminated.

QUESTION	ANSWER	ANALYSIS	REMINDER
29	A	bias	The flat statement, lacking proof, is obviously bias. Choice D is a provable assertion of fact (whether true or not). C is a possible choice, indicating, perhaps, that the author is biased toward self. But choice A is more obviously biased and therefore the best choice.
30	B	tone	Given the emotional, somewhat satiric approach, *outspoken* is the best choice.
31	B	valid/invalid	The implication is that all people are alike, and they are not.
32	B	conclusion	The passage is obviously anti-censorship.
33	B	fact/opinion	In the same way that this statement is obviously biased (question 29), it is also obviously opinion.
34	A	pattern	The author is clarifying a particular point of view concerning censorship.
35	C	author's purpose	The sentence brings into question the idea of censorship by suggesting that if subversive books are going to

QUESTION	ANSWER	ANALYSIS	REMINDER
			damage some people, then they are going to damage the censor as well.
36	B	valid/invalid	The assumption that the after-school jobs *cause* the avoidance of trouble with the police is illogical.
37	C	central idea	The other choices are details. The major point discussed has to do with the structure (lack of idle time) offered by TV.
38	B	details	Arguments are not mentioned.
39	A	word meaning	The word *rapid* might lead you to choose *movement* as a logical choice, but the remainder of the sentence should lead you to choice A.
40	B	author's purpose	The word *found* indicates that the passage will deal with something that Kubey determined (by means of the survey).
41	D	pattern	The passage is a listing of the survey findings.
42	A	fact/opinion	This can be validated; records were kept.

QUESTION	ANSWER	ANALYSIS	REMINDER
43	A	tone	The tone is very straightforward and analytical.
44	C	conclusion	The passage does not suggest that TV has *no* impact on other viewers. B may be true in some cases, but the passage does not suggest it. Choice C is logical because we have perhaps not realized the impact shown by the survey.

SCORE: _____ (number of correct answers)
TIME: _____

REVIEW GUIDE

IF YOU MISSED QUESTIONS	REVIEW SECTIONS
	Literal Comprehension
1, 21, 37	1. central idea (p. 139)
2, 22, 38	2. details (p. 142)
3, 4, 39	3. word meaning (p. 144)
	Critical Comprehension
5, 23, 35, 40	1. author's purpose (p. 148)
6, 24, 34, 41	2. organizational pattern (p. 150)
7, 25, 33, 42	3. fact/opinion (p. 153)
8, 26, 29	4. bias (p. 155)
9, 27, 30, 43	5. tone (p. 158)
12, 13, 14, 16	6. relationship within sentence (p. 161)
15, 18, 19, 20	7. relationship between sentences (p. 162)
10, 17, 31, 36	8. valid/invalid (p. 164)
11, 28, 32, 44	9. conclusion (p. 166)

MATHEMATICS TEST

ANSWER KEY

1. (D)	13. (B)	24. (A)	35. (D)	46. (C)
2. (C)	14. (B)	25. (C)	36. (B)	47. (B)
3. (B)	15. (B)	26. (B)	37. (B)	48. (C)
4. (C)	16. (C)	27. (D)	38. (C)	49. (D)
5. (A)	17. (A)	28. (C)	39. (C)	50. (C)
6. (C)	18. (B)	29. (C)	40. (C)	51. (D)
7. (D)	19. (C)	30. (C)	41. (C)	52. (D)
8. (C)	20. (C)	31. (B)	42. (C)	53. (C)
9. (C)	21. (C)	32. (D)	43. (B)	54. (C)
10. (C)	22. (C)	33. (D)	44. (B)	55. (D)
11. (B)	23. (C)	34. (D)	45. (B)	56. (B)
12. (C)				

SCORE: _____ (number of correct answers)

TIME: _____

ANALYSIS

1. (D) Competency 1. To add two numbers with the same sign, add the numbers and keep the same sign. (Remember to convert the mixed numbers to improper fractions and to convert both fractions to common denominators.)

$$-\frac{7}{3} + \left(-\frac{5}{4}\right) = -\frac{28}{12} + \left(-\frac{15}{12}\right) = -\frac{43}{12} = -3\frac{7}{12}$$

2. (C) Competency 2. To divide fractions, turn the second fraction upside down (invert) and then multiply. Reduce, if necessary. (Remember to convert the mixed number to an improper fraction.)

$$\frac{1\cancel{5}}{1} \times \frac{3}{\cancel{10}_2} = \frac{3}{2} = 1\frac{1}{2}$$

3. **(B)** Competency 3. Remember, when adding two numbers with the same sign, add the numbers and keep the same sign. Don't forget to align the decimals.

$$
\begin{array}{r}
-1.840 \\
+ -\ .031 \\
\hline
-1.871
\end{array}
$$

4. **(C)** Competency 4. There is a *total* of 5 digits to the right of the decimal in the top portion of the problem. Therefore, there must be 5 digits to the right of the decimal in the answer.

$$
\begin{array}{r}
1.89 \rightarrow 2 \text{ digits to right} \\
\times\ -.023 \rightarrow 3 \text{ digits to right} \\
\hline
-.04347 \rightarrow 5 \text{ digits to right}
\end{array}
$$

Remember that $+ \times - = -$.

5. **(A)** Competency 5. First find 25% of 32: $32 \times .25 = 8$. To decrease 32 by 25%, or 8, simply subtract: $32 - 8 = 24$.

6. **(C)** Competency 6. The problem asks for the nearest $\frac{1}{4}$ inch. The pictured triangle measures $1\frac{7}{16}$ inch, which is closer to $1\frac{1}{2}$ inch than it is to $1\frac{1}{4}$ inch.

7. **(D)** Competency 7. The distance around is the same as the perimeter.

$$
P = \text{sum of all sides}
$$
$$
P = 4.5 + 3.5 + 8 + 7 = 23 \text{ meters}
$$

The problem asks for centimeters.

$$
100 \text{ centimeters} = 1 \text{ meter}
$$
$$
23 \times 100 = 2300 \text{ cm}
$$

8. **(C)** Competency 8. $A = \frac{1}{2}bh = \frac{1}{2}(6)(4) = 12$ sq cm.

9. **(C)** Competency 9. $\sqrt{18}$ and $\sqrt{2}$ are not like terms, so they cannot be subtracted as is. But $\sqrt{18}$ can be simplified to $3\sqrt{2}$ as shown below, and then they are like terms.

$$
\sqrt{18} - \sqrt{2} = \sqrt{9 \times 2} - \sqrt{2} = \sqrt{9}\ \sqrt{2} - \sqrt{2} = 3\sqrt{2} - \sqrt{2} = 2\sqrt{2}
$$

10. (C) Competency 10. To divide by a radical, use the steps shown below to eliminate the radical from the denominator.

$$\frac{4}{\sqrt{3}} = \frac{4}{\sqrt{3}} \times \frac{\sqrt{3}}{\sqrt{3}} = \frac{4\sqrt{3}}{\sqrt{9}} = \frac{4\sqrt{3}}{3}$$

11. (B) Competency 11. Working from *left* to *right:* (1) do all operations in the *grouping symbols,* (2) do all *exponents* (*powers*), (3) do all multiplication and division, (4) do all addition and subtraction.

$5t - (3t \times 2) + (18t^2 \div 3) \times 2 = 5t - 6t + 6t^2 \times 2 =$
$5t - 6t + 12t^2 = 12t^2 - t$

12. (C) Competency 12. (1) Multiply the numbers together to get the first figure.

$$1.4 \times 5.2 = \underline{7.28}$$

(2) Add the powers of 10.

$$-4 + 7 = \underline{3}$$

$7.28 \times 10^3 = 7280$ (7.280 moved 3 places to right because the power of 10 is 3)

13. (B) Competency 14. To work with an inequality, treat it exactly like an equation, *except,* if you multiply or divide *both* sides by a negative number, you must *reverse* the direction of the sign.

$$3b - 5 \geq 5b + 3$$
$$3b - 5b \geq 3 + 5$$

$$\frac{-2b}{-2} \geq \frac{8^4}{-2}$$

$$b \leq -4$$

14. (B) Competency 15. Replace F with 45° and simplify:

$$F = \tfrac{9}{5}(45°) + 32° = 81° + 32° = 113°$$

15. (B) Competency 16. Substitute -2 for x in the given equation and solve.

$$f(-2) = (-2)^3 - 3(-2)^2 - 2(-2) =$$
$$-8 - 3(4) + 4 = -8 - 12 + 4 = -20 + 4 = -16$$

16. (C) Competency 17. The factors are $(2x + 1)(4x - 3)$. Check by multiplying out.

$$(2x + 1)(4x - 3)$$

first term $= (2x)(4x) = \underline{8x^2}$

middle term $=$ the sum of $(2x)(-3) = -6x$

$(1)(4x) = \underline{4x}$

$\underline{-2x}$

last term $= (1)(-3) = \underline{-3}$

$8x^2 - 6x + 4x - 3 = 8x^2 - 2x - 3$

17. (A) Competency 18. Write the equation as $8x^2 - 2x - 3 = 0$. Factor and rewrite the equation as

$$(2x + 1)(4x - 3) = 0$$

Solve the equations that result from setting each of the factors equal to zero.

$$2x + 1 = 0 \quad \text{or} \quad 4x - 3 = 0$$
$$2x = -1 \quad \text{or} \quad 4x = 3$$
$$x = -\frac{1}{2} \quad \text{or} \quad x = \frac{3}{4}$$

18. (B) Competency 19. The scale for 1985 falls midway between 2 and 3 inches.

19. (C) Competency 20. The *mean* is the average of all the scores.

$$\text{mean} = \frac{54}{9} = 6$$

20. (C) Competency 21. This is an arrangement, or permutation, problem. There are 4 job openings with 9 applicants available for the first opening, 8 applicants for the second opening, 7 applicants for the third opening, and 6 applicants for the fourth

opening. Therefore, $9 \times 8 \times 7 \times 6 = 3024$ ways to fill the 4 job openings.

21. (C) Competency 22.

C is true.

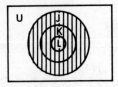

The shaded area shows elements in set J which also include all elements in sets K and L.

A is false.

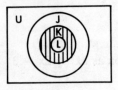

The shaded area shows elements in set K which are not members of set L.

B is false.

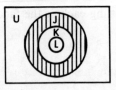

The shaded area shows elements in set J which are not members of set K.

D is false.

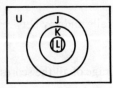

The shaded area shows elements which are members of all four sets J, K, L, and U.

22. (C) Competency 23. The exponent rule that applies is

$$(xy)^a = x^a y^a$$
$$(6 \cdot 4)^2 = (6)^2 (4)^2 = (6 \cdot 6)(4 \cdot 4)$$

23. (C) Competency 24.

$$4 \quad 2 \quad \underline{0} \quad 3 \quad 1 \text{ (base 5)}$$
$$5^4 \quad 5^3 \quad \underline{5^2} \quad 5^1 \quad 5^0 \text{(place value)}$$

24. (A) Competency 25.

$$25\overline{\smash{\big)}19.00}^{\,.76}$$

25. (C) Competency 26. ⅕ is a positive number, so it is larger than $-\frac{2}{3}$, a negative number.

26. (B) Competency 27. Remember, the problem asks for an estimate of the total weight of the herd.

$\left.\begin{array}{l} 35 \times 500 = 17,500 \\ 35 \times 12,000 = 420,000 \end{array}\right\}$ 350,000 is the only answer that falls between the two.

27. (D) Competency 28. Choice D is correct.

A is false: $\angle Q = 55°$ (vertical angles are equal)

$\angle O = 60°$ (alternate exterior angles are equal)

$\angle O + \angle P + \angle Q = 180°$

$\angle P = 65°$

B is false: $\angle S = \angle Q = 55°$ (corresponding angles are equal)

C is false: $\angle W = \angle P + \angle Q$ (corresponding angles)

28. (C) Competency 29. An isosceles triangle has two equal sides, and the angles opposite the equal sides are congruent. All angles in an acute triangle are less than 90°.

29. (C) Competency 30.

$$\frac{DE}{CA} = \frac{EB}{CB}$$

$$\frac{5}{7.5} = \frac{2}{CB}$$

$$5CB = 2(7.5)$$

$$\frac{\cancel{3}CB}{\cancel{3}} = \frac{15}{5}$$

$$CB = 3$$

30. (C) Competency 31. Area is measured in square units. Remember, surface area refers to polyhedrons [a three-dimensional closed surface whose faces (sides) are polygons].

31. (B) Competency 32. The associative property regroups.

32. (D) Competency 33.

i. $3\left(\dfrac{1}{5}\right) - \dfrac{4}{5} < 0$ ii. $\left(\overset{2}{\cancel{10}} \cdot \dfrac{1}{\cancel{5}_1} - 3\right)\left(\cancel{5} \cdot \dfrac{1}{\cancel{5}_1} + 4\right) = 5$

$\quad\dfrac{3}{5} - \dfrac{4}{5} < 0$ $(2 - 3)(1 + 4) = 5$

 $-1(5) = 5$

$\quad -\dfrac{1}{5} < 0$ $-5 \neq 5$

 false

      true

iii. $\cancel{5}\left(\dfrac{1}{\cancel{5}_1}\right) - 3 = -\overset{2}{\cancel{10}}\left(\dfrac{1}{\cancel{5}_1}\right)$

$\quad 1 - 3 = -2(1)$

$\quad\;\; -2 = -2$

 true

33. (D) Competency 34. The distance traveled remains the same, and since D = RT, then D = 90(8) and D = 65t; therefore, 90(8) = 65t. The only ratios that will cross multiply correctly are D.

$$\frac{90}{65} = \frac{t}{8}$$

34. (D) Competency 35. Choice D is correct.

A shows $x \geq 3$ and $y \geq 0$
B shows $x \geq 0$ and $x \leq 3$
C shows $x \geq 0$, $x \leq 3$, and $y \leq 0$

35. **(D)** Competency 36. The *mode* is the most frequent (greatest number). In the graph, the mode is 1. The *median* is the score in the middle, and the graph shows that the height of the 7 bar is in the middle of the ratings. The *mean* is the average of the scores. In the graph, the mode is 1, the lowest number rating, and the median is 7, the highest number rating. Therefore, the mean (average) has to be *between the mode and the median.* You can see that the following answers are false.

mode 1   ⎫   A. The mean is less than the mode.
mean between ⎬   B. The mode is greater than the mean.
median 7   ⎭   C. The median is less than the mode.

36. **(B)** Competency 37. A biases the sample by choosing customers. C leaves it to chance that *all* customers surveyed will mail in their preferences. D can be eliminated because they are not customers.

37. **(B)** Competency 38. The probability that the first ball drawn is not yellow is 10/12 because there are 10 balls that are not yellow and 12 balls altogether. After the first ball is drawn, there are 9 balls out of 11 balls left, a probability of 9/11. The probability that both balls are not yellow is

$$\frac{10}{12} \times \frac{9}{11}$$

38. **(C)** Competency 39. The sentence is in the form "if p, then q," which has a negation of "p and not q."

39. **(C)** Competency 40. The sentence is in the form "if p, then q," which is equivalent to "if not q, then not p," "not p or q," and "q or not p." Choice C does not fit any of these forms.

40. **(C)** Competency 41. This is the only answer which can be deduced.

41. **(C)** Competency 42. C is an invalid argument in the form

$$\frac{\begin{array}{l} p \to q \\ \sim p \end{array}}{\therefore \sim q}$$

Choices A, B, and D are all valid forms of

$$p \rightarrow q$$
$$\sim q$$
$$\therefore \sim p$$

42. (C) Competency 43. Each term is multiplied by $-\frac{2}{3}$ to find the next term.

$$-\frac{2}{3} \times \frac{16}{9} = -\frac{32}{27}$$

43. (B) Competency 44. The distributive property distributes the number on the outside of the parentheses to each number on the inside.

$$a(b + c) = ab + ac$$

Let a = .63, b = 47.1, and c = 2.5.

$$.63(47.1 + 2.5) = .63(47.1) + .63(2.5)$$

44. (B) Competency 48. The only answer involving addition is B.

45. (B) Competency 49. x = 25 is the mean and *median*. x = 19 is the *median*. Since the first two have the median in common, the answer asked for is the median.

$$16 + 12 \div 2 = 14$$

46. (C) Competency 50.

$$\overset{p}{\text{Jane is } \underline{\text{going to college}}} \text{ or she is } \overset{q}{\underline{\text{going to get a job}}}.$$

$$\overset{\sim}{\text{Jane is } \underline{\text{not}}} \overset{q}{\underline{\text{going to get a job}}}.$$

$$\text{Therefore, she is } \overset{p}{\underline{\text{going to college}}}.$$

$$p \vee q$$
$$\sim q$$
$$\therefore p$$

47. (B) Competency 51.

$$\underset{p}{\underset{none}{\text{There are } \underline{\text{no dogs}} \text{ that } \underline{\text{are not}} \underline{\text{animals}}.}} \text{ (None are not p.)}$$

$$\underline{\text{All}} \text{ dogs } \underline{\text{are}} \text{ animals. (All are p.)}$$

48. (C) Competency 52.

$$\begin{array}{r} \$50 \text{ profit} \\ \times \quad 5 \text{ chairs sold} \\ \hline \$250 \text{ profit earned} \end{array}$$

49. (D) Competency 53. The problem asks for the amount of gas *saved*. Ken saved 36%.

$$150 \times .36 = 54$$

50. (C) Competency 55. Change all figures into inches or feet. Then subtract the area of the inside dimensions from the area of the outside dimensions to find the area of the frame.

$$\begin{array}{l} 42'' \times 2\frac{3}{4}' = 42'' \times 33'' = 1386 \text{ sq in} \\ 33'' \times 2' = 33'' \times 24'' = \underline{-\ 792} \text{ sq in} \\ \hphantom{33'' \times 2' = 33'' \times 24'' =} 594 \text{ sq in} \end{array}$$

594 sq in ÷ 144 sq in = $4\frac{1}{8}$ sq ft

51. (D) Competency 56. Use the Pythagorean theorem to solve.

$$\begin{aligned} a^2 + b^2 &= c^2 \\ a^2 + 6^2 &= 10^2 \\ a^2 &= 10^2 - 6^2 \\ a^2 &= 100 - 36 \\ a^2 &= 64 \\ a &= 8 \end{aligned}$$

52. (D) Competency 57. The value of the equipment after 6 years is found by finding the average depreciation per year and subtracting 6 times that amount from the original cost.

$2340 − $456 = $1884 ÷ 10 = $188.40 (depreciation per year)
6 × $188.40 = $1130.40 (loss of value in 6 years)
$2340 − $1130.40 = $1209.60 (value after 6 years)

53. (C) Competency 58. C is true; odd × odd = odd.

54. (C) Competency 60. The probability that an event will occur is 1 minus the probability the event will not occur.

$$1 - \frac{3}{8} = \frac{5}{8}$$

To change probability to odds *in favor*:

$$\frac{\text{probability will}}{\text{probability won't}}$$

$$\text{odds in favor} = \frac{\frac{5}{8}}{\frac{3}{8}} \quad \text{or} \quad \frac{5}{8} \div \frac{3}{8} = \frac{5}{1\cancel{8}} \times \frac{\cancel{8}^1}{3} = \frac{5}{3}$$

55. (D) Competency 61. Choices A, B, and C are not valid because they don't follow logically from the premises.

56. (B) Competency 54. The numbers 3, 7, and 21 fulfill the requirements. 65 ÷ 3 = 21, remainder 2. 65 ÷ 7 = 9, remainder 2. 65 ÷ 21 = 3, remainder 2. 22 ÷ 3 = 7, remainder 1. 22 ÷ 7 = 3, remainder 1. 22 ÷ 21 = 1, remainder 1.

LIST OF SOURCES

We would like to thank the copyright holders acknowledged below for their permission to quote from their material in the reading sections of this book.

Brief excerpts were taken from the following publications:

The New Book of Popular Science, copyright 1979 by Grollier, Inc.; *Student's Book of College English,* by David Skwire and Frances Chitwood, copyright 1975 by Glenco Publishing Co., Inc.; *The Cousteau Almanac,* by Jacques-Yves Cousteau, copyright 1981, by the Cousteau Society, Inc., by permission of Doubleday & Company, Inc.; *The Moon and Its Exploration,* by Necia H. Apfel, copyright 1982 by Franklin Watts Publishers; *Physical Science: An Inquiry Approach,* copyright 1977, Harper & Row, Inc.; *Psychology: An Introduction,* 4th ed., by Charles G. Morris, copyright 1982 by Prentice-Hall; *Swimming,* by Betty Vickers and William J. Vincent, William C. Brown Company; *How to Learn and Study in College,* by Victor P. Maiorana, copyright 1980, Prentice-Hall; *Perceiving the Arts: An Introduction,* 3rd. ed., by Dennis J. Sporre, copyright 1981, Prentice Hall; *The United States,* Combined 5th ed., copyright 1982, Prentice-Hall.

Longer passages used in the tests are reprinted by permission of the following:

Reading Pre-Test

Passage 1: Conniff, Richard. "We Shed 50 Million Skin Cells a Day; They Make Good Scents to a Hound." *Smithsonian* June 1986: 65.
Passage 2: Russell, George. "Trade Face-Off." *Time* 13 April: 35.
Passage 3: Barry, Dave. "You Can Avoid Fashion Victimization." *The Bradenton Herald* 14 June 1987: C 10.

Passage 4: Tyndale, Katie. "Nasal Addiction." *Insight* 4 May 1987: 53.

Passage 6: Tyndale, Katie. "Of Heft and Sex." *Insight* 4 May 1987: 53.

Passage 7: Lagowski, J.J. "The National Teacher Certification Board." *Journal of Chemical Education* May 1987: 385.

Passage 10: "Less Means More." *Nursing Life* May/June 1987: 14.

Passage 11: Spock, M.D., Benjamin. "Are Your Kid's Friends Bad Influences?" *Redbook* June 1987: 22.

Passage 12: Goode, Stephen. "Muzzles and Miranda." *Insight* 4 May 1987: 55.

Passage 13: Goode, Stephen. "Priest Loses Lawsuit." *Insight* 4 May 1987: 55.

Passage 15: Roberts, Marjory. "Patient Knows Best." *Psychology Today* June 1987: 10.

Reading Post-Test

Passage 1: "A Miraculous Sky Rescue." *Time* 4 May 1987: 26.

Passage 2: Challem, Jack, and Renate Lewin. "Beta Carotene." *Let's Live* June 1987: 10.

Passage 4: Cox, James A. "Being Snuck Up On By 'Sneaker Chic.'" *Smithsonian* January 1986: 168.

Passage 5: Theroux, Phyllis. "The Great Escape." *Parents* July 1987: 55.

Passage 6: Trippett. "Down and Out in L.A." *Time* 22 June 1987: 23.

Passage 7: Will, George. "Consideration to Be Unconsidered." *Sarasota—Herald Tribune* 21 June 1987: F 2.

Passage 9: Lacayo, Richard. "Problems of Crime and Punishment." *Time* 21 June 1987: 60.

Passage 10: "The Creation Story." *Sarasota—Herald Tribune* 21 June 1987: F 2.

Reading Sub-Test

Passage 1: Starrett, Sylvia. "Why I Love Teaching The Gifted." *English Journal* May/June 1987: 56.

Passage 2: "NASA Forms Office To Study Manned Lunar Base, Mars Mission." *Aviation Week and Space Technology* 8 June 1987: 22.

Passage 4: Jones, Howard Mumford. "The Fetish of the Classics." *English Journal* April 1987: 14.

Passage 6: "More Violent Hurricanes?" *Time* 20 April 1987: 69.

Passage 7: "And to keep Our Honor Clean." *Time* 20 April 1987: 20.

Passage 8: Hays, Arthur. "Should Libraries Restrict the Use of Subversive Publications?" *English Journal* April 1987: 15.

Passage 9: Goetz, Jill. "Television: Idle Comfort." *Psychology Today* June 1987: 10.